KU-371-586

Contents

Preface

If you want to know what social science research is all about and how to do it, this book is for you. In accessible language it will lead you into the world of research and give you confidence that you know how to design a research study, how to carry it out and how to report on your research. You will become aware of the range of possible approaches and what each offers. You will learn how to decide what approach suits the issue you want to study, the question you want to answer. You will also become alert to some of the pitfalls as well as learning the 'tricks of the trade'.

The logic of research is presented in such a way as to enable the novice to prepare research proposals and to conduct research. The essential logic of scientific research is the same for physicists as it is for sociologists. It is the same for beginners as for masters of the art. This book introduces this essential logic of research, that is, the kind of disciplined thinking that scientific research requires. Designing and conducting a research project requires clear and disciplined thinking.

While there are many kinds of research, and research projects seem at first to take many forms, it is a mistake to assume that there is no pattern to the process. The second mistake is to sheepishly follow one pattern.

This fifth edition of *The Research Process* is aimed at tertiary students who are enrolled in an introductory research methods subject, or who want to learn how to do the kinds of research required for jobs in marketing, social policy, social work, politics, communications and community work. It assumes that readers have only a vague understanding of 'social science' and little knowledge about doing research. The text begins in a leisurely way, introducing concepts one at a time, with examples. It takes a non-statistical approach, presenting the essentials of the research process in an understandable manner. Both quantitative and qualitative methods are introduced. While these methods are different in some ways, there are many issues common to these important ways of gathering evidence for understanding the social world we live in.

This is not a book on the philosophy of science or social science. The last few decades have witnessed a hotly contended set of debates about the aims, the achievements and the very possibilities of the sciences. In the meantime, researchers have continued their basic task of describing the way aspects of our world work and testing theories by relating evidence to propositions about the state, nature and operation of the universe. The essential philosophical questions apply to all researchers—chemists, physicists, social psychologists, demographers and others.

The approach

We approach research methodology as a process involving a sequence of activities, each preparing students for the next. When doing social science research, some questions are best answered before others are raised. The reasons for this sequencing of the questions are explained to readers and several common pitfalls are pointed out.

The process of social science research is divided into three phases.

Phase 1 involves:

1 selecting a problem (including narrowing and clarifying the problem) and restating the problem as a hypothesis for quantitative research or a research objective for qualitative research
2 defining variables and determining ways of measuring them
3 choosing a research design
4 choosing a sample.

Phase 2 is the data-collection stage. This book includes discussion of researchers' ethical responsibilities; understanding these will be helpful in securing the approval of a Human Research Ethics Committee to conduct your research.

Phase 3 involves the analysis and interpretation of data and writing the report.

Several examples in each chapter demonstrate how the research process progresses. In addition, there are exercises and questions throughout the text to provide practice in the methods discussed. Each chapter ends with questions to test your comprehension of chapter material.

The Research Process is designed to develop research skills important for living and working in our world—a world in which information is becoming one of the most valuable commodities and in which the ability to handle information is one of the most valued and marketable skills. A skill that is critical to getting a job today.

Gary D. Bouma
Rod Ling

February 2004

Acknowledgments

To Donald H. Bouma

This book is dedicated to my father—sociologist, community leader and opinion shaper. I learned research as a child. I learned the importance of having evidence to support an argument and how evidence-based argument could be a powerful tool for liberation. For him it was used in support of the Black civil rights movement in the United States. For me it has been used to advance other liberations and the analysis of the shape and management of religious diversity in postmodern societies.

We would like to thank all those who have attended workshops and seminars on 'research methodology'. The questions you raised, the ideas you shared and the enthusiasm you had for the topic led to the writing of *The Research Process*. Particular thanks are due to Mary Sinclair for her assistance in opening her classes to learn about research using early versions of this material, and for her general support.

We are indebted to the hundreds of students who have taken 'The Research Process' as a research methods subject at Monash University. Their comments on the text, its examples and shortcomings have greatly helped shape the progress of new editions.

I am deeply indebted to the many PhD, Masters and Honours students who have come to me for supervision. I hope they have learned as much about research from me as I have from them.

I also wish to thank the thousands who have been participants in research projects I have conducted. Whether it was quantitative or qualitative research, I depended absolutely on their willingness to tell me about themselves in some way.

I have enjoyed working with Rod Ling on this major revision of the book for the fifth edition. He had assisted with the fourth edition and I decided it was time to make the teamwork evident in giving him author status.

Gary D. Bouma

I send my deepest thanks and love to my parents, Rex and Heather, who gave me everything.

Rod Ling

Every effort has been made to trace the original source of material contained in this book. Where the attempt has been unsuccessful, the publisher would be pleased to hear from the author or publisher to rectify any omission.

Introduction

How we know what we know and how we know we know

Have you ever had an argument with someone? She said one thing and you said another. She claimed she was right because she read it in a book. You defended your position by pointing out that a doctor told you and a doctor should know. So arguments go. But how do they stop? How can these points of view be tested to determine which is correct? How do we know when we are right or wrong? How do we know what we know?

We are confronted by questions all through life. What is the best diet for weight loss? What is the impact of job loss on the rate of marital breakdown? What is the solution to child poverty, or homelessness? Is tertiary education worthwhile? Is coeducation better for males than it is for females? We may spend a lot of time debating the issues raised by these and similar questions, but how do we find reliable answers to our questions? How do we get the knowledge we seek?

Knowledge can be defined as a description of the state or operation of some aspect of the universe upon which people or groups are prepared to act. If I 'know' that it will rain, I am likely to take my umbrella, or wear a raincoat. If I 'know' that completed tertiary education is reliably associated with higher levels of income, I am more likely to make some effort to attend and graduate.

Knowledge does not hang in space; it is a product of social processes. The production of knowledge usually begins when the public, governments or groups of experts recognise that the state of knowledge in a particular area is inadequate. Next, funding bodies, corporations and universities accept research proposals and decide which are the most relevant and deserving of support. Successful proposals are carried out by teams of researchers who produce findings through their combined experience and skills. Research findings are communicated and endorsed by professional organisations who decide what research should be published and how it should be presented. Finally, communities and governments 'have a say' in how new knowledge is applied by debating and legislating for its appropriate uses. In this way knowledge is both a product and the property of social groups.

Answering our questions

One of the first issues is whether we will answer questions ourselves or rely on others for the information we need. If we want to know whether it is raining outside we can look ourselves or ask someone else. If we want to know what Australians think about politicians we can either ask ourselves or look at the recent polls. Whatever the question, we are faced with roughly the same choice. We can do research, that is, collect the evidence ourselves, or consult an authority.

Consulting an authority as a way of knowing

Usually when we have a question, we look up the answer in an encyclopaedia, 'surf' the Internet, ask a friend who 'knows', or ask an expert—a medical practitioner, a lecturer, a religious leader, the police, a lawyer or an umpire, as appropriate. We refer to articles in journals or the newspaper, or look for a book, a web site or a CD-ROM on the subject. The most common way in which we get answers to our questions is by consulting authorities. As long as the authority consulted knows the answer, this is the most efficient way to answer a question.

People can have at least two kinds of authority: authority due to position and authority due to knowledge. The kind of authority that is most useful to answer our questions about the nature and operation of the world—particularly the social, biological and physical world—is authority derived from knowledge.

The problem with consulting authorities is selection. On what bases do we select authorities? When we are looking for an answer to a question or problem, the essential guideline should be that the authority has the knowledge we need. However, other reasons sometimes influence our choice.

We are sometimes influenced by a person's position, popularity or appearance. The critical point is that no matter how prominent the person, no matter how much authority or power they have, their opinion on a subject is of no more value than any other person's unless they have expertise in the area. A bishop, a physician, a judge or an Olympic gold medallist may hold opinions about unemployment, taxation, the way families should be raised, or the role of government in foreign aid. These opinions, unless based on special knowledge of the issue in question, are no more valid than those expressed on the same topic by anyone else.

Inevitably, a problem with consulting authorities will arise—two recognised authorities in the same field will disagree. For example, it is very common to encounter conflicting opinions regarding the extent of unemployment, gender discrimination and racial discrimination; the benefits and costs of domestic welfare programs, foreign aid and affirmative action policies; and the incidence of infections and work-related injuries. Authorities also fail us when they cannot answer questions with assurance. Sometimes their opinions are unconvincing. On many issues that are or appear to be new, there may be no authorities at all.

Research as a way of knowing

To evaluate the opinions of authorities, we review their research. For this, we need to understand the 'research process'—the generally adopted approach to doing research. Then we can make informed inquiries and judgments of authorities. Has the authority chosen the most appropriate research method? Have all stages of the research been conducted properly? Does the authority's research address the relevant aspects of the question? Has the authority made a valid interpretation of the research findings? What are the limitations of the research?

When authorities cannot answer our questions or we are dissatisfied with their opinions, we conduct research ourselves. To obtain findings in which we can have confidence, we must be familiar with the research process.

The research process is guided by rules and principles for making confident statements about knowledge of the world based on our observations. As the rest of this book will show, the research process is a not an activity that we know intuitively and can just 'go and do'. It is an activity that others have spent much time developing through practice and critical discussion. You will not become familiar with the research process unless you study and practise it.

Following are examples of the types of important questions that face groups in today's societies. To pursue valid answers to such questions, knowledge of the research process is essential.

1 Corporations need to have an informed idea of public preferences for products or services. Will the public accept changes in packaging or product performance?

2 Social workers need to know what it is like to live under certain conditions, with certain levels of ability, or in certain ethnic groups and subcultures in order to design appropriate service delivery systems.

3 Professionals such as doctors need to assess the validity of theories that have consequences for the way they practise. Does taking a regular low dose of aspirin reduce the incidence of cardiovascular disorder?

4 Governments need to know about the effects of policies. What have been the consequences of the immigration policies of the past two decades? What are the consequences of prison terms for juvenile offenders?

If the subject of the research is controversial, it will encounter considerable scrutiny. The researchers will be challenged to provide solid and carefully collected evidence. If the results of their research are clear they may be able to settle the controversy, not by appeal to authority, but by appeal to the evidence they have collected and are able to show to others.

Summary

Research is done to settle disputes about the nature and operation of some aspect of the universe. The research process is a disciplined way of coming to know something about our world and ourselves.

Questions for review

1 When is research carried out?

2 In what ways is the expertise of an authority limited?

3 Discuss some of the problems involved in consulting authorities in order to answer questions. Who would you consult about child-raising techniques? Who would you consult about the impact of explicitly violent television on the play routines of children?

4 List the authorities you regularly consult. How do you know they know? What characteristics of these authorities are important to you? Gender? Age? Social position?

5 Is it possible to live without accepting the word of authorities?

Suggestions for further reading

Chalmers, A. F. (1999), *What is This Thing Called Science?*, 3rd edn, University of Queensland Press, St Lucia.

Denzin, Norman K. and Yvonna S. Lincoln (eds) (2000), *Handbook of Qualitative Research*, 2nd edn, Sage, London.

Wallace, W. (1971), *The Logic of Science in Sociology*, Aldine, Chicago.

Waters, Malcolm and Rodney Crook (1993), *Sociology One*, Longman Cheshire, Melbourne, chapters 1–3.

Research as a way of knowing

Science can be defined as a discipline that collects, weighs and evaluates the empirical evidence for accepting a particular theory or explanation. The *goal of science* is to produce a widely acceptable description of the nature or operation of some aspect of the universe. Science, whether social, psychological, biological or in the field of physics, does this by collecting and analysing sensory evidence in such a way that others looking at the same evidence in the same way would draw the same conclusions, or at least understand that it is possible to see what the researcher was examining in that way. *Scientific research* involves the attempt to gather evidence in such a way that others can see why particular evidence was gathered, how that evidence was gathered, and what the findings were; they can then draw their own conclusions on the basis of that evidence.

This chapter explores the practical meaning of this definition of science. How does scientific research go about trying to produce knowledge that is supported by empirical evidence, that is, by physical, tangible evidence? What are the several kinds of disciplined activities involved in the research process?

Scientific research is done to find ways of understanding, describing, and making more predictable, or controlling, the behaviour of some aspect of the universe. The results of research may be used to develop remedies for problems, strategies for projects and plans for action. Problems like youth homelessness, projects to improve levels of education and plans to combat or contain diseases like SARS all require information that does not exist and must be researched.

We also engage in research to settle conflicting claims or differences in opinion, or to test ideas about the world we live in. Take the following simple case:

Georgina: The fastest way to drive from Melbourne to Mildura is through Castlemaine and Maryborough. It cuts out that Bendigo traffic.

Frank: No way! You don't save a thing! It's faster to go straight through Bendigo. The route is more direct.

The conflict between Georgina and Frank can be settled by scientific research. They both have 'theories' about the fastest way to drive from Melbourne to Mildura. It is possible to collect evidence to test their competing 'theories'. This example will be developed through this chapter.

Research as a process

Doing research involves a process or a series of linked activities moving from beginning to end. The research process is not absolutely rigid, but there is a sense in which it will be weakened or made more difficult if the first steps are not executed carefully.

Those who have done a lot of research develop their own style of going through the phases of the research process. Each researcher will be able to describe a pattern or a regular way they do their research. When their patterns are compared, a 'normal' sequence begins to emerge—normal, not in the sense of being a strict set of steps but as an order of basic phases, with related issues considered at each phase.

The following outline of the research process has helped many students to learn the necessary skills and avoid the major pitfalls involved in research. It is not the only way of doing research, just one useful way.

Outline of the research process

Phase 1: Essential first steps
The researcher clarifies the issue to be researched and selects a research method.

Phase 2: Data collection
The researcher collects evidence about the research question.

Phase 3: Analysis and interpretation
The researcher relates the evidence to the research question, draws conclusions about the question and acknowledges the limitations of the research.

Phase 1 of the research process involves five essential steps, each concerning a separate issue. Failure to satisfactorily address these issues will render the rest of the research process more difficult or impossible—therefore, the steps are essential. While qualitative and quantitative research designs both follow these steps, there are differences in the way they do. These differences will be noted as we go along.

Phase 1: Essential first steps

1   Select, narrow, and formulate the question to be studied.
2   Select a research design.
3   Design and devise measures for variables.
4   Set up tables for analysis.
5   Select a sample.

Step 1: Focus and narrow the research problem. Initially, a research problem may start with an observation like 'Most people who are unemployed seem to be young.' One approach to developing a research problem from this observation would be to ask 'What is it like to be young and unemployed?' This would probably lead to qualitative research guided by a research objective. Another approach would be to test the validity of this observation. To do this, it is necessary to be clear about what has to be tested. The observer claims that there is a relationship between two varying aspects (variables) of their general social experience, 'unemployment' and 'age'. They are really saying that according to their general observations, 'The lower a person's age, the more likely they are to be unemployed.' This is one way of moving from the observation to articulating a relationship to be tested. Each of these approaches clarifies the focus of the research.

Step 2: Select a research design. The first choice here is between qualitative and quantitative research. Your observation might motivate you to ask 'What is it like to be young and unemployed?' or 'Is being unemployed different for young men compared with young women?' Such questions are usually answered using qualitative research methods.

On the other hand, you might want to test a more quantitative question such as 'What percentage of youth are unemployed?' or 'Is youth unemployment greater now than in the 1980s?' or 'Is youth unemployment more prevalent in Bankstown than in Vaucluse?' The first question about the relationship between 'age' and 'unemployment' could be tested in a single social environment such as a social club or a suburb. The results would be based on information gathered in one environment. The subsequent questions require that the relationship be examined in several social environments such as different points in time or several suburbs and the results for each be compared, providing the desired results.

Step 3: Select ways of measuring changes in variables. If you choose to take a quantitative approach you will select variables and find measures for them before you gather evidence. For example, to measure changes in 'unemployment' you might select the government's official 'unemployment rate'.

However, if you take a qualitative approach you will decide which prompts to use to enable your interviewees to tell their stories, or select certain aspects of human behaviour to observe and record.

Step 4: If you choose to take a quantitative approach you design tables to be used in summarising your data in a manner that makes later reporting and analysis straightforward. If you take a qualitative approach you may have a set of tentative themes in mind that you expect to explore, but you remain open to your experience in data collection to shape the approach you take in analysing your observations or interview transcripts.

Step 5: Select a sample. Research is always done on a sample; hardly ever is everyone included. The extent to which you wish to generalise your findings will shape your selection of a situation or group of people for your research. In qualitative research, situations or people are selected to represent dimensions of interest to the researcher. To learn what it is like to be young, unemployed and female/male it makes sense to talk to some young males and females who are unemployed. On the other hand, if you wish to test the relationship between age and unemployment in your local area, then you will want a sample that represents the population of the area—a more systematic sample is required.

These steps provide a basis for the successful conduct of the research, in three ways. First, they articulate the problem and narrow the focus of the research. This allows the researcher to undertake the practical aspects of their project with a clear awareness of what has to be tested or studied. Second, these steps immediately introduce discipline to research procedure. This discipline is necessary to keep the project focused and to maintain rigour in data collection and analysis. Lastly, the steps provide a structure to evaluate the progress of a research project. If something goes wrong, or the project gets bogged down, revisiting the steps will probably tell the researcher where the project went off the rails.

A quantitative example

We now return to the argument about which route from Melbourne to Mildura is faster. Both Georgina and Frank have a hunch, or a 'theory'. Let's test these theories. We commence with Step 1 of Phase 1 by focusing the question and narrowing it to a specific set of circumstances. For this particular problem, consideration must be given to the following issues:

- Are normal or special cars to be used?
- Are cars to be driven by normal or specially trained drivers?
- Are speed limits to be observed? One route may be faster only if the speed limit is exceeded.
- At what time of the day and on which day of the week do we want to make the test?
- Will we be satisfied with a single test or will more than one be required? How many?

- Will any other routes be considered?
- Will any allowances be made for time lost to accident, breakdown or road hazard (like a stone through the windscreen)?

Step 1 requires us to focus, clarify and narrow the research problem. Let's say that we decide to consider the two routes at a certain time of day, for particular drivers and cars, under certain rules, between certain points of departure and arrival. We will run the test cars leaving a starting line at the Melbourne General Post Office with instructions to obey all road safety laws. The first car to arrive at the Mildura General Post Office will be declared to have taken the faster route.

The research question is no longer 'Which is the faster route from Melbourne to Mildura?' It has become 'Which is the faster route for equivalent cars and drivers to drive legally from Melbourne General Post Office to Mildura General Post Office on a Friday afternoon in May?'

Our variables have also been defined. The first variable is 'route'. There are two routes: Georgina's route and Frank's route. The second variable is 'journey speed'. There are two journey speeds—the 'faster' journey speed and the 'slower' journey speed. Frank is saying that if Georgina changes her route, her journey speed will change from the 'slower' to the 'faster'. This is one way of considering the relationship we have to test.

For Step 2, we select a research design. We are going to use a simple research design, where we compare the routes under the given conditions on one occasion.

In Step 3, the measures for each variable are selected. The measure for the variable 'route' is straightforward—it is simply the 'route' assigned to each car. Car A takes Georgina's route and Car B takes Frank's route. The measure for 'journey speed' is 'order of arrival'. The car that arrives 'first' will be designated as having the faster journey speed, the car that arrives 'second' will be designated as the one with the slower journey speed.

For Step 4, we design a table for easy analysis and data collection, such as Figure 2.1.

Figure 2.1 A simple table designed for easy collection and analysis of research results

	Georgina's route (Car A)	**Frank's route (Car B)**
Order of arrival		

In Step 5, we select a sample. In this case, we are sampling the entire population under review, that is, the two routes.

Phase 2: Data collection
1   Collect data.
2   Summarise and organise data.

Although many have the impression that data collection is the major enterprise in research, this is not strictly correct. Preparation (Phase 1) takes the most time, and drawing conclusions and writing the report often take more time than data collection. Data collection often takes the least time, especially in quantitative research.

For Step 1, we will collect data about the cars' 'order of arrival', which is the measure for the variable 'journey speed'. Let's say that Car A arrived in Mildura first, beating Car B.

For Step 2, we summarise the data (see Figure 2.2).

Figure 2.2 Completed table

	Georgina's route (Car A)	**Frank's route (Car B)**
Order of arrival	First	Second

Now we are ready for Phase 3, analysis and interpretation. In this phase, we relate the data collected to the research question and draw conclusions. It is really quite simple, as long as the research problem is articulated and made clear in Phase 1.

Phase 3: Analysis and interpretation
1   Relate data to the research question.
2   Draw conclusions.
3   Assess the limitations of the study.
4   Make suggestions for further research.

For Step 1, ask yourself, 'How does the data relate to the research question? What can the data tell us about the two routes?'

In Step 2, we draw conclusions. Given the data in Figure 2.2, what would you conclude? Is Frank's assertion that his route offers a faster journey supported?

In Step 3, we acknowledge the limitations of the research. You may be able to see some limitations in our study. It applies only to one Friday in May under certain conditions. Only one trial was made. The outcome might have been the result of an accident along Frank's route that held up traffic for three-quarters of an hour. Different drivers, cars or days might produce different results. What other limitations should be mentioned in the research report?

In Step 4, we suggest further research that should allow us to answer the research question in more detail. You should propose and plan another piece of research that would clarify any questions raised by the limitations. For example, the research was conducted under only one type of weather conditions—those that occurred on the day of the test. This raises the question, 'Are the results the same under different weather conditions?' To research this, the test should be repeated on a day when weather conditions are different from those of the first test.

As shown in this quantitative example, research is a process by which ordinary questions are focused upon, in which data is collected in such a way that the research questions are answered on the basis of observable evidence.

Most research projects raise new questions and in this sense the research process is a continuous one, with the end of one project becoming the beginning of another.

A qualitative example

Phase 1: Essential First Steps. The first step requires that we decide what to observe and state what it is in the form of a research objective. This is necessary to focus our attention and to screen out what is only of incidental or passing interest. In practice, we all tend to get distracted by things that have some personal interest.

Take the observation mentioned above about youth and unemployment. You might decide to take as your research objective 'How does it feel to be unemployed for young men as compared to young women?'

In Step 2 you decide to do an in-depth interview study involving young men and women from one social club. This will keep a number of background characteristics similar while allowing access to both genders. This is a case study.

In Step 3 you decide to ask interviewees to tell you about being unemployed. What is it like? How do people respond when they learn of their situation? Do they try to pretend to be employed? If one topic gets them going, let them follow it—it is probably important to them.

Step 4 will involve identifying themes for analysis. These might include parents' reactions, friends' reactions, dealing with employment agencies, and others. But mostly you will wait till your informants have told their stories to code the responses.

Step 5 involves selecting those whose stories you will collect. This will depend on who is available and willing. It will also depend on characteristics that you may have identified as potentially important—length of unemployment, marital status, whether living at home or on their own.

Phase 2: Data Collection. You go to the club and put up a poster saying you want to talk to people about their experiences of being unemployed. You sit in a corner and people talk with you. You may audio record what they say or you may make notes and write it up afterwards. Whichever way, your data will be conversations with unemployed young people, male and female.

Phase 3: Analysis and Interpretation. This is where the really hard work begins in qualitative research. You pore over the interviews and begin to code them and identify themes. As you read and re-read the interviews you will begin to appreciate and understand what it is like to be young and unemployed. You will also begin to detect differences between males and females. They may not be what you expected, but that is why we do research—to find out what we do not already know. Then you are ready to write your report.

Research as a discipline

Research requires discipline, clear thinking and careful observation. The first and probably the hardest discipline required by the research process is learning to ask the right questions. The problems that motivate us to do research are often enormous. How to prevent nuclear war? How to save the economy? How to prevent cot death? How to improve the quality of life for all people? The first discipline is to move from these 'global' questions to researchable questions.

Researchable questions have two basic properties. First, they are limited in scope to certain times, places and conditions. A researchable question is usually a small fragment of a larger question. One of the hardest things for a researcher to do is to confront a large, burning issue by tackling only one small, manageable part of it. Failing to do so, of course, would mean that the work would be doomed because the problem addressed would be larger than the time, energy or other resources available to the researcher. It is better to answer a small question than to leave a large one unanswered. Perhaps by piecing together a number of small answers a large answer may be discovered.

For example, the question 'What factors affect decision-making within Australian families?' is very large. Many factors are involved and these may vary depending on the type of family observed. A more manageable question would be, 'Among single-parent families in Melbourne, are choices of breakfast food influenced by the parent's gender?' Similarly, in order to be researched, the question 'Does parents' education affect scholastic achievement of children?' would have to be focused, narrowed and limited.

The best and probably the only way to learn the skill of narrowing and focusing a broad issue so that it becomes a research question is to practise. Try limiting the question 'Does parents' education affect scholastic achievement of children?'

To help you get started, let us look at the question. As it stands, it looks like a simple question requiring a 'yes' or 'no' answer. To become a research question it needs to be made more specific. It helps to ask, 'What are the main things, ideas or activities in the question?' The question asks something about the *relationship* between 'parents' education' and 'scholastic performance'. What do we mean when we use the term 'parents' education'? In what aspects of 'parents' education' are we specifically interested?

- The stage at which they finished their education (secondary school, TAFE, university)?
- Their standards of academic achievement at school, TAFE or university?
- The types of schools (public/private) they attended?
- The prestige of the schools or universities they attended?

Similarly, we should ask ourselves, 'What do we mean by "scholastic performance"?'

- Final grades in all subjects?
- Consistency in high grades across subjects? Overall 'place in class'?
- Quality of their school reports?
- Level of participation in important school activities such as school prefecture and sport?

The results are some focused research questions using the focused versions of our original concepts, 'parents' education' and 'scholastic performance':

- Does the type of school attended by parents affect children's final grades?
- Does the stage at which parents finish their education affect children's overall place in class?
- Do parents' levels of academic achievement affect the quality of children's school reports?

Now try your hand at limiting these questions:

1 What factors are important in family decision-making? (Hints: Try listing some factors, for example, economic, social life, extended family commitments. Limit the area of decision-making.)

2 Can we promote the development of a positive self-image among handicapped teenagers? (Hints: What do you know about self-image? What are key factors that lead to a healthy self-image or to a negative self-image?)

The first property of a researchable question is that it is limited in scope, narrowed in focus and confined to a certain time, place and set of conditions. While frustrating and difficult, the discipline required to focus the research question is one of the most important in the research process.

The second property of a researchable question is that some observable, tangible, countable evidence or data can be gathered that are relevant to the question. There must be something that can be observed by you and others. That is, the question must be answerable through observation of some aspect of the universe we live in. Some refer to this as 'empirical research'. Empirical research can only deal with the observable, measurable aspects of the questions we want to answer. For example, questions about morals are not answerable by the kind of research we are talking about. Research cannot determine whether an action is 'right' or 'wrong'. The question 'Is it morally right to allow terminally ill patients to die?' is not answerable by empirical research. Empirical research can be either qualitative or quantitative. Empirical research only seeks to answer those questions that can be answered by reference to sensory data. Sensory data are data that can be seen, heard, touched, recorded, measured or counted.

> *empirical* Based on, guided by, or employing observation and experiment rather than theory. From the Greek word *empeirikos* meaning experience, skilled.
>
> *Shorter Oxford English Dictionary*

While empirical research cannot answer the moral question 'Is it right or wrong to allow terminally ill patients to die?', it can answer the question 'How many students in a particular university seminar think that it is right or wrong to allow certain types of terminally ill patients to die?' One of the disciplines associated with doing research is learning to ask questions to which there are measurable, sensory, countable answers—that is, questions that can be answered in terms of observations and experiences.

There are other kinds of questions to which there are no empirical answers—for example, questions of beauty. Is the Taj Mahal more or less beautiful than the Cologne Cathedral? Is Melbourne more beautiful than Sydney? Is the Sydney Harbour Bridge more beautiful than the Golden Gate Bridge? These are questions of aesthetics, not empirical questions.

Of course, they can be turned into empirical questions. We can make up an empirical question relating to one of the aesthetic questions above. For example, 'How many Adelaide TAFE students consider this picture of the Sydney Harbour Bridge to be more beautiful than this picture of the Golden Gate Bridge?'

The same issues can be raised about other questions of taste, fashion, etiquette, morality, religion and political ideology. Empirical research cannot determine which table setting is 'most tasteful' or which jacket is 'most fashionable'. These are not empirical questions. Empirical research can answer such questions as 'Which table setting is judged the most tasteful by a sample of interior decorators?'

Similarly, empirical research cannot answer questions of religious faith. Does God exist? It can, though, answer questions such as 'How many lecturers at the Australian National University believe that God exists?' or 'What social characteristics are found among believers in God?'

In summary, the first discipline required by the research process is to ask the right kind of questions. Researchable questions are limited in scope and very specific. It can be a real challenge to devise a clear, specific, narrow question. This skill can be learned. You can learn to take a general question and formulate a research question from it. You will get more practice at this in the next chapter.

Honesty and accuracy

The second major discipline required by research is to be honest and accurate. Honesty and accuracy should be characteristics of any intellectual enterprise, and require a degree of self-control. We often have in mind an outcome we wish to arrive at. For example, we might believe that more students should consider the Sydney Harbour Bridge to be more beautiful than the Golden Gate Bridge. But discipline in doing research compels us to be as objective as possible, to make sure that there is no bias in the way we ask questions, to ensure that we correctly record the data and are honest in reporting the results. What is wrong with the following examples?

■ 'Here are two pictures of bridges. You really don't think the one on the left (Sydney Harbour Bridge) is more beautiful, do you?' Write an unbiased version of this question.

■ 'Only 70 per cent of those asked thought the Sydney Harbour Bridge was more beautiful than the Golden Gate.' Write an unbiased statement of this research finding.

If we are disciplined and accurate in our reporting of research findings, then we increase the reliability of the research process. Some research has fallen into disrepute because researchers have not been disciplined, accurate and honest. Have you ever read about controversy over scientific work in which bias has been suggested? An example would be Eysenck's research into racial differences in intelligence. Some people have forced their data to fit their theory by falsifying results, by not recording data accurately, or both. Research is useful only to the extent that the researchers have been disciplined, accurate and honest.

Record-keeping

A third discipline is recording what was done in such a way that someone else can see exactly what was done and why. There are two reasons for this. First, this safeguards the reliability of the research process. If what was done is reported accurately and in adequate detail, then another person can repeat the research. If they get the same results, then what was found originally becomes even more certain. If they do not get the same results then the original findings are less certain.

The second reason is to provide a record for yourself. It is amazing how quickly we forget what we did and why. At the end of a research project you need to be able to refer to your research notes and refresh your memory. This is a great help when you are writing about the limitations of the study.

Assessing limitations

The fourth and final discipline of the research process involves assessing the limitations of the research. If you study only one family, you cannot apply your findings to all families. If you study a group of 10-year-old boys, your findings apply to that group and that group only. It is a great temptation to over-generalise, to make claims that apply beyond the data collected.

Similarly, if you did your research on an empirical question derived from a non-empirical question, your conclusions apply only to the empirical question.

For example, if your initial question was 'Is the Sydney Harbour Bridge more beautiful than the Golden Gate Bridge?' but your research question was 'How many Adelaide TAFE students consider the Sydney Harbour Bridge to be more beautiful than the Golden Gate Bridge?', the data you collect will answer the empirical question, not the question of beauty. Keeping your conclusions at the level of the question asked is part of the discipline of accepting the limitations of the research process.

In summary, doing research requires discipline. The right kind of questions must be asked. Questions must be narrowly defined because only empirical questions can be answered by empirical research. Second, honesty and accuracy in asking questions and reporting findings are required. Third, careful record-keeping and accurate reporting are needed. Finally, you must assess the limitations of the research process and your particular research question.

Theory and data

A research question can come from anywhere. We may just be curious: I wonder how that works? I wonder why some people do this or that? Does it make any difference? Curiosity can begin the research process.

On the other hand, it may be a problem that motivates us to ask a researchable question. How is the problem of teenage malnutrition best handled? How can I make my father understand me? How can I improve my health? How can the incidence of drink–driving be reduced? Problems such as these and many others motivate people to ask researchable questions.

Arguments are a frequent starting-point. The example of Georgina and Frank is typical. I might have one idea about how things are and you might have another. It may be possible to design a piece of research to see whose idea is supported by evidence. Research is often started by controversy.

Magellan sailed around the world. Was this evidence uniformly accepted as proof that the earth was not flat and that sailors who ventured too far would not fall off the edge? No. Even after Magellan's circumnavigation of the earth, many people continued to believe that it was flat. Perhaps satellite photographs of the earth taken from great distance provide the most compelling evidence available to date that the earth is not flat.

As with Magellan and the flat-earth theory, evidence does not always stop the controversy that motivated research. Some people do not accept the evidence. Some argue that the research was not properly conducted. Some argue that research questions were not properly defined. In such cases, the research process usually continues, with more evidence being collected to test more carefully defined questions. Part of the fun of doing research is to see how each question leads to more questions. The research process is continuous.

The research process is a disciplined process for answering questions. Another way of putting this is to say that the research process is a disciplined process for relating theory and data. At this point, we will try to clarify and simplify the terms 'theory' and 'data'.

Theory

Put most simply, a theory is a guess about the way things are. Georgina had a theory about the fastest route to Mildura from Melbourne. A theory is an idea about how something works, or what it is like to be something, or what will happen if… It may be an idea about what difference will be made by doing or not doing something. Theories are ideas about how things relate to each other.

There are many ways of expressing theories. Some are very formal, others are informal. Some theories are very elaborate and complex, yet simplicity and clarity are often desirable features of theories. Put simply, theories are ideas about the way other ideas are related. Theories are abstract notions about the way concepts relate to each other. This will become clearer as you proceed through this book. Here are some examples of crude theories:

- a hunch about the fastest route between Melbourne and Mildura
- an idea that putting a cup of salt into a litre of soup will make it too salty for your liking
- a guess that the more reassurance you give to small children that they are valued, cared for and wanted, the more likely they are to develop healthy images of themselves
- the idea that more education produces more reliable, more productive, more contented people.

A theory asserts a relationship between concepts. It states that some 'things' are related in a particular way. It is a statement of how things are thought to be. A theory is an idea, a mental picture of how the world might be.

The research process is a disciplined process for answering questions. It is a way of testing theories, a way of determining whether there is any evidence to support a mental picture of the way things are. The evidence collected in the research process is called data.

Data

datum (singular), *data* (plural)   Latin, neutral, past participle of *dare*, to give. A thing given or granted; something known or assumed as fact, and made the basis for reasoning or calculation.

Shorter Oxford English Dictionary

Data are facts produced by research. Data, like facts, by themselves are meaningless. They acquire meaning as they are related to theories. For example, the fact that Car A arrived in Mildura 30 minutes and 20 seconds before Car B is meaningless. The fact takes on meaning when it is related to the two theories about which route is the faster from Melbourne to Mildura. The fact becomes part of the data by which these theories can be tested.

Data are empirical facts. They are readings on thermometers. They are records of events (Car A arrived before Car B). They are counts (100 students thought the picture of the Sydney Harbour Bridge was more beautiful than that of the Golden Gate Bridge). They are tapes of conversations or transcripts of interviews. They are written observations. Data are records of the actual state of some measurable aspect of the universe at a particular point in time. Data are not abstract; they are concrete, they are records of events, they are measurements of the tangible, countable features of the world. While theories are abstract mental images of the way things may be, data are measures of specific things as they were at a particular time.

There are two kinds of data used in social science: quantitative and qualitative. Quantitative research tends to answer questions such as: How much? How many? How often? Quantitative data are usually expressed in numbers, percentages or rates. In contrast, qualitative research tends to answer questions such as: What is it like to be a member of that group? What is going on in this situation? What is it like to experience this or that phenomenon? Hence qualitative data tend to be expressed in the language of images, feelings and impressions; they describe the qualities of the events under study. The research process is somewhat different for each type of research. Quantitative styles of research are dealt with first because they require the most preparation during Phase 1, while the efforts in qualitative research tend to be concentrated in the data collection and interpretation phases.

The challenge of the research process is to relate theory and research in such a way that questions are answered. Both theory and data are required. When we are faced with a question we formulate a theory about its answer and test it by collecting data—that is, evidence—to see if our theoretical answer works. Data cannot be collected without some theory about the answer to the question. Theories alone are unsatisfactory because they are unproven, untested. To answer our questions we need both theory and data.

The result of the research process is neither theory nor data, but knowledge. Research provides answers to researchable questions with evidence that is collected and evaluated in a disciplined manner. This is how we know. We ask questions, propose answers to them and test those answers. We ask what it is like and go and find out. Doing research in a disciplined way is 'how we know we know'.

Questions for review

1 Why do we undertake research?

2 It is claimed that research is a process. What is a process?

3 What is the normal sequence of the research process? In what way is it normal?

4 What are the essential first steps of the research process? Why are the first steps so important?

5 What is done in Phase 2 of the research process?

6 List the four major disciplines involved in the research process.

7 What are the two major properties of a researchable question?

8 What are theory and data? What role does each play in the research process?

9 What are the two major kinds of research? What is the main difference between them?

10 Find a newspaper article or an article in a recent magazine that reports a controversy over research findings. What was the nature of the criticism of the research?

Suggestions for further reading

Babbie, E. R. (2003), *The Practice of Social Research*, 10th edn, Wadsworth Publishing, London.

Chalmers, A. F. (1999), *What is This Thing Called Science?*, 3rd edn, University of Queensland Press, St Lucia.

de Vaus, D. A. (2002), *Surveys in Social Research*, 5th edn, Allen & Unwin, St Leonards, NSW, chapter 2.

Denzin, Norman K. and Yvonna S. Lincoln (eds) (2000), *Handbook of Qualitative Research*, 2nd edn, Sage, London, Introduction.

Giddens, Anthony (2001), *Sociology*, 4th edn, Polity Press, Cambridge, chapter 20.

Kumar, Ranjit (1999), *Research Methodology: A Step by Step Guide for Beginners*, Sage, London, chapters 1–2.

Minichiello, Victor, Rosalie Aroni, Eric Timewell and Loris Alexander (1995), *In-Depth Interviewing: Principles, Techniques, Analysis*, 2nd edn, Longman Cheshire, Melbourne, chapter 1.

Wallace, W. (1971), *The Logic of Science in Sociology*, Aldine, Chicago.

Waters, Malcolm and Rodney Crook (1993), *Sociology One*, Longman Cheshire, Melbourne, chapters 1–3.

PHASE 1

Essential First Steps

Selecting a problem

CHAPTER OUTLINE

The first step in Phase 1 of the research process is the selection and focusing of a research problem. This step involves decision-making, sorting, narrowing and clarifying. It requires clear thinking and at times the discarding of favourite topics for more focused ideas. This chapter describes the skills involved in developing an initial question into a practical research problem.

Starting-points

The research process begins when our curiosity is aroused. When we want to know something, we begin formally or informally to engage in research. An observation, something we read, a claim someone made, a hunch about something—each may be a stimulus to begin the research process. This chapter presents several examples to develop your skills for moving from starting-points to focused researchable questions.

Here are some examples of starting-points for research projects.

An observation
Some students get better marks than others.

An observation like this may prompt someone to ask the following questions: Why? Which students? Is it the way papers are marked? An observation may trigger the inquiring mind to ask questions and the research process has begun.

An important family decision
The Wright family has to decide whether to send their daughter to a state school or to a private school.

Someone who knows of this situation might be prompted to ask such questions as these: What difference would it make? Is there a difference in terms of her chances of being accepted into university? What kinds of factors do the Wrights consider important as they arrive at their decision? A situation like an important family decision may stimulate the asking of questions and the research process is under way.

A news report
News reports often raise questions for research. Read your daily news-paper, or tune into radio and television news, and pay attention to the headlines for titles to research projects: 'Divorce Rate Steady for a Decade', 'Crime Rate on Increase', 'Single Mums in Poverty Trap', '1 in 10 Unemployed Seriously Depressed', 'Teenage Suicide Rate Increases', 'Plight of Homeless Worsens', 'More Females Studying Law'. Each of these could lead to a research project to gain more knowledge about some aspect of social life, or to test some idea about what is happening in the world.

News reports usually contain a lot of 'facts' about patterns in society, but less clear and explicit interpretation of those 'facts'. You may be prompted to ask questions: How does the pattern presented in this report compare with the situation 5, 10 or 15 years ago? Why is this pattern happening? What factors might be affecting changes in such things as the tertiary choices women are making, the teenage suicide rate, the age at first marriage, or the effects of unemployment? Questions like these, prompted by your reading of news reports, can be the start of research projects.

A policy issue
The state government is concerned about the provision of proper care in homes for elderly people.

Think about this issue. What questions does it raise? What is the current state of affairs in homes for elderly people? What do elderly people need? Again, the inquiring mind is prompted to ask questions that might lead to research.

It makes little difference where you begin the research process: the first step is to narrow the focus and clarify the issues involved in the problem.

None of the above starting-points provides a sufficiently focused research question. The first step in the research process is to move from an ordinary everyday question to a researchable question by focusing on one aspect of the issue arousing your interest.

Narrowing and clarifying the problem

Our goal in this step in the research process is to produce a clear statement of the problem to be studied. A statement of a problem must explicitly identify the issues on which the researcher chooses to focus. How do we do this? There are no rules or recipes. This skill is best learnt by practice.

Once we examine most starting-points, we quickly realise they suggest research problems that are too unclear and unfocused for practical research. To clarify and focus a problem we have to 'unpack' it—that is, list the issues that make up the problem. We can then choose the issues on which to focus our attention.

The following general questions can be used to unpack a problem:

■ What are the major concepts?
■ What is happening here?
■ What are the issues?
■ Is one thing affecting, causing or producing a change in something else?
■ Why is this so?

Such questions may isolate issues of interest. Take the example of the observation, 'Some students get better marks than others'. Begin with the question 'Why does this observation occur?' Here are four possible explanations:

1 Some students are smarter than others.
2 Some students study more than others.
3 Some students eat better meals than others.
4 Some students enjoy study more than other students do.

Relying on your own experience, write down four other possible explanations of why some students get better marks than others.

Did you think of factors such as exercise, parents' education, social life, family income? If so, you have begun to unpack the issue. You have begun to isolate factors and possible explanations.

You now have eight possible factors. You can begin narrowing the research question by selecting just one. However important other factors may be, it is usually necessary to focus on very few.

Our general observation of the differences in student marks can now be focused to a choice of research problems. These problems can be described in direct questions about the issues they address:

- Are students' marks affected by the amount of study they do?
- Are students' marks affected by the nutrition of the meals they eat?
- Are students' marks affected by their enjoyment of study?
- Are students' marks affected by the status of their parents' occupations?

Another way to narrow and clarify a problem is to consult research relevant to issues raised by the starting-point. This is called 'reviewing the literature'. What have others found? Look at previous research for factors and approaches to the problem you have not considered.

In unpacking the observation 'Some students get better marks than others', you might consult your lecturer. A reference librarian might be able to suggest a few articles or books for you to read. These may include reports of previous research in this area. More ideas will come to you. Reading about the topic of your research will help to clarify your thinking.

Since this step in the research process is so important, let us take another example. Remember, the goal is a clear question for research. To do this you unpack your starting-point. List everything that comes to mind about the subject. Do some reading. Consult some people who know—the more ideas the better. Then select one factor, one idea and one small problem for your research.

Take the example of an important family decision. The Wright family has to decide whether to send their daughter to a state school or to a private school. Remember that the aim is to isolate a question for research, not necessarily to find an answer to the problem faced by the Wright family. What issues are suggested? There are no right or wrong answers here. You are working toward a research question.

Here is a list of some of the issues raised by this starting-point:

1   Is one system of education demonstrably better than another:
    - in terms of sport?
    - in terms of test results?
    - in terms of social life?
2   How do families make decisions like this?
    - What factors do they consider?
    - Do the children participate?
3   Do socio-cultural factors shape these family decisions?
    - Is gender an issue?
    - Do ethnic groups differ?
    - Is social class a factor?

What issues, further questions and factors occurred to you? Write them down. What resources do you have that might help you with this question? Do you know someone who might have ideas on the subject? You could ask your librarian for material on family decision-making or you could ask for information on public versus private education. Are there other things you can use to help identify the issue here? List some other resources.

At this point, the key tasks are to identify issues, to select one to pursue in depth and to leave the rest behind.

We have seen that there are many issues, ideas and factors that might be raised by the decision to send a daughter to a state or private school. Your research will probably be able to treat only one. The rest must be left for other studies. It is the mark of a clear thinker and a good researcher to be able to identify and note the many issues and to make the choice to study one. People reading your report will realise that you are aware of the complexity of the issues involved but are sufficiently disciplined to address yourself to only one.

Stating the problem

The next task is to restate the issue as a researchable question. This is a skill in itself. Two basic forms will be discussed: *hypothesis* and *research objective*. Most other forms can be seen as variations of either a hypothesis or a research objective.

The hypothesis

A hypothesis is a statement that asserts a relationship between concepts. A concept is an idea that stands for something, or that represents a class of things or a general categorisation of an impression of something. If we watch a chess game and decide that chess is an 'intellectual activity', we are describing, both to ourselves and others, our impressions of chess in terms of the concept 'intellectual activity'. Concepts are categories or descriptions of our world and experience. We use concepts to make sense of the world for ourselves and others.

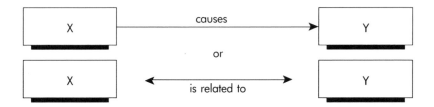

The usual form of a hypothesis

The key feature of a hypothesis is that it asserts that two concepts are related in a specific way. Usually a hypothesis takes the form 'Concept X causes concept Y', or 'Concept X is related to concept Y.' Return to the example we have been using. We began with the observation 'Some students get better marks than others.' We have unpacked this observation by listing issues that come to mind. We thought of the possible impact of factors such as amount of study, nutrition and students' enjoyment of particular subjects. We talked to our lecturer and read material given to us by the librarian. When that was all done, suppose that we decided to do some research into the impact of the amount of study on marks. We have two concepts: 'study' and 'marks'. We also have an idea about how these two concepts are related. We suspect that the more somebody studies, the better their marks will be.

Having done our preparation, we are in a position to write a hypothesis to guide our research. For example:

The more a student studies, the better will be the student's academic performance.

Note that a more general concept, 'academic performance', has been selected in place of 'marks'. Our observation was of a difference in marks, but the general issue or problem is variation in 'academic performance'. It sometimes helps to become more general before focusing on concepts. For example, this will enable a wider variety of measures of academic performance to be considered.

This hypothesis states that two concepts, namely amount of study and academic performance, are related in such a way that more of one (study) will produce or lead to more of the other (academic performance). This hypothesis could be represented or 'diagrammed' as follows:

The two concepts are in boxes. The boxes are linked by an arrow going from one concept to the other. The arrow indicates that one concept (amount of study) does something to the other concept (academic performance). The plus sign indicates that the relationship is seen as a positive one, that is, that more of the one will lead to more of the other.

Diagramming hypotheses is a very useful device to promote clear thinking. If you cannot diagram your hypothesis, it may be because it is not yet clear to you.

Take a different example. We have diagrammed a positive relationship between two concepts. How about a negative relationship—that is, when more of the one concept leads to less of the other, and vice versa. Look over your list of factors that might affect academic performance. Would you say that increases in any of them lead to lower academic performance? How about the number of parties attended? The hypothesis would be stated:

The more parties a student attends, the lower will be the student's academic performance.

It would be diagrammed as follows:

A hypothesis states that there is a relationship between two concepts and specifies the direction of that relationship. The above hypothesis states that there is a negative relationship between parties attended and academic performance. The greater the number of parties attended, the lower is academic performance.

Continue with the 'factors affecting marks' example. Suppose that in doing your literature review on the factors affecting marks you came across an article that claimed that the kind of breakfast students ate had an effect on their academic performance. Write a hypothesis derived from this article.

Now diagram this hypothesis in the form below:

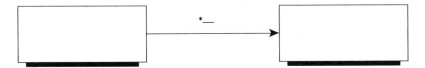

* Is the relationship proposed by the hypothesis positive or negative? If it is positive, place a plus sign in the blank. If it is negative, place a minus sign in the blank.

The best way to develop skill in deriving hypotheses is to practise. Do the following exercises and then derive hypotheses relevant to other topics and issues.

1   Here is a hypothesis: 'As fewer people have involvement with churches, there will be an increase in the number of couples choosing to live in de facto marriages.' What are the concepts?

■ church involvement

■ de facto marriages.

What relationship between these concepts does this hypothesis assert? Diagram the hypothesis here:

* Is the relationship proposed by the hypothesis positive or negative? If it is positive, place a plus sign in the blank. If it is negative, place a minus sign in the blank.

2   Suppose you decide to compare the happiness of couples in de facto relationships and formal marriages. You might propose the following hypothesis:

> Couples who are formally married enjoy more marital satisfaction than couples in de facto relationships.

In this example, the relationship between the concepts cannot be described as positive or negative because the independent concept, 'relationship', is a special type, the categorical concept. A *categorical concept* is one that is rigidly divided into two or more exclusive categories. Examples of categorical concepts include:

- marital status (formal marriage vs de facto marriage)
- gender (male vs female)
- social class (upper class vs middle class vs lower class)
- occupational status (white-collar vs blue-collar)
- school education (state school vs private school)
- wealth (poor vs rich)
- spiritual belief (atheist vs believer).

Changes in categorical concepts are not described as 'more' or 'less' of the variable, but as 'one category' or 'another category'. You don't usually classify people as 'more female' or 'less female' but as either 'male' or 'female'.

In the above example, we cannot say that more or less of the independent concept 'relationship' leads to more or less 'marital satisfaction'. The independent concept does not vary in terms of 'more' or 'less'. It takes the form of either of its categories, 'formally married' or 'de facto'.

Diagram this hypothesis here:

3   If you read some of the literature on marital satisfaction you would have discovered that there are many factors in reported marital satisfaction. Some of these factors are:

- values shared
- emotional health of partners
- common backgrounds
- number of friends
- economic security
- length of the relationship
- security in the relationship.

One hypothesis that could be derived from these factors is this:

> Couples in formal marriages feel more secure in their relationships than de facto couples.

Diagram this hypothesis:

4 Derive another hypothesis from the above list of factors and write it out concisely.

As you can tell from doing these exercises, developing a hypothesis requires that you identify one concept that causes, affects or has an influence on another concept. The concept that does the 'causing' is called the *independent concept*. An independent concept 'causes', produces a change in, or acts upon something else. The concept that is acted upon, produced or 'caused' by the independent concept is called the *dependent concept*.

Writing a hypothesis requires that you identify an independent concept and a dependent concept. In the examples above, amount of study, parties attended and nutrition were independent concepts. These concepts were seen as 'causes' of changes in academic performance.

List the independent concepts in the exercises you have just done. For example:

Exercise 1: church involvement
Exercise 2: marital status
Exercise 3:
Exercise 4:

In terms of the diagram, the independent concept is the one from which the arrow is drawn.

The dependent concept is the thing that is caused, acted upon, or affected, the thing in which a change is produced by the independent concept. List the dependent concepts in the exercises you have just done. For example:

Exercise 1: de facto marriages
Exercise 2: marital satisfaction
Exercise 3:
Exercise 4:

In the pattern of diagramming introduced above, the dependent concept is the one to which the arrow is drawn:

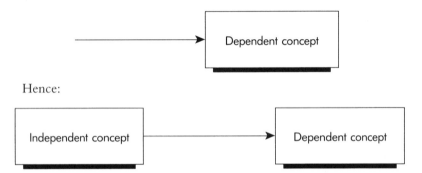

Hence:

In its usual form, a hypothesis states that something about the independent concept produces a change in the dependent concept.

Some of the confusion about independent and dependent concepts arises from the fact that it is possible for the same concept to take the *independent* role in one hypothesis and the *dependent* role in another. Just because a concept is independent in one case does not mean that it should always be treated as independent. For example, here are some concepts:

- academic performance
- nutritional adequacy of breakfast
- study
- party-going
- intention to go to university.

These concepts can be linked in a variety of ways. Many hypotheses can be derived from this list. We have seen that:

Which of the above concepts is the independent concept? Which is the dependent? We have also seen that:

Which of the above concepts is the independent concept? Which is the dependent?

But it also makes sense to derive the following hypothesis using two of the concepts in the above list:

The greater the academic performance of a high school student the more likely it is that the student will intend to go to university.

This hypothesis would be diagrammed as follows:

In this case, what had been a dependent concept (academic performance) in one hypothesis becomes an independent concept because going to university is dependent on academic performance, whereas, earlier, academic performance was dependent on study. Whether a concept is independent or dependent depends on your theory. Focusing and diagramming hypotheses helps to clarify theories.

The research objective

Not all research is best guided by a hypothesis. Some research, such as qualitative research (see chapter 10), is done to find out what is 'going on' in a situation. Sometimes it is not possible or desirable to specify the relationship between concepts before making observations. There are times when developing a *research objective* is a more desirable way to focus a research project. For example, if the general area of your study relates to child development or skill acquisition, you might use the following research objective to guide your research:

Objective: To observe a particular child, four years of age, for a specified period of time, in order to observe patterns of skill acquisition through play.

When the goal of the research is descriptive rather than explanatory, a statement of an objective can serve to guide the research. Consider this example:

Objective: To describe what factors the Wright family took into account in deciding whether to send their daughter to a state or a private high school.

The intent of this research is to describe what happened, not to explain what happened. At the end of the study the researcher will be able to specify the factors that emerged in this family discussion. Who raised which issues? Who responded and in what ways? These observations can lead the researcher to formulate a hypothesis that attempts to explain the family's actions, to be tested later.

A starting-point dealing with the policy issue of care for the elderly might prompt research that is primarily descriptive. When you want to describe what is 'going on', an objective will help to focus your efforts. Here are some examples of research objectives related to care for the elderly.

Objective: To determine the number and percentage of elderly people in a particular community who require special accommodation.

The goal of this study is to ascertain a community need. There are no influencing factors under study. There is no attempt to test the impact of anything or to ascertain whether special accommodation is needed.

Objective: To discover the existing policy on admission to homes for elderly people.
Objective: To discover the government's policy on funding for homes for elderly people.

As long as your aim is to describe what is, rather than to test explanations for what is, a research objective will be the preferred guide to your research. The next two chapters show how to convert a research objective into a statement that will be able to guide your research effectively, whether you adopt a qualitative or quantitative approach. Chapter 10 describes the way in which qualitative research is done.

Summary

The research process may be started from any point. Curiosity, claims of others, reading, problems—all these can begin the process. Once begun, the first step is to clarify the issues and to narrow your focus.

In order for your research to succeed, a clear statement of the problem or issue must guide it. The two most common forms of such statements are the hypothesis and the research objective. A hypothesis is developed to guide research intended to test an explanation. A research objective states the goal of a study which is intended to describe. Without a clear statement of the problem the research will be confused and ambiguous. It is impossible to satisfactorily proceed to the next stage of the research process without such a statement.

Questions for review

1   List six common starting-points for the research process.

2   What are the reasons for reviewing the literature on a particular subject?

3   Why is it essential to identify the issues or factors involved in a subject, topic or problem being considered for a research project?

4   Why is it necessary to select one issue from among the issues identified?

5   What is a hypothesis? Give an example. Diagram a hypothesis.

6   What is a negative relationship? Give an example. How is it diagrammed?

7   What is a positive relationship? Give an example. How is it diagrammed?

8   What is an independent concept? What is a dependent concept? Which of the following are independent concepts? Which are dependent concepts?

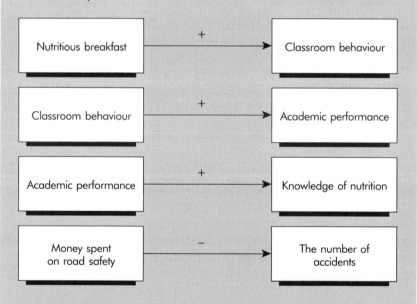

9   Write out fully each of the above diagrammed hypotheses.

10 Diagram the following:
- The greater the proportion of sweets in the diet, the greater the incidence of dental cavities in children.

- The introduction of a module on management theory will improve the quality of decision-making among students.
- The greater the age gap between parents and children, the greater will be the degree of difficulty in communication they experience.

11 What is a research objective? How is it different from a hypothesis? For what kinds of research is it appropriate?

Suggestions for further reading

Babbie, E. R. (2003), *The Practice of Social Research*, 10th edn, Wadsworth Publishing London, chapter 3.

Bessant, Judith and Rob Watts (2002), *Sociology Australia*, Allen & Unwin, St Leonards, NSW, chapter 3.

de Vaus, D. A. (2002), *Surveys in Social Research*, 5th edn, Allen & Unwin, St Leonards, NSW, chapter 3.

Giddens, Anthony (2001), *Sociology*, 4th edn, Polity Press, Cambridge, chapter 20.

Judd, C. M., E. R. Smith and L. H. Kidder (1991), *Research Methods in Social Relations*, Holt, Rinehart & Winston, Fort Worth, chapters 1–2.

Kumar, Ranjit (1999), *Research Methodology: A Step by Step Guide for Beginners*, Sage, London, chapters 3–4.

Wallace, W. (1971), *The Logic of Science in Sociology*, Aldine, Chicago, chapter 3.

Waters, Malcolm and Rodney Crook (1993), *Sociology One*, Longman Cheshire, Melbourne, chapters 1–3.

4

Selecting variables

CHAPTER OUTLINE

As you will recall from chapter 2, the act of doing research involves reducing conceptual problems to empirical questions, that is, questions about 'things' that can be measured, counted, recorded or in some way observed. Finding ways of measuring concepts demands creativity and skill. It is one of the more challenging aspects of doing research.

Concepts and variables

Concepts are categories into which ideas, impressions and observations of the world can be placed. So far, we have dealt with concepts such as academic performance, study, nutrition, and marital happiness. While concepts are critically important in the initial stages of research, they have limited use when difficult or impossible to measure. Some are elusive to define, mean different things to different people and lack definite boundaries. Often, concepts are not perceived by touch, sight, smell or hearing and direct measurements are not possible.

Take the concept 'happiness'. How could you define or describe the essential aspects of happiness? The problem is that an infinite number of experiences, observations and impressions are included in the concept. A simple definition that includes all your impressions of happiness is impossible to produce. This task becomes even more difficult to imagine when you attempt to account for other people's impressions of happiness. Finally, what are the boundaries of happiness? When does happiness become its opposite, unhappiness? Often we feel that we are neither happy nor unhappy. If we don't know, then there must be 'in-between' emotional states where we would be unsure of whether we were attempting to measure happiness or unhappiness.

It is clear that the concept of happiness has a wide range of meanings, is not readily measurable and is difficult to observe. How then can happiness be observed and measured in a way that is acceptable to you and most others? These same problems are encountered when trying to research most concepts.

Variables

If we are going to do empirical research that others can follow and evaluate, we have to make our abstract concepts observable and measurable. The conventional procedure for doing this is to replace abstract concepts with measurable concepts, referred to as 'variables'. What is a variable? A variable is a type of concept, one that varies in amount or quality. A variable is something that it is possible to have more or less of, or something that exists in different 'states' or 'categories'. The variables that interest us are those that vary not only in amount or kind but that are also measurable.

For example, the concept 'heat' can be measured by measuring the variable 'temperature'. To measure temperature, we read a thermometer and document the measurement it indicates. We generally take the measurement of temperature to be an indicator of the level of heat.

Someone might say that 'love' is a variable—you can have more or less of it and there are different kinds of love. However, love is not directly measurable. If we want to measure love we have to find suitable and measurable variables to use. Some might choose such measurable variables as the number of kisses received from their lover or spouse, the frequency and quality of flowers received, the number of hugs, or the failure to remember important dates such as birthdays and anniversaries. Although love itself is not directly measurable, we can use measurable variables to assess whether we are loved or not.

Specifically, the primary function of any variable is to enable measurement of changes in its corresponding abstract concept. When we pose a hypothesis, we argue that changes in one abstract concept occur as a result of changes in another. When we test a hypothesis we use variables to allow us to measure changes in the abstract concepts. To be measurable substitutes for abstract concepts, variables must have the following characteristics:

1   Variables must validly represent an abstract concept being studied. This will mean that changes in variables validly represent changes in abstract concepts. A valid variable for the concept 'academic performance' is 'final

grades' because most people would be confident that changes in final grades represent changes in academic performance. Generally, though, the concept of academic performance does not extend to 'batting average' or 'popularity rating', which would not in this case be valid variables for detecting changes in academic performance. This point is expanded later in this chapter, in the section 'The question of validity'.

2   Variables must have at least one range of 'possible states'. For example, a range of possible states for the variable 'final grade' is 'distinction', 'credit', 'pass' and 'fail'. (Another range is 0–100 per cent. Some educational institutions use the range 'A', 'B', 'C', etc.) As a variable has a range of states, then it can change and these changes can be taken to indicate change in the abstract concept represented by the variable. A positive change in a student's final grades (variable), from credit to distinction level, indicates a positive change in academic achievement (abstract concept).

3   Variables have 'states' that are observable and measurable. You can only detect changes in a variable if you can observe and measure it. For example, the variable 'final grades', which represents the abstract concept 'academic performance', can be observed and measured by checking students' reports or asking their teacher. If you cannot observe and measure a variable, then you cannot detect changes in the variable and you cannot detect changes in the abstract concept it represents. Say the abstract concept 'happiness' is given by the variable 'inner peace'. This would be unsatisfactory because you cannot observe or measure 'inner peace'. Consequently, it would be a useless variable for the concept 'happiness'.

The activity of finding measurable variables for concepts is called 'operationalisation'. An operational definition of a concept goes beyond a usual dictionary definition. It defines a concept in terms that can be measured, that is, it defines a concept in empirical terms.

The basic question that guides this activity is 'How can I measure that?' That is, what can I take as an indicator of what is going on? Let's continue our sample hypothesis. When we last left it, it looked like this:

This hypothesis says that two concepts, study and academic performance, are related in such a way that the more there is of one, study, the more there will be of the other, academic performance. The question we now face is, 'How shall we measure study and academic performance?' or 'What measurable, tangible, observable things can we take as indicators or variables of study and academic performance?'

Take academic performance first. We are so familiar with ways of measuring academic performance that we often forget the concept being measured. The measures with which we are most familiar include:

- final grades
- test results
- essay marks
- examiners' reports
- project assessments.

Academic performance is the abstract concept. Marks and test results are variables related to the concept of academic performance.

What about study? How shall we measure study? What variables can be taken as indicators of study? It is hard to measure such things as concentration, or the absorption of material. But we can measure the amount of time a student spends 'studying'. Hence, an operational definition of the concept 'study' might be:

- time spent in revision
- time spent practising.

It is now possible to state our hypothesis in two forms, in a conceptual form and in an operational form.

Conceptual form of the hypothesis

In its conceptual form, the hypothesis describes a relationship between the concepts 'study' and 'academic performance'. Study is the independent concept and academic performance is the dependent concept.

Operational form of the hypothesis

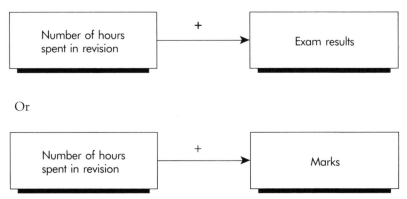

The operational form of the hypothesis asserts that there is a relationship between variables, that is the number of hours spent in revision and exam results or grades. Number of hours spent in revision is the independent variable and exam results, or marks, is the dependent variable.

Any hypothesis can be stated at both the conceptual (abstract or theoretical) level and at the operational (empirical or measurable) level. At the conceptual level, a hypothesis asserts a relationship between concepts and at the operational level it asserts a relationship between variables. We will practise deriving variables as appropriate measures of concepts, then we will discuss the problem of the relationship between concepts and variables.

Finding variables for concepts: hypotheses

There are no set ways or even useful guides for finding variables that are appropriate measures for concepts. This is an area for creativity and experimentation. Doing research involves a great deal of inventiveness and a willingness to think in new ways. You have to search for variables. Variables must be measurable and relate in some accepted way to the concept in question. Beyond those two rules, the task (or fun) of finding variables is up to you. Here is another conceptual hypothesis:

> Better nutritional status leads to better academic performance.

Diagrammed, the hypothesis looks like this:

If we are to test this hypothesis, we must find a variable that relates to nutrition and another that relates to academic performance. We already have some ideas about academic performance—test results, marks, examiners' reports, etc. What variables might give an indication of a student's nutritional status? What about:

- how many meals per week include vegetables?
- whether breakfast includes fruit?
- the percentage of recommended daily allowance of nutrients in foods eaten each day?

List others you can think of.

Taking one of the variables associated with nutrition and one of those associated with academic performance, restate the hypothesis in operational form.

Higher nutrition of meals leads to higher final grades.

Now in diagram form:

In this case, what is the independent variable and what is the dependent variable?

For further practice, take two other variables, one related to nutrition and another related to academic performance. Develop an operational hypothesis and write it out. Then diagram it.

Now let us try an entirely new hypothesis. Take the area of family life. We are concerned about the relationship between the abstract concepts 'family resources' and 'family happiness'. We may have the theoretical hypothesis:

The more resources available to a family, the happier that family will be.

Diagram this theoretical hypothesis:

Think of variables that might be useful indicators, or specific measures, of family resources—things such as:

■ family income
■ relatives
■ time
■ social status
■ quality of housing.

Now, what variables might be taken as indicators of family happiness? Happiness is one of those concepts that are not directly measurable. But we can get some indication. How? How about:

■ absence of divorce
■ presence of observable signs of affection—hugs, kisses
■ self-reported happiness
■ the result on a test of marital happiness?

Think of other indicators of family happiness. One operational hypothesis that can be derived from the above lists of variables is:

Greater family income leads to less divorce.

This could be diagrammed as follows:

Note that although the conceptual hypothesis asserts a positive relationship between two concepts, this operational hypothesis asserts a negative relationship between two variables. This is not a problem. Divorce is taken as a negative indicator of marital happiness. Here is another possible operational hypothesis:

The more time a family spends together, the more likely are members of the family to report that they are happy with the family.

This hypothesis would be diagrammed:

Gain some practice by deriving other operational hypotheses from the above lists of variables and diagram them.

Let us take a final example, this time with a categorical variable. Some family researchers believe that intimacy between parents and their infants is a very important factor in successful infant development. The independent concept in this example is 'parent–infant intimacy', and the dependent concept is 'infant development'.

A variable for 'parent–infant intimacy' could be 'feeding intimacy', a categorical variable with two states, 'breastfed' and 'bottlefed'. The first half of a diagram of an operational hypothesis, the part showing the independent variable, will look like this:

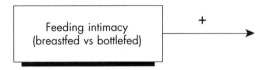

The problem now becomes selecting some measure of 'infant development'. Infant development is a very wide concept. To arrive at a suitable variable, let's consider some 'subconcepts' of infant development that might be affected by feeding preference:

■ infant growth
■ motor development
■ physical health
■ emotional health.

Add some of your own.

Let's take 'infant growth' as a substitute for infant development. The developed conceptual hypothesis would be:

Greater feeding intimacy leads to increased infant growth.

This would be diagrammed:

But this is still at the conceptual level. It is now necessary to think of variables that are indicators of infant growth. What variables might be associated with infant growth? There is weight accumulation. You can have lower or higher weight accumulation. 'Weight accumulation' is a variable. The operational hypothesis could now be phrased as follows:

Feeding intimacy influences infant weight accumulation.

This hypothesis would be diagrammed:

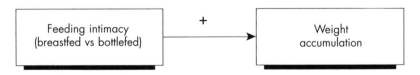

Alternatively, you might have preferred to use the subconcept 'physical health' instead of 'infant development'. In that case, the conceptual hypothesis would be stated:

Parent–infant intimacy influences a baby's physical health.

How can this hypothesis be operationalised? What variables can you think of that relate to physical health? Here are a few:

- absence of colic
- absence of infectious disease
- normal growth pattern
- appropriate development
- physician's report.

Add to this list.

To gain more practice in selecting variables, look through your notes, identify some issues, formulate conceptual hypotheses and then try to identify appropriate variables.

Finding variables for concepts: research objectives

When developing research to meet our objectives it is still necessary to clarify our concepts and to select variables appropriate to these concepts. For example, the research objective might be:

To learn about infant growth and development.

'Growth' and 'development' are the concepts. The question that needs to be answered is, 'What variables relate to growth and development?' Growth is fairly easy—weight, height, length of limbs are all variables that relate to growth. By observing changes in these variables we can measure growth.

What variables relate to development? We can now see that the above objective is still very broad. What kind of development—social, behavioural, psychological? For each of these and other kinds of development there are well-established variables to observe. Specific abilities, or patterns of behaviour, are taken as evidence of certain kinds of development.

Research objectives are used to guide research that seeks to *describe* rather than *explain* what is happening. While this means that there will not be independent and dependent concepts and variables, it is still necessary to operationalise the concepts in the research objective. Variables must be selected to serve as indicators for the concepts being studied.

An objective presented in the previous chapter was:

Objective: To discover the existing policy on admission to homes for elderly people.

'Policy' is a fairly general concept. How might admission policy vary from home to home? How do policies relate to:

- age
- health
- financial status
- family status?

All of these are variables related to the concept 'policy'. Put differently, they are aspects of admission policies of homes for the elderly, which can vary. By thinking through these issues before beginning your data collection, you ensure that the research is focused and clarified. Some background reading—reviewing the relevant literature—will help you identify variables that might be related to the concepts being studied.

Another example of a research objective may help to demonstrate further the idea that both hypotheses and research objectives deal with concepts.

Objective: To observe the classroom behaviour of school students.

What aspect of the concept 'classroom behaviour' is to be observed? What are some variables related to the classroom behaviour of students? Some of the following might be considered:

- attention span of each student
- noise level in classroom
- frequency of discipline
- attention span of the whole class
- frequency of disruptive behaviour
- length of time taken to settle down at beginning of lesson.

Before beginning an observational study it is necessary to decide what is to be observed. This involves selecting a few variables related to the concepts being studied.

The question of validity

The most critical consideration in choosing variables is 'validity'. When measured, does the variable adequately reflect our understanding of the concept? This is the issue of validity. We must question all the variables we use to provide indicators of our theoretical concepts. How good is each possible indicator? Does it adequately represent our concept? Is it not quite the same thing?

Many arguments arise over the issue of validity. Take the case of IQ testing. Are such tests valid indicators of intellectual ability? Or do they test something else? Take the issue of academic performance. Do exam results validly reflect academic performance? Or do they measure something else? Can the absence of disease be taken as an indicator of health, as one of our hypotheses suggested? Can the absence of divorce be taken as an indication that a family is happy? Were you satisfied with the variables suggested as measures of love—number of kisses or hugs, flowers, and anniversaries remembered?

Whenever we feel dissatisfied with the variables chosen to measure a concept we raise the issue of validity:

- Is a low noise level a valid indicator that a class is learning? Or is the class just well disciplined?
- Is the fact that a baby gains a great deal of weight quickly a valid indicator of its health, or does it simply indicate the kilojoule content of its diet?
- Is an expressed opinion a valid indicator of the way a person will act?
- Is church-going a valid indicator of depth of spirituality? Or is it an indicator of conformity? Or of something else?

These are examples of issues regarding the validity of chosen variables. Such issues are inevitable because the act of choosing variables involves finding a concrete expression of abstract (i.e. conceptual) ideas. Not everyone will agree with your choice of variables. Some people will question your research based upon your variable choices.

Another problem raised by questions of validity is that concepts are often multidimensional and impossible to represent with a single variable. For such concepts, a single variable has to be chosen on the basis of its being the 'least inadequate' option. For example, 'social class' is a concept with a range of dimensions—income, wealth, education, ownership/control of the factors of production, gender, etc. When choosing a variable for 'social class' you can have only one of these factors. Obviously any single factor is inadequate as a variable. Therefore, you have to choose the variable that is the 'least inadequate'. The inadequacy of your chosen variable is a limitation of your research. The only thing that can be done about it is to describe the inadequacies of your chosen variable in your research report.

Usually, you cannot find the 'perfect' variable for a given concept. There are no perfect variables. Variable selection is a matter of finding an adequate variable and being honest about its shortcomings.

An overview of the research process

What have we learnt so far? It is important that we keep the various threads of development together.

When we encounter a problem, or a question about which we want to do some research, we first try to express that concern in a research objective or a hypothesis. This activity focuses our attention. It clarifies our interest. When stated as a hypothesis, our focal question or statement of concern asserts a relationship between two or more concepts. When stated as a research objective, our focal question defines, using concepts, our area of interest. We examined such sample hypotheses as:

More study leads to better academic performance.
Better nutrition leads to better academic performance.
Greater family wealth leads to greater family happiness.

These hypotheses are all stated at the conceptual level. Each hypothesis states a relationship between ideas.

By now we can see that regardless of whether our research is guided and focused by a hypothesis or by a research objective, we select variables as observable indicators for the concepts we are studying. One of the more challenging and creative tasks in the research process is the discipline of finding measurable, observable, sensory variables that relate to the concepts that concern us. The following may help to clarify the steps in the research process we have learnt so far:

Step 1
Select, narrow and focus the problem to be studied.
State the problem as either a hypothesis or research objective.
Step 2
Select variables that relate to the concepts in the hypothesis or research objective.

As we go along we will fill in the additional steps that have to be taken. Figure 4.1 lays out some of the examples we have developed.

Figure 4.1 Concepts and their related variables

Concept	Variables related to concept
Academic performance	Marks Exam results Essay evaluation Examiner's reports
Nutritional adequacy	What is eaten for breakfast Contents of lunch
Growth	Height Weight Length of limbs
Classroom behaviour	Attention span Degree of disruption

For each concept we have identified several related variables. For each idea we have suggested two or more measurable, observable indicators.

If a variable relates appropriately to the concept being studied it is said to be a valid variable. The problem of validity deals with the success of our efforts to find measurable indicators of our theoretical concepts. One of the limitations usually discussed in research reports is the validity of the variables selected. How valid is this variable as an indicator of that concept? For example, how valid are test results as indicators of intelligence? How valid are changes in height and weight as indicators of growth, or the contents of someone's lunch as an indicator of the nutritional adequacy of their diet?

Questions for review

1   What is a concept? Give three examples.

2   What is a hypothesis?

3   What is a variable?

4   Why are variables selected?

5   Figure 4.2 lists a number of concepts. For each one think of at least two variables.

Figure 4.2 Finding variables for concepts

Concept	Related variables
Health	
Marital happiness	
Nutritional adequacy	
Maturity	
Socio-emotional development	

6   What is the difference between a hypothesis and a research objective? Why must variables be selected for both?

7   To what does the question of validity refer?

8   What is an operational definition? State the following hypothesis in an operational form:

The better a student's nutritional status, the better will be that student's classroom behaviour.

Suggestions for further reading

de Vaus, D. A. (2002), *Surveys in Social Research*, 5th edn, Allen & Unwin, St Leonards, NSW, chapter 3.

Giddens, Anthony (2001), *Sociology*, 4th edn, Polity Press, Cambridge, chapter 20.

Judd, C. M., E. R. Smith and L. H. Kidder (1991), *Research Methods in Social Relations*, Holt, Rinehart & Winston, Fort Worth, chapter 2.

Juredini, Ray and Marilyn Poole (2003), *Sociology: Australian Connections*, Allen & Unwin, St Leonards, NSW, chapter 12.

Kumar, Ranjit (1999), *Research Methodology: A Step by Step Guide for Beginners*, Sage, London, chapter 5.

Wallace, W. (1971), *The Logic of Science in Sociology*, Aldine, Chicago, chapter 3.

Finding a variable's measurements

CHAPTER OUTLINE

The general task of empirical research is to 'observe' for changes in variables. When testing hypotheses, we observe for changes in at least two variables, to see if they change together in the manner we predict. When pursuing research objectives, we focus our attention on certain variables, observing either how they appear or how they change.

So how do we know when variables have or have not changed? We 'measure' variables in different situations, such as two points in time. If the measurements are different then we recognise that a change has occurred. If the measurements produce the same results, then we recognise that no change has occurred. But how do we 'measure variables'? This is the main subject of this chapter.

The logic of measurement

The logic of measurement is something we take for granted. For instance, we frame many of our everyday perceptions in standard systems of measurement—thinking of distances in kilometres, the outdoor temperature in degrees Celsius and the cost of petrol in cents per litre. Also, we constantly use measuring instruments such as watches, speedometers, thermometers, rulers and gas meters. Generally, we don't question the validity of these measuring systems and instruments—we tend to take their validity for granted.

In a research situation, where we set out to measure variables, we need to be more conscious of the logic of measurement. In deciding how variables should be measured, we face three major issues that require careful consideration:

1   What is it that varies in the variable?
2   By what instrument are we going to measure the way(s) the variable varies?
3   In what units are we going to report our measurements of this variation?

Figure 5.1 uses the example of physical growth to show the relationship between concept, variable, measuring instrument and units of measurement. This relationship is basic to all empirical research. To measure a variable, we need both a measuring instrument and units of measure in which to report variations in measures taken of the variable.

Figure 5.1 Measurement: the example of physical growth

Concept	Variable	Measuring instrument	Units of measurement
Physical growth	Length	Metre stick Ruler Tape measure	Metres, centimetres
	Weight	Scales	Kilograms, grams

Figure 5.2 clearly shows the order in which the problems facing you, as a researcher, should be handled. First, clarify the problem by defining the concepts to be studied. Second, identify variables associated with each concept.

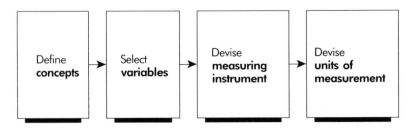

Figure 5.2 The logical order of issues to be decided in measurement

Select one or two variables for each concept. Third, for each variable, devise or select a measuring instrument. Fourth, select or devise units of measurement.

Some additional examples may help to clarify the logical flow of the issues related to measurement. As you look at the examples in Figure 5.3 try to think of other ways of measuring each variable, or of other units of measurement.

Figure 5.3 Examples of the logical order of issues to be decided in measurement

Concept	Variable	Measuring instrument	Units of measurement
Physical growth ⟶	Height ⟶	Ruler ⟶	Centimetres
Physical growth ⟶	Weight ⟶	Scales ⟶	Grams
Heat ⟶	Temperature ⟶	Thermometer ⟶	Degrees Celsius
Fever ⟶	Temperature ⟶	Thermometer ⟶	Degrees Celsius
Vehicle performance ⟶	Speed ⟶	Speedometer ⟶	Kilometres per hour
Drink-driving ⟶	Level of alcohol in blood ⟶	Breathalyser ⟶	Percentage by volume of alcohol in the blood
Tyre performance ⟶	Pressure ⟶	Pressure gauge ⟶	Kilopascals

Variable measurement in the social and behavioural sciences

For most variables studied in the 'natural sciences' (physics, chemistry and biology), there are generally accepted units of measurement and measuring instruments. Length is measured in metres, volume of sound in decibels, time in seconds and the strength of an electric current in amps. Clocks are standard instruments for measuring time, speedometers commonly measure speed and so on. This is because natural scientists have established some agreement on the nature of many of their common variables, like velocity, current, salinity, etc. Since they generally agree on *what* they are measuring, they have general agreement on *how* variables are to be measured.

Agreeing on what is to be measured makes agreement on how to measure easier. For example, if you and your friends generally agree that the variable 'height' is the physical distance from the floor to the top of a standing person's head, then agreeing on how to measure 'height' is not so difficult, because at least there is general agreement on what has to be measured to obtain a value for 'height'.

In the social and behavioural sciences, however, researchers do not enjoy the same levels of agreement about the nature of common variables such as class, status and poverty. Consequently, they have not reached general agreement on how common variables ought to be measured.

For example, any two social researchers will probably agree that there is such a variable as 'standard of education'. However, many would disagree about the nature of this variable. One researcher might think of 'standard of education' in terms of a scale of the highest level of formal education a person has completed (none/primary/secondary/tertiary). Another might think of it in terms of the number of years in full-time education. Different ideas about the nature of the variable would lead different researchers to adopt different measures because they would have different notions about *what* they were measuring.

Life as a researcher would be simpler, although perhaps less interesting, if there were generally accepted and standard ways of measuring the following common social and behavioural variables:

- social class
- academic performance
- political preference
- quality of teaching
- marital satisfaction
- sexuality
- ethnicity
- motivation
- race
- racial tension
- status
- social integration.

Given this situation, researchers need to take great care when devising their own measures for variables. This process is one of the challenging aspects of doing research in the social and behavioural sciences.

The importance of measuring variables in the social and behavioural sciences

The practice of adopting measures for variables strengthens several areas of the research process. First, it focuses data collection. Most variables are vague and might be measured by a large number of empirical phenomena. Marital satisfaction might be measured by frequency of sexual activity each month, average amount of time spent together, number of incidents of infidelity, etc. Given the confusion that can occur due to so many choices, researchers need to clarify variable measures for their own benefit. Researchers must limit their choices and focus their data collection on those choices. If they don't, they lack direction in their data collection and have less chance of carrying it out coherently.

Second, since data collection becomes focused, it can also become more streamlined and efficient. Data-collection devices such as interview schedules and tally sheets can be designed so that the data is collected clearly and is easily organised for analysis.

Third, selection of measures allows for disciplined and consistent observation of variables in different situations and therefore allows for disciplined and consistent observation of changes in variables. If you apply the same measure of the variable 'unemployment', such as the official national unemployment rate, in two consecutive years, you can compare the measurements and ascertain if 'unemployment' has changed. If you take different measures of unemployment for two consecutive years, for example the official national rate in the first year and one of the unofficial rates in the second, you could not compare those measurements to ascertain if unemployment had changed.

Fourth, variable measurements are a context in which data analysis and findings can be expressed clearly.

A report on the findings of a study into unemployment that has no consistent measure for unemployment could read: 'Given what they observed in welfare offices, job agencies and the newspapers, the researchers judge that the level of unemployment has increased significantly over the past two years.' This statement gives little indication of how the researchers analysed the data or how the finding was reached. It is vague because it lacks a rigorous context.

Alternatively, the report might say, 'The national level of unemployment increased significantly during the period investigated. At the beginning of year 1, the official national unemployment rate was 8.2 per cent. Subsequently the rate increased by an average of 0.1 per cent every 3 months for the next 2 years. By the end of year 3, the official unemployment rate had increased to 9 per cent.' These findings are expressed in a context that readers should be able to understand, that is, the context of the official unemployment rate, which is the measure for unemployment. Readers have a clear rigorous context in which to consider the researchers' analysis and findings.

Measuring variables through data collection

Once a measure for a variable has been identified, data collection for the measure can be organised and conducted. The collection of such data is the process of variable 'measurement'. Imagine you have decided to research the variable 'patriotism' among male and female adults in your street. You decide that the measure of patriotism for each gender group will be the 'percentage of males/females who can sing the national anthem'. When you collect data on this measure, you are taking measurements of the variable 'patriotism' among males and females. Therefore, such directed data collection is variable measurement. From this point, the term 'data collection' will be used to signify 'variable measurement'.

There are three basic data-collection techniques that researchers use for measuring variables. The first is 'observation', where researchers observe what is 'going on' and record what they observe. The second technique is interviewing, where researchers ask people questions and record the responses. The third technique is examining records and documents. Each technique provides quantitative data for variables, that is, data that can be counted or measured.

As described above, the measurement of variables has two major steps, which occur in the following order:

1 choosing an appropriate measuring instrument
2 choosing units of measurement.

In the social and behavioural sciences, this procedure is often less rigid. After selecting a variable, social and behavioural scientists often develop their measuring instruments and units while they interact with their subjects. This process can be seen in the following descriptions of data-collection techniques.

Using observation to measure variables

To conduct 'observation' is simply to 'watch what happens'. However, all research observation is guided by a research question. Researchers do not just go and 'have a look' at their subjects—they look for something in particular that is stated or alluded to in their research hypothesis or objective. More importantly, what the researcher is looking for is best determined before the observation commences. Let's examine the requirements of a proper observational study, where the measure of the variable has been decided before data collection commences.

First of all, decide what to observe and state what it is. This is necessary because, in practice, we all tend to get distracted by things that have some personal interest. The following experiment should demonstrate this.

Take a look
This exercise is best done with a group. It can be fun for three or more people. Go with the group to some place: a milk bar, a classroom, a playground, a street, an intersection, a footy match—almost any place will do. Let everyone look at the scene selected for two minutes. This should be done quietly, with no sharing of views. Then ask each person to write down everything they observed. After each person has finished writing, share your observations. Then ask:

■ What did you find?
■ Was there much similarity in what was seen?
■ Were there many differences in what was seen?

The results of your exercise will probably show that different observers focused their attention on different things. If observation is not directed by the hypothesis or research objective, then we are likely to become distracted and gather irrelevant data. Therefore we need to discipline ourselves, and any other researchers we are working with, to observe only those 'things' that are relevant to the hypothesis. We do this by identifying the focus of our observations before we begin observing.

Next is an example of an observational study where the observation is directed by the research hypothesis. You are assigned the task of studying the behaviour of car drivers in the pre-Christmas period. As a good researcher, you have decided to focus on the concept of 'illegal driver behaviour' to keep the study manageable. Further, you have decided to study this concept at a busy city intersection for the weeks of December leading up to Christmas Day. Your research objective is clearly stated as follows:

To observe 'illegal driver behaviour' at one city intersection over a four-week period.

You have decided to use 'traffic light infringements' as the measurable variable to indicate changes in illegal driver behaviour. Hence, the operationalised restatement of your research objective would be:

To observe 'traffic light infringements' at one city intersection over a four-week period.

You would not just occasionally look at the traffic and guess if there were more or fewer drivers 'running the lights'. Rather, you would observe the intersection at specified times and ask 'How many motorists are driving through red lights?' The measure of your variable would be 'the number of motorists who drive through red lights at specified times'.

You might observe the intersection each Thursday during December (assume that 1 December is a Thursday). Each observation session takes place during the peak traffic period, 4 pm to 7 pm. You could record the data for each observation session on a data-collection sheet such as that shown in Figure 5.4.

Figure 5.4   Data-collection sheet

Illegal driver behaviour — data-collection sheet

Date: 1 December   **Time:** 4 pm–7 pm

Traffic light infringements (place a tick for each observation):

✓✓✓✓✓✓✓✓✓✓

Daily total: 10

Next, you would place the totals for each observation session on a data-summarisation form, which might look like Figure 5.5.

Figure 5.5   Data-summarisation form

Weekly observation	Date	Total traffic light infringements
1	1 December	10
2	8 December	16
3	15 December	22
4	22 December	30

This summarisation form provides a systematic record of observations. It shows a steady increase in traffic light infringements from week to week, which would support the hypothesis that drivers become increasingly reckless as Christmas Day approaches. From the table, you can construct graphs, charts, tables or other presentations of your data.

If you studied more than one intersection, you would have a separate summarisation form for each. You would also keep a different set of weekly tally sheets for each intersection. It would be essential to record data separately for each intersection in order to make comparisons later.

From the above example, you can see that to prepare for data collection you need to:

1 select concepts
2 select variables
3 select a means for measuring those variables
4 design a means for recording the measurements you will make.

If all this is done before you begin to collect data, then data collection and analysis will proceed more smoothly and easily. Failing to measure and record your data properly will jeopardise the rest of the research process. Think back over the above example. Ask yourself the following questions:

■ What concept was studied?
■ What variable was selected?
■ How was the variable measured?
■ In what unit of measurement was variation in the variable reported?
■ What data-recording devices were developed?

The concept was 'illegal driver behaviour'.

The variable was 'traffic light infringements'.

The variable was measured by observing traffic at a given intersection, at a given time, and by noting the total number of drivers who had driven through the intersection when the red light was showing.

The unit of measurement was 'traffic light infringements'.

Two recording devices were developed. The first was a 'data-collection sheet' on which daily traffic light infringements were recorded and later totalled. The second was a 'data-summarisation sheet' on which the total observed infringements at every observation session were recorded so that comparisons for each week could be made.

The research process has a set of steps. The first two steps—defining concepts and selecting variables—must be done in the order shown in Figure 5.2. However, in the social and behavioural sciences, the fourth step of the process—devising units of measurement—often occurs while data is being collected. This is demonstrated in the next example.

You may hear a teacher make the following statement about the students at their school:

Boys behave better in the classroom than girls.

You decide to research this claim. The concepts of the hypothesis are 'gender' (independent) and 'classroom behaviour' (dependent). The independent variable can remain as 'gender'. The dependent variable can be 'disruptive behaviour'. 'Gender' is easy to measure; our problem will be to find measures for 'disruptive behaviour'.

This is a difficult variable to measure because there are many types of disruptive behaviour, which occur spontaneously, and we cannot know for certain which ones will occur when we conduct our observation. Therefore, deciding on a single measure before entering the class could be a waste of time.

A possible approach would be to devise a checklist of disruptive behaviours before observing the class. The total occurrences of all such behaviours would be the measure for this variable. Data could be collected separately for each gender group. Each time any such behaviour is observed in a class, we would place a tick after the behaviour in the appropriate column, 'boy' or 'girl'. If girls exhibited more total disruptive behaviours than boys, the hypothesis would be supported by the data collected. Our completed observation checklist might look like that shown in Figure 5.6.

The data, which is now organised to clearly represent measurements of the variables, indicates that in this particular class our measurement for disruptive behaviour was greater for girls than for boys. The hypothesis that 'boys behave better in the classroom than girls' is supported by measurements of the variables.

As can be seen from Figure 5.6, an observation checklist focuses observation of the indicators of change in the variable and records these observations as data, rendering them 'countable'.

The results make it possible to move from an impression to facts when describing observations. Instead of saying 'It was my impression that the girls

Figure 5.6 Observation checklist for classroom behaviour

Class: 10A	Date: 13/4/2004
Observer:	Reece Ercher
School:	Australia High
Teacher:	G. Roo
Subject:	Social Etiquette

Behaviour	Boy	Girl
1 Pokes neighbour	1	0
2 Talks out of turn	1	3
3 Whispers	0	6
4 Interrupts	5	0
5 Gets out of desk	2	3
6 Dozes	1	0
7 Throws something	2	2
8 Teases	1	3
9 etc.	etc.	etc.
10 etc.	etc.	etc.
Total disruptive behaviour in this classroom	24	32

were more disruptive in class than the boys', you would be able to say, 'The girls were observed to engage in a greater number of disruptive acts than the boys.'

To recap: observation is the most basic data-collection technique available to researchers. The first difference between casual observation and scientific observation is that scientific observation is guided by a clearly stated question. The second difference is that researchers systematically measure and record their observations in ways that make the phenomenon being studied countable. Instead of impressions, researchers record numerical data:

Not: I think that drivers are breaking the rules more often in the month before Christmas.

But: In observations conducted at a certain intersection between 4 pm and 7 pm on each Thursday of December, the number of motorists who drove through red light signals increased from 10 to 30.

Not: It is my impression that boys are better behaved in the classroom.

But: In one-hour observations conducted in each of six classrooms
at such-and-such school, girls were found to exhibit an average
of 16 disruptive acts per hour while boys exhibited 12 such acts.

Thus, one way of measuring a variable is by systematic observation.

Some further examples of research using systematic observation to measure a variable may help to develop your skills in observation. Suppose you
were interested in the area of sex role differences. Your background reading in
this area has indicated that the opinions of women are frequently given less
weight, ignored or ridiculed by men. Moreover, you suspect that this occurs
frequently in discussions involving family members. You decide to observe a
family interacting in order to test the hypothesis that:

The evaluation of contributions to a conversation within a family will
be affected by the gender of the contributor.

This can be diagrammed:

Gender is a categorical variable. A person is either 'male' or 'female'. The
dependent variable poses a greater challenge. But you, the researcher, have
decided to focus on the evaluation of opinions expressed in a family context.
You will explore the variable by asking the following questions while observing a family conversation:

- Is the opinion ignored?
- Is the opinion discussed further?
- Is the opinion ridiculed or scorned?
- Is the opinion discounted?
- Is the person expressing the opinion interrupted?
- Is the person expressing the opinion ignored?

This is a list of indicators of a negative evaluation. You will measure each
during the family conversation.

How can you conduct the study? Assume that you have received a family's
permission to record its meal-time conversation.

The Sloan family consists of father, mother and two children: John, who is
18, and Helen, who is 16. Once you have the tape of their conversation, you
and perhaps others can observe what was going on and fill out an observation
checklist (such as Figure 5.7) for each person in the conversation.

Figure 5.7 Observation checklist for analysing a conversation

Person: Helen

Type of conversation: Meal time   Fate of opinion

	Location on tape	Opinion	Rejected	Ridiculed	Ignored	Interrupted	Discussed	Praised	Adopted
1	137	re: Weather	✓						
2	236	re: Football match		✓					
3	etc.	etc.							

The question is, 'What happens to each member's contribution to the conversation?' On the checklist, note where on the tape the contribution began (using the counter on the tape recorder). Note the speaker. Then note what happened to the opinion.

By using a tape recording you can go back over the event and check it. You can also have other people observe the event and compare assessments. For example, let us assume that you recorded a family meal-time conversation. Part of the conversation might have gone:

Helen   (Trying to get a word in) I've got a problem.
John   You always have problems. (He continues speaking about Saturday's football match.)

In this instance Helen's comment was ignored. The conversation continues:

Helen   Look, I've got to talk to you about…
Father Be quiet and let John finish.

Here Helen is interrupted and stopped by her father. If this pattern continued throughout the conversation, there would be some evidence to suggest that male members of the family did not take Helen seriously.

Once you have filled out a checklist for each person in the conversation you can compare the fate of each member's contributions. You can compare parents with children, males with females, mother with father and son with daughter. By comparing the number of negative fates (being ignored, discounted, ridiculed or interrupted) with the number of positive fates (discussed further, praised, adopted, taken seriously) it is possible to assess differences in the variable 'evaluation of contributions to a conversation'.

Thus, one way to measure a variable is by systematic observation. The following questions should be answered in order to ensure that the proposed observation will yield useful results.

A checklist for research involving observation

1 Have you clarified and narrowed your hypothesis or research objective? What are the key concepts?
2 What variables are to be studied?
3 How is each variable to be measured?
4 Have you devised an observation checklist, or some other means of systematically recording your observations?
5 Have you practised using your checklist?
6 In what units will the results be reported?

If you can answer these questions, you are probably ready to conduct your observations. You are not ready until you can do so.

Using interview schedules and questionnaires to measure variables

The second common data-gathering technique involves asking people questions, that is, interviewing. In an interview, the researcher asks the respondent (the person being questioned) questions in a face-to-face situation or over the telephone using an 'interview schedule'. A 'questionnaire' is used when the respondent reads and answers the questions separately from the interviewer. Interview schedules and questionnaires measure variables by gathering answers to questions.

Interview schedules and questionnaires must collect data, which are measurements of variables. This is extremely important. Each question must be relevant to one of the variables you are studying. These techniques are not 'fishing' expeditions, in which all sorts of 'interesting' questions are asked.

There are two practical issues concerning the relevance of interview questions. First, remember that you are selecting questions for the purpose of measuring variables, not to satisfy simple curiosity. Resist the temptation to include a question just to satisfy curiosity. Such questions do not generate useful data and often confuse respondents.

The second issue concerns your planning and preparation. Never attempt to compensate for inadequate preparation by including questions that have only potential relevance to your variables. You must be honest with yourself about this. Before including a question, always ask yourself, 'What do I plan to do with the data collected with this question? Which variable am I measuring?' If you cannot answer, then your preparation is inadequate and even if you get reliable data you will have no framework for data analysis. You will not be able to articulate *what* you have measured and your analysis will be very weak. If you realise that your preparation is inadequate, repeat the steps of the research process and ask yourself the above questions again.

When consideration is given to what must be asked to measure the variables in a study, the choice of questions becomes straightforward and the number of questions can be kept to an acceptable limit. It is hardly necessary to say that a short questionnaire is easier to answer and analyse than a long one. Identify which questions must be asked in order to measure a variable adequately, and discard the rest.

It is important to realise that most hypotheses and research objectives can be researched using more than one technique of data gathering. For example, the observational study of car-driver behaviour discussed earlier could have been done using interview techniques. The same data-recording form would be used, but in each week the interviewer would visit or telephone the relevant police station and ask 'How many traffic light infringements were recorded by the cameras this week at "X" intersection?'

Take another example. Remember this hypothesis:

More study leads to greater academic performance.

One of the operational forms of this hypothesis developed in chapter 4 was:

More revision leads to more satisfactory exam results.

This hypothesis was diagrammed as follows:

You have been assigned to do some research related to this hypothesis. How are you going to measure the variables? The problem is straightforward in this case. You can count hours of revision easily and examination results can be recorded. You need to have a record, for each student involved, of only two things—the number of hours they spent revising and their examination marks.

Assume that your history tutorial group is to have a one-hour examination in a month's time. You could ask each student to keep a record of the time spent studying history. Then get each student's examination marks. One way of doing this would be to give each student a mini-questionnaire such as the one in Figure 5.8.

Figure 5.8 Questionnaire on time spent in revision

Student name (or identification number*): 2155260

I would be most grateful if you could help me with my research project. It will not take much time.

We are to have an examination on 8 May. During the month between now and then please keep an account of the time you spend in revising.

	hrs	mins		hrs	mins
April	_____		April	_____	
8	1 ___10 ___		24	_____	
9	1 ___10 ___		25	_____	
10	etc. _____		26	_____	
11	_____		27	_____	
12	_____		28	_____	
13	_____		29	_____	
14	_____		30	_____	
15	_____		May	_____	
16	_____		1	_____	
17	_____		2	_____	
18	_____		3	_____	
19	_____		4	_____	
20	_____		5	_____	
21	_____		6	_____	
22	_____		7	_____	
23	_____				

Total time spent in revision: 45 hrs 30 minutes

After the examination place your result in this blank.

Examination result: 49%

Return the questionnaire to me.

Thank you.

Harry Doolittle

History 101

Australian University

---

* Researchers sometimes assign numbers to people or to groups to preserve anonymity or to organise their data when names are not important.

This questionnaire measures the variable 'hours spent in revision' by asking each student to keep a record. It assumes that students will be honest in reporting both the time spent revising and marks. You could check with the tutor to ensure that the marks were honestly reported. One problem of using questionnaires is that you depend on the honesty of the respondents.

Once you have collected all the questionnaires, create a form to summarise your data. In this case you have data on two variables, 'time spent in revision' and 'examination result', for each student. Using a form like the one in Figure 5.9 may be useful to summarise and organise your data. It will be particularly helpful when it is time to analyse your data. The data-summarisation form preserves all the data required by this study for later analysis.

Figure 5.9 A suggested data-summarisation form

Student name or number	Hours spent in revision	Examination result (%)
2155	45.5	49
2156	47.5	51
2157	48	53
etc.	etc.	etc.

Here are some helpful hints for writing questionnaires that ask the respondent questions of fact rather than questions about opinions or attitudes:

1 Clarify exactly what it is you want to know. It is also important to ask yourself why you are asking the question. How does this question relate to your hypothesis and your variables?

2 Be direct and simple when asking questions. For example, if you wished to ask some people about the number of vacations they had taken in the last two years, you could design your question in this very indirect and complex way:

> In the last 24 months, on how many occasions have you taken a leave of absence from your usual activities in your home and your place of work to take up temporary residence in another locality for the purposes of recreational activities, relief of stress and a conscious perception of a change in environment?

This question is very comprehensive but the basic theme of its inquiry is not directly stated or easy to understand. A simple, direct question would be much more likely to get a clear answer. For example:

> In the last two years, how many times have you taken a vacation away from your home and paid job?

3 In most research, some questions are asked in order to obtain background information. They are often referred to as 'face-sheet' questions because they often appear on the front pages of questionnaires. These questions

request information about such things as the respondent's age, sex, religion, marital status, education, income and number of children. Only ask those that are directly related to your project.

4 Make sure that each question is clear and elicits a simple response of fact and not one of evaluation as well. Rather than asking a mother how she feels about the amount of television her child watches, a question such as 'How many hours did your child spend watching television last night?' will provide a clear and simple factual answer.

5 Address questions to the right person. If you wish to know how many hours a worker spends doing their job while in their workplace, don't ask their employer or their workmates, who might not know. Ask the worker—the person you are researching.

6 If you are asking for a response about a quantity of something, discourage the respondent from giving vague, general answers such as 'often', 'a great deal', 'quite a lot'. Give a clear indication that the response should be in terms of your choice of variable measurement. For example:

How much time per week do you spend watching television?
(in hours)_____
How often do you watch the news? (Circle your answer.)
once a day   three times per week   once a week   never

7 Be sure that respondents are willing to answer your questions. Questions that are deeply personal, offensively worded or ask respondents to give secrets or unpleasant information are not likely to be answered. For example, respondents are often uncomfortable about revealing their income.

8 Avoid informal terms, informal titles and abbreviations. The question 'Who would you vote for at the next election, the ALP or the conservative parties?' contains a set of initials, 'ALP', and an informal title, 'the conservative parties'. Don't assume that respondents are familiar with such expressions. Formal terms, formal titles and unabbreviated names are more likely to be familiar to respondents.

9 Avoid asking questions that raise more than one issue. Take the question, 'Should there be an increase in income tax and, if so, should the increase in tax revenue be spent on arts projects?' This question raises two issues: 'Should there be an increase in income tax?' and 'Should an increase in revenue be spent on arts projects?' If you wish to research two issues, then ask two separate questions and you will collect clearer information about respondents' positions on each issue.

10 Try not to use colourful or emotional language in writing questions. Here is an example:

Do you agree that white sugar is 'white death'? Yes/No

This is an emotionally written question and should be stated in a more balanced way that does not attempt to motivate a 'No' response. For example:

Sugar is bad for health. Do you agree/disagree? ____

11 Do not word questions in such a way that the respondent is placed in an impossible situation—for example, 'Have you stopped beating your wife?' or 'When did you stop cheating in your exams?'

12 Examine your questions for assumptions that may be wrong. If you asked a group of school children 'What does your father do for a living?', you would be making the assumption that each child in the group knows a person whom they think of as their father. Of course, many children grow up without knowing such a person and others have experienced the death of their father. For them, the question would be inappropriate or hurtful.

13 It is always a good idea to trial your questionnaire or interview schedule. Conduct a trial with people who are not in your sample but are like the people you plan to study. If respondents give you the wrong information or cannot answer or understand your questions, then your questions and interviewing method need refining. Ask for their comments on the relevance and coherence of each question. This will help to ensure that your questionnaire gives you the information you want. When you do the real survey, the number of questionnaires containing useless responses will be reduced.

Attitudes

The questions examined to this point have been designed to gather facts from the respondent. How much does your baby weigh today? How long have you studied? What was your result on the history examination? Questionnaires and interviews are often also used to assess the respondent's attitudes, values, beliefs or opinions. The construction of a questionnaire to measure opinions, attitudes, beliefs and values is much more complex than simply asking questions of fact. Consider the following hypothesis:

Males who have gone to single-sex schools are more sexist in their attitudes than males who have attended coeducational schools.

The concepts involved in this hypothesis are:
- social development environment of school
- sexism.

Note that the first concept emphasises the social development aspect of the schooling situation. Students experience social development 'only among boys' or 'among boys and girls'. This is what the researchers were thinking about when they constructed the hypothesis. The concept does not emphasise the enrolment policy of the school attended, which is the most obvious essential difference between 'all boys' and 'coed' schools. The essential difference considered by the researchers was 'social environment'. The variables are:

■ independent variable—school social environment (single-sex vs co-educational)
■ dependent variable—sexist attitudes.

The independent variable is a categorical variable and is easy to measure. Respondents' school social environment is either single-sex or coeducational. Those who have experienced both contexts can either be put in a third category (mixed) or eliminated from the study.

One of the first questions to be included in an interview schedule or a questionnaire designed to measure this variable would be:

Have the schools you have attended from the time you began school until now been (tick one):
____ a   coeducational
____ b   single-sex
____ c   both (coeducational and single-sex schools)?

Now comes the more difficult part. How do you propose to measure the dependent variable—sexist attitudes? This is a very complex variable. The abstract concept 'sexism' refers to the idea that one sex is in some way inferior or superior to the other. You could not measure this variable by asking the direct, simple question 'Are you sexist?' This approach would only measure the respondent's self-perception. What is required is a series of questions or statements (called 'scales') designed to evoke reactions from the respondents that, taken together, provide an indication of the respondent's sexist attitudes. While there are other kinds of scales, the attitude scale is one of the easiest to construct and analyse.

In this case the respondent is presented with a series of short statements and is asked to agree or disagree with each statement. The questionnaire shown in Figure 5.10 is an example.

Why is this called an attitude scale? It is a device to measure variation in an attitude. Its values range between two points and all respondents can be placed on that scale according to their responses to the questionnaire. It is also called a Likert scale, after the person who invented it. In a Likert scale the respondent is asked to indicate agreement or disagreement with a series of short statements on a given (usually five-point) range of responses.

How does a Likert scale work? The responses are turned into a numerical scale by assigning numerical values to each response and summing up the results. The scale can be made to run from a low number (indicating a low degree of sexism) to a high number (indicating a high degree of sexism) by assigning low numerical values to those responses indicating non-sexist responses and high values to sexist responses. In Figure 5.10, agreement with

Figure 5.10 A questionnaire designed to test for sexist attitudes among males

Name/identification number: _____	
Date: _____	
1 Have the schools you have attended since you began school been (tick one):	**Do not write in this area**
_____ a coeducational	1
_____ b single-sex	
_____ c both (coeducational and single-sex schools)?	
2 Please indicate your agreement or disagreement with the following statements by circling the response that most nearly coincides with your own. SA = Strongly Agree; A = Agree; U = Uncertain; D = Disagree; SD = Strongly Disagree	2
a A woman would never make a good judge. SA A U D SD	a
b Women are not as good at sport as men. SA A U D SD	b
c Women should be encouraged to seek leadership positions. SA A U D SD	c
d Men should not have to do any washing up. SA A U D SD	d
e Men should be left to make money decisions. SA A U D SD	e
Total	

statements **a, b, d** and **e** indicates a sexist attitude; so does disagreement with **c**. The numerical values assigned to each response in this case would be:

For **a, b, d, e**: SA = 5, A = 4, U = 3, D = 2, SD = 1

For **c**: SA = 1, A = 2, U = 3, D = 4, SD = 5

The highest numerical value on this scale would be 25. To get 25 a respondent would have to indicate strong agreement with items **a, b, d** and **e** and strong disagreement with item **c**. If this scale accurately measures sexist attitudes, such a person would be sexist indeed. The lowest score on this scale would be five. To get a score of five a respondent would have to indicate strong disagreement with items **a, b, d** and **e** and strong agreement with item **c**. Respondents who failed to answer all the items would have to be eliminated from the analysis. By adding the numerical equivalents to each response the respondent's total score can be calculated. Each respondent will have a score between 5 and 25.

If you were satisfied that responses to the statements you used gave an adequate indication of whether a person held sexist attitudes, this scale would be all you would need to test the hypothesis above. You now have a measure for each variable. The measure for the dependent variable is an attitude scale. The measure for the independent variable is provided by a single question related to the respondent's schooling. If you were to use a data-summarisation sheet it might look like the one in Figure 5.11.

Figure 5.11 Data-summarisation sheet for a study of sexist attitudes among males

Name or identification number	Type of social situation in school	Score on sexism scale
David	Single-sex	20
Johnny	Coed	10
etc.	etc.	etc.

Remember to ask only questions that are expected to collect data that measure variables. It may be intriguing to ask other questions, but they are not relevant to your study. For example, it may have occurred to you that other questions could be included in a study on sexism. You might have wanted to know such things as:

■ Does the respondent's mother work?
■ Has the respondent any sisters?
■ What does the respondent's religion say about sexism?
■ Have all the respondent's teachers been males or females?

While these are useful questions in themselves, because of the limitations of time and energy and the need to focus the study the sole independent variable was the type of educational context. Questions dealing with other issues were not raised. The fact that you considered these factors potentially relevant but were not able to include them in your study should be noted in the limitations to your study.

Scales like the one above can be developed for nearly everything. There are some basic rules that should be followed for designing attitude scales. The following suggestions state an ideal approach and include compromises that are acceptable for student projects, which must be kept manageable so that skills can be learnt:

1 The usual procedure is to begin with hundreds of items and, through testing and critical feedback, to narrow the number to between 20 and 50. Student projects should have no more than 15 items.

2   Each item should state one issue clearly. Here are some examples of what not to do. The following items have more than one key element:

- Women are smarter and better behaved than men.
- Men should not do washing-up and women should not keep the cheque book.
- Men are stronger but women are more spiritual.

It would be much better if each item were split:

- Women are smarter than men.
- Women are better behaved than men.
- Women are better at washing up.
- Men are better at keeping cheque books.
- Men are stronger than women.
- Women are more spiritual than men.

3   For a group of items to constitute a scale, each item must be related to a single theme. Each item should pick up a different aspect of the theme. For example, the items listed above all relate to the theme of the respective abilities of males and females. It would add a totally different dimension to the scale to add items on respective social roles.

4   The range of response categories must be designed very carefully. They must be in one dimension (e.g. 'agreement') and provide responses across the whole range of the dimension. Although research is done using a wide variety of response categories, several conventions have emerged. The five-point Likert-type response category is most frequently used. These response categories are strongly agree, agree, undecided, disagree, and strongly disagree.

5   The more specific the response categories, the more accurate and precise the information that will be provided. For example:

Australia should have nuclear armaments.
SA   A   U   D   SD

How often do you go to church?
Never   Yearly   Monthly   Weekly   Daily

How long did you study for this quiz?
Two hours   One hour   Half-hour   Quarter-hour   Not at all

Next are examples of unspecific response categories. These are examples of what not to do.

Australia should have nuclear armaments and use them only when necessary.
Agree   Maybe   Perhaps   Not sure   Possibly not

Immigrants should be allowed to express their unique cultures.
In principle   Sometimes   Only on Sundays   As long as no one
                                              is offended

Here is a method for constructing a list of items. First, select and list a large number of items arbitrarily. Include any items that you believe to be even partially relevant to your variables. Then, begin sifting through the list by eliminating or rewriting items and retaining those that you believe to be relevant. Sift through the list with friends or other students. Also give the whole list to a group of people similar to those for whom the questionnaire or interview is being designed. Talk to them afterwards about what you are trying to measure. They may have useful suggestions.

Try the following exercise to gain more experience in constructing a scale to measure an attitude. Suppose that you have been asked to do a study related to nuclear disarmament. Your dependent variable is 'attitude towards nuclear disarmament'. Assignment: construct a five-item scale measuring attitude towards nuclear disarmament. Remember that you must not only write the items but also decide what attitude dimension to measure and the range of responses to offer. Then you will be able to specify the highest and lowest possible scores. Now ask yourself:

1   How did I measure my dependent variable? How did I measure attitude towards nuclear disarmament? List the items.
2   What range of responses do I want to offer?
    a   Simple agree/disagree or a broader range?
    b   Will I include a neutral position, or will I force the respondent to make a choice?
3   Should the statements be collectively designed so that 'agreement' responses indicate an anti-nuclear disarmament attitude or a pro-nuclear disarmament attitude? Alternatively, should the statements be collectively designed so that agreement indicates an anti-nuclear armament attitude for some and a pro-nuclear armament attitude for others? Compare the following examples:

    a   There is no situation in which nuclear war is justified.
        SA   A   U   D   SD

    b   Australians should not mine uranium.
        SA   A   U   D   SD

    c   Nuclear-powered ships should be allowed to use our ports.
        SA   A   U   D   SD

    d   Development of nuclear-free areas is a waste of time.
        SA   A   U   D   SD

Agreement with **a** and **b** would be taken to indicate an 'anti-nuclear' response. However, agreement with **c** and **d** would indicate a pro-nuclear response. It is usually better to vary the response pattern in this way. This prevents people from getting into the habit of checking the same column. It helps to keep respondents awake and thinking.

4 What is the highest possible score on the scale constructed from the items you listed for Question 1? What is the lowest? This will depend on the number of items you included and the number of response categories you used. If you had five items and five response categories (SA/A/U/D/SD) then the highest possible score would be 25, and the lowest would be five.

Here is how the highest and lowest possible scores are calculated for the scale formed by responses to the four items relating to nuclear disarmament listed in Question 3.

Say that you wanted your scale values to run from high (indicating strong pro-nuclear disarmament attitudes) to low (indicating low pro-nuclear disarmament attitudes). In this case, the numerical values assigned to each response would be as follows:

For **a** and **b**

SA	A	U	D	SD
5	4	3	2	1

For **c** and **d**

SA	A	U	D	SD
1	2	3	4	5

The reason for this is that agreement with **a** and **b** indicates an anti-nuclear position. When agreement indicates the reverse position (pro-nuclear, as in **c** and **d**), the numerical values assigned to the response categories are reversed. In this case, the highest possible score would be given to the person who made which responses? What is the highest possible score? What is the lowest?

A scale is a set of values among which respondents can be positioned on the basis of their response to items on a questionnaire or an interview schedule. A scale is a device for measuring variation in a person's commitment to an attitude, or the strength with which an attitude is held. Although there are many complicated issues in the measurement of attitudes, values and beliefs, you should now be familiar with the basic logic.

There is one more form of questionnaire to be considered. This involves ranking options. Ranking is often used in research into values and preferences. Australian voters are asked to rank candidates. Respondents can be asked to rank options, candidates, preferences, commodities or values. Ranking forces respondents to express the relative strength of their attitude to all the options. It is important that all the options be of the same kind. Here is an example:

> Rank the following values from highest (1) to lowest (7) in terms of their importance to you:
>
> loyalty _____ independence _____
>
> excitement _____ equality _____

peace   _____   creativity   _____
security   _____

Here is another example:

Rank the following qualities from most important (1) to least important
(8) in terms of how you would assess a potential marriage partner:

_____ appearance	_____ sensitivity
_____ honesty	_____ ability to earn money
_____ integrity	_____ religiosity
_____ sense of humour	_____ flexibility

Respondents, or groups of respondents, can be compared in terms of the
way they ranked options. For example, you might find that a group of girls on
average ranked sensitivity higher than appearance, while a group of boys on
average ranked sense of humour above flexibility. Ranking options provides
another way of measuring respondents' values and preferences.

The questionnaire and the interview schedule are data-gathering techniques by which a researcher can measure the variables being studied.
Questions are asked in order to gain information. This information can be
factual: How did you vote? How old are you? How much does your baby
weigh? Or questions may be asked in order to determine respondents' attitudes, beliefs or values: Would you support a republic? Do you believe in
heaven? What is the most important thing in a relationship?

Examining records and publications to measure variables

The third common data-gathering technique is to measure variables by using
the information kept in records or official reports of organisations, government agencies or persons. Possibly the most familiar example of this kind of
data is the census. Government departments keep records of marriages,
divorces, deaths and financial transactions. Organisations keep records. Hospi-
tals have records of admissions, discharges and types of surgery performed.
Some churches retain documents about members, marriages, baptisms, and
amounts of money received and paid. Schools archive information about student numbers, student–teacher ratios and subjects taught.

The basic problem with using records to gather data is gaining access. Census material is available from the Australian Bureau of Statistics and in many
libraries and on the Internet. The yearbooks or annual reports of many organisations often give information on various aspects of the organisation.
However, sometimes researchers don't know the location or character of
records—whether they are computer files, bound annual reports or uncollated

documents in filing cabinets. Often there are occasions when a researcher doesn't know if records are available or even if they exist. Finding and gaining permission to access records can take a great deal of time.

The second problem is that the records often do not contain the exact information you want. They may be for the State of Victoria when you are interested in the City of Melbourne. Or they may be for the City of Sydney and you want Redfern. Information may be collected in one way in 1992, in another in 1996 and in yet another in 2000, making comparison difficult.

If you are interested in such information as trends in divorce, birthrate, population growth, the proportion of people of a certain age in the population, average age at first marriage, average age at divorce, the number of children affected by divorce in a given year, the incidence of teenage pregnancy or the percentage of weddings performed by civil celebrants, you can find answers in documents available from the Australian Bureau of Statistics.

If you belong to a tertiary institution, these kinds of documents will probably be available in or through your library or you can make direct inquiries to an office of the Australian Bureau of Statistics, which has a web site and publishes census data on CD-ROM.

Content analysis

Content analysis is a different way to examine records, documents and publications. It is very like an observation study. In a content analysis a checklist is developed to count how frequently certain ideas, words, phrases, images or scenes appear. However, in a content analysis what is being observed is a text, a film or a television program.

Recently a team of our students conducted a study of the perception of the aged in our society. This involved the researchers watching a night's television to observe the roles played by the elderly in television commercials. Another approach required that the researchers deduce the needs of the elderly on the basis of advertisements aimed at the elderly.

The procedure for a content analysis of a television or radio program follows the same lines as an observation study. Recording the program allows the researcher to go back over the material several times to complete and check the accuracy of the content analysis. It provides an opportunity for several people to do a content analysis of the same material, and it helps them examine the material to see what things can be observed and counted. The steps for preparing a content analysis of television or radio material are as follows:

1   Clarify and narrow your hypothesis or research objective. What are the concepts involved?

2   Identify variables related to the concepts under study. This may involve watching some television programs or listening to radio programs to become familiar with what there is to be observed.

3   Devise a way to measure the variables. Develop a checklist to count how often the things you have selected to observe appear, for example the number of advertisements featuring the elderly, or the number of advertisements in which women play roles of authority.

4   Decide what programs to examine. Decide whether your unit of analysis is a time period (e.g. two hours of Wednesday-night prime-time television) or a specific program, or a number of advertisements over a period of time (e.g. the first 10 advertisements screened after 6 pm on Channel 9 on Friday nights).

5   Devise a data-summarisation sheet.

6   Collect your data by doing the observations you propose.

7   Summarise the results on the data-summarisation form.

The content analysis of published material

Published material is a storehouse of material for content analysis. Magazines, periodicals, books, novels and textbooks—all can be subjected to content analysis. The logic of research using content analysis of published material is the same as the logic of other kinds of research. The first step is to clarify your hypothesis or research objective. Once the concepts under study have been identified, variables that are related to the concepts can be selected. Then the problem of how to measure and record variation in the variables can be tackled. Once measurement problems are settled, the units of measure in which to report findings can be decided. Remember this flow:

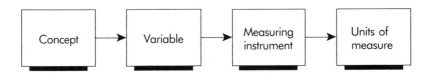

This same flow of issues occurs in designing research using the content analysis of written material. Let us assume that you are interested in the area of sex-role stereotyping. You are interested in the origin of sex-role stereotypes—where do they come from? One possible source would be children's books. This might lead you to ask whether there has been a change in the amount of sex-role stereotyping in children's books. How could you measure change in the amount of sex-role stereotyping over a number of years?

One possible way would be to examine the reading material used to teach reading to Year 1 students. What are Year 1 children reading today compared with 20 years ago? To do this you need access to the material used 20 years ago and the material used now. Second, you need to develop a set of indicators of role stereotyping. What roles do girls and boys play? What roles do men and women play? What activities characterise each sex? Do the illustrations promote sex-role stereotyping? Once you have begun to identify countable features you can devise a checklist on sex-role stereotyping in Year 1 books.

Or you might devise a set of questions like the ones in Figure 5.12.

Figure 5.12 A content-analysis questionnaire

	Place tick in appropriate column				
	Always	In over half the stories	Half and half	In less than half the stories	Never
1 Are boys shown to dominate girls?					
2 Are girls shown to win against boys?					
3 Is unisex clothing used?					
4 Are women shown in traditionally male roles (e.g. a female physician or female priest)?					
5 Does a male ask a female for help or directions or information?					
6 Are females shown to be helpless?					

In this way a scale of sex-role stereotyping in literature can be developed. By applying it to literature from different times, changes can be observed and systematic comparisons made.

Here is an example of research using content analysis of published material. Since the Second World War an increasing proportion of Australian married women have been employed. Has this movement into paid work outside the home had an impact on the publications directed at women? The hypothesis could be this:

As the proportion of women who are employed outside the home increases, there will be an increase in the attention paid to working women in the publications aimed at women.

This can be diagrammed as follows:

Since we know there has been an increase in the proportion of married women who are employed, we only need to find variables to provide an indication of change in the dependent concept—change in content of material published for women. Several approaches are possible.

First, the number of magazines published for women may have changed between 1945 and the present. Are there more or fewer now? Are some of the new ones directed mainly at employed married women? You might gain help from your library on the number and kind of women's magazines that have come and gone since 1945.

A second approach would be to select one title that has been published continuously through this time. For example, the *Australian Women's Weekly* and *Vogue* have been published continuously. It would be interesting to see if the number of articles that appeal to working women, or address the problems faced by working women, has changed. Here you must decide what to count. Do you count articles or the number of pages? Do you take just one issue or a year of issues? It would be better to deal with more than one issue in each year in case the issue you chose for a given year is atypical. Therefore, you might take one issue from each month. The results would be reported as the number of articles or pages per year appealing to working women.

A third approach would be to see if the magazine's attitude to the idea of married women working has changed. It is possible that the *Australian Women's Weekly* has devoted roughly the same number of articles or pages or proportion of space to the subject of employed married women, but that it has shifted from disapproval to approval. This would require not only counting articles or pages devoted to the subject but deciding whether each was favourable, unfavourable or neutral. Your record of research might look like Figure 5.13.

Let us say that 12 issues each for the years 1945 and 1996 were read. There would be 24 record sheets, one for each issue. The analysis would be by year.

The classification of the content of the articles as favourable, unfavourable or neutral would proceed on similar lines. Additional categories might need to be introduced after all the material was read.

Figure 5.13 A record sheet for a content analysis of articles dealing with employed married women

Magazine: _____   Issue: _____

Year: _____   Total pages: _____

Total no. of articles: _____

Title of article	Number of pages	Orientation expressed
Total no. of articles	Total no. of pages	

Figure 5.14 Data-summarisation sheet for content analysis

	1945	1996
Total pages		
Number of pages devoted to employed married women		
Proportion of total pages devoted to employed married women		
Total number of articles		
Number of articles devoted to employed married women		
Proportion of articles devoted to employed married women		

Content analysis can be fun. Popular music, movies and magazines are interesting to analyse.

Before you begin content analysis, refer to the following checklist:

1 Clarify the hypothesis. What concepts are involved?
2 What variables can be used to indicate change in or differences between the concepts?

3   How can this variable be measured using content analysis? What is to be counted—pages, words, articles, pictures or something else? Devise a record sheet for recording your data.

4   In what units are the results to be reported—pages per issue, words per year, articles per week or something else? Devise a data-summary sheet for reporting your data (for example Figure 5.14).

Validity

At the end of chapter 4 the problem of validity was discussed. This is concerned with how accurately a variable fits a concept. For example, is 'absence of disease' a valid indicator of health? Is a history test a valid way to test a student's grasp of historical material? Most variables can be questioned in one way or another.

The problem of validity is most acute in the construction of questionnaires or interview schedules to 'measure' a person's attitudes, beliefs or values. For example, it is necessary to ask whether the items used to measure variation in a person's attitudes to nuclear disarmament, developed earlier in this chapter, are valid. On reflection, only one item deals with nuclear war. The others deal with the use of nuclear material in other ways. It is quite possible for someone who is very much in favour of nuclear disarmament to also favour the peaceful use of nuclear material for the generation of power. The items do not focus clearly on the variable to be measured. Therefore, they lack validity.

It is important to be aware of the problems of validity. In professional research, a great deal of time and effort is spent ensuring validity. As a student there are things that you can do too. In addition to being very careful in your construction of measuring devices, record sheets, questionnaires and checklists, you can ask your friends and your lecturer to comment on your measures. This may help to increase their validity. Moreover, you can pretest scales using individuals known to exhibit extremes of the dimensions you are trying to measure. For example, what would it mean for the validity of your scale if someone whom you knew to be very sexist got a low score on a sexism scale which you had devised? Clearly, you would have to rework your scale! It is very important to pretest your research instrument to ensure that it is working properly before actually doing your research.

Reliability

The question of reliability is different from the question of validity. When someone asks if a measure is reliable, they are asking whether different researchers using the same measuring device would get the same results when measuring the same event. For example, will a group of 10 students who weigh the same baby, one after another, record the same weight? Is a baby-weighing scale reliable? This may depend on how difficult it is to hold the baby still, which is relevant to the reliability of a weighing scale. The basic question is whether the measurement device employed provides the same results when repeated. This is called test–retest reliability.

The reliability of observation techniques is often questioned. Will a group of observers report the same observations? This is also a problem in content analysis. Will several people agree that article X dealt with a topic related to the needs of working married women? Will they agree that it recognises the right of married women to work? The more agreement there is in coding observations on content analysis, the more reliable is the instrument.

A feature of recorded or published materials that facilitates the testing of their reliability is that others can review the exact material. Where there are differences, it is possible to sort them out with those who are evaluating the material. Was the daughter's comment ignored, or was it ridiculed? If you are unsure, you can go back to that section of the tape and check. The challenge to the reliability of a measure is that different researchers using the same measure may record different results.

Questions of reliability refer to problems in the accuracy of the measuring device. Questions of validity refer to the appropriateness of the measuring device. It is important for you to be aware of both these problems. It is appropriate to include questions about validity and reliability in any discussion of the limitations of your research.

Summary

Once you have clarified your hypothesis and selected variables for study, the issue of measurement must be considered. Three basic techniques for measuring variables have been discussed: observation techniques, questionnaires or interview schedules, and content analysis. The importance of developing systematic data-recording forms and data-summarisation forms has been emphasised. The fact that you collect data to measure variables in a hypothesis is the major emphasis of this chapter. Data are gathered to measure variables you have clarified beforehand.

Questions for review

1   What are the basic steps in preparing to do research involving observation as a data-gathering technique?

2   What is the purpose of a checklist for observation?
3   What is the purpose of a data-summarisation sheet?
4   What are the basic steps in preparing research involving the use of a questionnaire or interview schedule?
5   What is the difference between an interview schedule and a questionnaire?
6   How do you determine the highest and lowest possible scores on a scale framed by responses to items designed to measure a respondent's attitudes, values or beliefs?
7   What does it mean to reverse the polarity of response for an item? What impact does this have on the way the responses are scored for scale construction?
8   What are the steps involved in preparing to do research involving the use of content analysis?
9   What is the problem of validity?
10 What is the problem of reliability?

Suggestions for further reading

Babbie, E. R. (2003), *The Practice of Social Research*, 10th edn, Wadsworth Publishing, London, chapter 5.

de Vaus, D. A. (2002), *Surveys in Social Research*, 5th edn, Allen & Unwin, St Leonards, NSW, chapters 4, 6 and 7.

Foddy, William (1993), *Constructing Questions for Interviews and Questionnaires: Theory and Practice in Social Research*, Cambridge University Press, Cambridge.

Judd, C. M., E. R. Smith and L. H. Kidder (1991), *Research Methods in Social Relations*, Holt, Rinehart & Winston, Fort Worth, chapter 3, 7 and 10.

Kumar, Ranjit (1999), *Research Methodology: A Step by Step Guide for Beginners*, Sage, London, chapters 9–11.

Minichiello, Victor, Rosalie Aroni, Eric Timewell and Loris Alexander (1995), *In-Depth Interviewing: Principles, Techniques, Analysis*, 2nd edn, Longman Cheshire, Melbourne, chapters 2, 4 and 6.

Wallace, W. (1971), *The Logic of Science in Sociology*, Aldine, Chicago, chapter 2.

Selecting a research design

CHAPTER OUTLINE

A hypothesis states that a relationship exists between two or more concepts. In a research project, the hypothesis is the reference point on which researchers focus their activity. The role of a research objective is the same. Researchers should keep a statement of their hypothesis or research objective visible as a constant reminder of their specific task.

How does the hypothesis guide the research? The hypothesis claims that there is a relationship between concepts X and Y. Research is undertaken to determine whether there is evidence to support this claim. In order to carry out the research, two general tasks must be done. First, the concepts in the hypothesis must be defined in such a way that they can be measured. In chapters 4 and 5 we learnt how to select and measure variables that relate to concepts. However, research requires more than measuring the concepts in a hypothesis.

The second task is to find evidence that the relationship stated in the hypothesis actually exists. Measuring X and Y is one thing. Finding evidence that X and Y are related is another. While the issues concerning measurement of concepts are narrowed by the operational definitions, the existence of a relationship between X and Y is assessed by the research design.

Let us look at the diagram of a hypothesis again:

This hypothesis states that a change in X will produce a change in Y and that the nature of the relationship between X and Y is such that an increase in X will produce an increase in Y. One of the hypotheses we have been using as an example states:

More study leads to increased academic performance.

The conceptual form of this hypothesis was diagrammed:

A number of variables for each of the concepts were identified (if you cannot remember, turn back to chapter 4). The selected variables were 'number of hours spent in revision' for the concept 'study', and 'exam results' for the concept 'academic performance'. The hypothesis can be restated in its variable form as follows:

In chapter 5 we devised measures for each variable. Students were asked to keep a record of the time they spent revising and to state their result for the history exam. The operational definition of the hypothesis—the statement of the hypothesis as a relationship between measures—would be as follows:

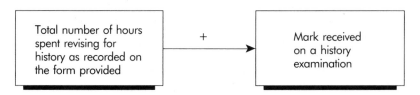

You may well be thinking, 'Surely that is enough!' But it is not. You do not have a measurement of the relationship between study and academic performance. How do you know that, generally speaking, it was the amount of study that produced the examination result? How do you know that a change in the independent variable produced a change in the dependent variable?

What kinds of relationships can there be among variables? There are three basic types:

1 The variables are causally related, that is, a change in one variable will produce a change in the other variable.
2 The variables are only associated, that is, they change together but this happens through no perceived causal relationship and, in the absence of contrary evidence, could be a coincidence.
3 The variables are neither causally related nor associated.

It is relatively easy to determine whether two variables are associated. It is more difficult to determine that X (independent variable) causes Y (dependent variable). In order to establish that two variables are causally related it is necessary to show that:

1 X and Y are associated.
2 Changes in the dependent variable, Y, always occur after changes in the independent variable, X.
3 All other variables that might produce changes in Y are 'controlled', that is, their possible effects on Y are accounted for.

As we shall see, the experimental research design is the only design truly adequate for testing a causal hypothesis. Given that an experimental design is not always possible, practical or permissible, other designs are used to approximate an experimental design or to provide some information relevant to the test of a causal hypothesis.

Choosing a research design is one of the most important and difficult parts of doing empirical research. For example, you may feel certain that an increase in study will produce an increase in academic performance. But how do you prove that these concepts are related in this way? How do you design your research to answer this question?

There are five basic types of research design. Each type is appropriate for a different general kind of research question or problem and the type you select depends on your hypothesis or research objective. In this chapter, we will examine the five types of research design by using each to examine the relationship between study and academic performance. Although one design may be more desirable than another, each can make a contribution to our knowledge about the relationship.

One way to become familiar with the logic of research design is to understand that each type of research design asks a different kind of question or confronts a different type of research problem. The five basic types of research design can be grouped according to five different sets of questions:

1   **The case study**
     What is going on?
     Is there a relationship between variables X and Y in entity A?
     (An 'entity' is a group, social situation, text or other focus of research.)

2   **The longitudinal study**
     Has there been a change?
     Is the relationship between variables X and Y in entity A the same or different at time 1 and time 2?

3   **The comparison study**
     Is Group A different from Group B?
     Is the relationship between variables X and Y the same in entities A and B?

4   **The longitudinal comparison study**
     Has there been a difference between Group A and Group B over time?
     Has there been a change over time in the relationship between X and Y in entity A compared with entity B?

5   **The experiment**
     Why are Groups A and B different?
     Is the difference in Y (dependent variable) between Group A and Group B due to a change in X (the independent variable)?

     We will develop each design in detail so that you can see the value and limitations of each.

1 The case study

The case study can answer the question 'What is going on?' The key element of the case study design is that it focuses on a single 'case' or 'entity', which might be one person, one group, one classroom, one town or a single nation. The single case or entity is studied for a period of time and the results recorded. The aim of the case study is to find out if there is a relationship between variables X and Y within the entity.

People who discuss research design have given the term 'case study' several meanings. Some limit the use of the term to an exploratory study in which no hypothesis is tested. For example, you might be interested in the factors a particular group of families considers when planning meals. You simply want to know what is 'going on' inside the entity (i.e. the group of families being studied). You are not testing a hypothesis. You are not comparing one group of families with another.

Researchers may also carry out exploratory case studies to ascertain relevant variables for further research. Such studies might also be done to formulate hypotheses for later study. An exploratory case study takes a very broad look at the phenomenon being investigated. The purpose is to gather information to build a description of what is 'going on'.

Other researchers use case studies to make initial tests of hypotheses. It is often useful to check whether two variables show an association before doing more rigorous testing. The sort of hypothesis that can be tested by a case study could take this form: 'There is an association between variables X and Y.' Case studies are not usually appropriate for testing causal relationships. This is to due to the fact that case studies usually bring the researcher into environments where several variables are operating, and the case study design is not structured to isolate the influence of any individual variable.

Our example concerns the relationship between study and academic performance. What can a case study tell us? It can test for an association between the variables, hours of study and exam marks, within the case being studied. Given the results, we can decide whether a more complicated test for a causal relationship between the variables is likely to show a causal relationship.

A case study designed to discover whether there is any relationship between study and academic performance might take this form. The questionnaire on time spent revising, developed in the last chapter, would be given to a specific history class who are the 'case' being studied. The measurement is carried out once. The results are assessed once for one class and one examination. The data would then be analysed. While we will deal with data analysis in detail later, let us say that you discovered that the amount of study time was positively associated with the marks achieved. Your graph might have looked like Figure 6.1.

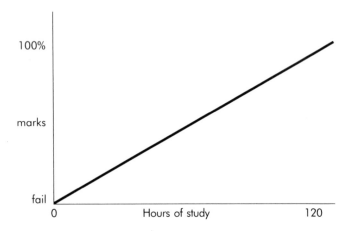

Figure 6.1 A sample graph of possible results from a case study

What would your graph have looked like if you found that the amount of time spent studying related negatively to the marks achieved? What could you have concluded from this study if you had done it as described and obtained results like those in Figure 6.1? You could conclude that in the group of students examined there was a positive relationship between amount of study and academic performance as measured by the instrument devised. You could not conclude that greater amounts of study caused higher marks. All you know is that in one case (i.e. the class studied), at one point in time, the hypothesis was supported (by an observed association). This observation is very interesting but it may well have occurred by chance. Also, you cannot rule out alternative explanations. For example, the students who studied longer might also have sat at the front of the room and paid better attention. What caused the differences in result—study or attention?

You might be prompted by your curiosity to test other factors or to compare test results from other groups of students. Knowing what happened in one case may prompt you to try other cases. Or it might persuade you to test whether it really was the amount of time spent in revision that produced the results (by repeating your research with an experimental design).

Consider now the following example. You are an occupational health and safety (OH&S) officer at a large worksite. You are concerned that the nutritional status of the company's workers may affect the frequency of injuries on the job. You arrange for a guest speaker to talk to groups of workers, during working hours, about nutrition. You hope this will motivate the workers to eat healthier food. You have also decided that you want to evaluate the effectiveness of the speech. How can you do so? What can a case study tell you? A case study can tell you 'what is going on'—whether the speech had the desired effect. You have the impression that the speech has not had the desired effect and that workers are continuing to choose less nutritious food. But you have no evidence to support that belief. You can check this impression by doing a case study.

Your research objective for a case study related to the issue of food selection might be:

To discover what snack-food choices a particular group of workers makes at the company cafeteria.

To measure this concept, variables will have to be selected and a measuring instrument devised. You talk with the manager of the cafeteria. She agrees to let you observe the selections made at the cafeteria. You decide to devise a checklist with which to record your observation of the food selections made by a particular group of workers, for example, machine operators on A-shift. It might look like the chart in Figure 6.2.

Figure 6.2 A checklist for observing the snack choices of machine operators on A-shift

Sweet	Fruit	Other

In this case study, you would be recording the total choices for the whole shift. The way you gather your data depends on whether you are asking about individual selections or the pattern for the group. Here our interest is the pattern of snack decisions for all machine operators on A-shift. Figures 6.3 and 6.4 present some hypothetical results. What would you conclude from each?

Figure 6.3 A table of hypothetical results from a case study of the snacks selected by machine operators on A-shift

	Sweet	Fruit	Other	Total
Number of selections	24	3	3	30

Figure 6.3 gives the numbers of selections made in each category. The workers appear to select less nutritious foods, such as sweets, more often than nutritious items, such as fruit. Figure 6.4 presents the same findings as percentages. The use of percentages helps in making comparisons among groups of different size. It is also a very common way of showing the pattern of a variable for a group within a case study.

Figure 6.4 Percentage of snacks selected by a class of machine operators on A-shift

	Sweet	Fruit	Other
Percentage of selections	80	10	10

In a case study, you could collect data showing the distribution of worker food selections at the cafeteria. What proportion of the selections were nutritious foods, such as fruit, or non-nutritious foods, such as sweets? There would be little point in pursuing a major study if in this simple case study you discovered that, contrary to your impression, most workers selected fruit for their snacks.

The case study is the basic building block of research design. In a case study, a variable or set of variables is measured for one entity at one point in time. The other research designs involve the study of more than one entity, or compare studies of the same entity at different points in time. In a sense, all other research designs facilitate hypothesis testing by comparing additional case studies designed to isolate the influences on the variables under study.

2 The longitudinal study

The longitudinal research design involves two or more case studies of the same entity with some time between each case study. The basic question posed by a longitudinal study is 'Has there been any change over a period of time?'

The longitudinal research design tests for an association between two variables in the same entity at different points in time. It asks, 'Has there been any change in the level of association between the variables over a period of time in entity A?' The answer is 'yes' or 'no'. If the answer is 'yes', the research design should also indicate the nature or size of the change. Given that longitudinal studies are really comparisons of case studies, they cannot identify and isolate the causes of changes in associations. The longitudinal design can be diagrammed as follows:

Figure 6.5 A diagram of a longitudinal study involving two measures of one group, entity or individual A, at more than one point in time

To do a longitudinal study you:
1 select variables relevant to the concepts under study
2 devise a way of measuring those variables
3 develop a data-recording device
4 measure the same variables in the same way in one group (or for one person) at two or more times.

Longitudinal research designs are often employed in analyses of national data. You may hypothesise that increased female participation in the workforce leads to a general increase in the age at which women have their first child. A possible way of investigating this would be to analyse national statistics as measures for the variables 'female workforce participation' and 'average age at first birth', at a number of points in time.

Figure 6.6 Females: workforce participation and average age at birth of first child

	Workforce participation rate (%)	Average age at first birth (years)
1993	52.2	26.8
1996	53.8	27.2
2000	54.5	27.8

Source: ABS cats. 1301.0; 3301.0

Figure 6.6 compares the relationship at three points in time—1993, 1996 and 2000. As can be seen, the two variables are associated because measures (national statistics) for both variables have risen throughout the period under study. Therefore, the hypothesis is supported by the research.

You could also do a longitudinal study of the population growth rate of your suburb and its relationship to the number of people attending church in your suburb for the last 10 years. Think of a longitudinal study you could do using the position of your favourite football team at the end of each of the last 10 seasons as a dependent variable.

Another common form of the longitudinal study is the 'before and after' study. Some lecturers give 'before and after' tests to see if their lessons have had any effect on their students' knowledge. Studies of the impact of diet on physical characteristics frequently use a 'before and after' longitudinal research design: 'He weighed 96 kg before following our strict diet and exercise regime and three months later he weighed 80 kg.'

Taking our example of the relationship between study and academic performance, we can ask, 'What additional information would a longitudinal study provide?' In the section on the case study, we suggested that the result of the research was that amount of time spent in revision and the mark on a history test were positively related. The more time a student spent in revision, the better was that student's mark. One possible longitudinal study would be to repeat the same case study for the next history test to see whether the relationship continued to hold. This would help to find out whether the result in the first study had been a fluke. If the result occurred again, our confidence in the finding and in the worth of the hypothesis would increase.

The study of workers' snack selections at the cafeteria lends itself to a 'before and after' style longitudinal research design. Let us assume that when the OH&S officer conducted the case study it was discovered that 70 per cent of the workers' choices were for sweets and only 10 per cent were for nutritious foods such as fruits. The OH&S officer decided to invite a guest speaker to speak to the machine operators on A-shift about nutrition. After this had taken place the initial research would be repeated to see if there were changes in workers' food selections.

What could the OH&S officer conclude if the results looked like those in Figure 6.7? Would it be valid to conclude that the talk was a success? Could the OH&S officer conclude that as a result of the talk there had been a shift in workers' snack selections toward more nutritious food?

Figure 6.7 Hypothetical results of a longitudinal study of workers' snack selections

	Before	After
Sweets	70%	50%
Fruit	10%	30%
Other	20%	20%

The only valid conclusion is that workers were selecting more nutritious food, that is, more fruit. While it is likely that the speech had some impact, only an experimental design (see below) could test whether the speech produced the results.

There may have been other factors that caused the change in food selections, quite unrelated to the speech. For example, the stock at the cafeteria might have changed. The price of sweets might have gone up. Neither the simple case study nor the longitudinal study can control the influence of these other factors.

3 The comparison study

In a comparison study, the research question is 'Is the relationship between variables X and Y the same in entities A and B?' A comparison study compares

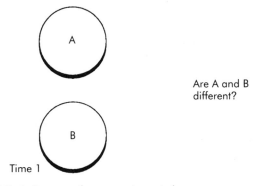

Are A and B different?

Time 1

Figure 6.8 A diagram of a comparison study

case studies of the relationships between the same variables done for different entities at the same point in time. The comparison study can be diagrammed as in Figure 6.8.

A great deal of research is of the comparative type. Basic examples are 'Is the relationship between "contraception availability" and "youth pregnancy" the same in Geelong and Adelaide?'; 'Is the relationship between "ethnicity" and "sports achievement" the same in both the local girls' and boys' soccer teams?'; and 'Is the relationship between "family type" (one parent/two parents) and "academic achievement" the same for students at Caulfield Grammar and Collingwood High School?'

Comparison studies are undertaken for two main reasons:

1 To investigate a relationship further by testing it within different types of entities. This practice might be called 'doing the same test under different conditions'. Car tyres are tested under different conditions, such as dry roads, wet roads, sealed roads, gravel roads, etc. A social-relationship hypothesis can be tested under the same principle, with tests conducted for the same point in time or time period for different social entities. If we hypothesise that there is a relationship between 'ethnicity' and 'sports achievement', we may wish to test this relationship under different 'gender conditions' to see if the relationship is affected by the variable 'gender'. A possible way to do this would be to test the relationship in similar entities of different gender composition, such as the local girls' and boys' soccer teams.

2 To investigate a relationship further by testing it within similar types of entities. This practice might be called 'doing the same test under similar conditions', where the tests are conducted for the same point or period of time. Such studies are done to test the reliability of research and to examine the effects of outside variables. If we accept that Geelong and Adelaide are similar cities, we could use them to study the relationship between 'contraception availability' and 'youth pregnancy'. If our research demonstrates a relationship between the variables in both places, then the reliability of the research is supported. However, if our research shows a relationship in Adelaide but not in Geelong, then our research method could be unreliable and in need of re-evaluation. There may also be an unconsidered but critical difference between the two cities that is affecting the relationship—that is, there could be a 'third' variable in the relationship. If we strongly suspect this, then further research needs to be carried out to identify the mystery third variable.

Let's explore this last point with an example. Suppose you postulate a relationship between the variables 'English proficiency' and 'unemployment'— that is, groups with lower English proficiency experience higher levels of unemployment. You decide to compare this relationship in two suburbs of Melbourne, Carlton and Preston.

Suppose your research yields different results for the two suburbs. In Carlton, the results support your hypothesis because you find that adults with low English proficiency do experience high unemployment. On the other hand, the research carried out in Preston does not support your hypothesis. In Preston, adults with low English proficiency have a rate of unemployment that is unexpectedly low. Therefore, the hypothesis that English proficiency is related to employment would not be supported for all suburbs of Melbourne. Consequently, the simple theory would need to be refined or challenged. This refinement would usually begin with the question, 'What are the differences between the suburbs Carlton and Preston that change the relationship between English proficiency and employment?'

Further research could confront this question by pursuing the research objective 'To observe patterns of employment acquisition' in Preston. It might be observed that the language spoken most frequently by adults in Preston is Russian. As a result, most local employers (given that they do business with local residents) tend to hire people proficient in Russian rather than English.

A more complete view of the relationship between English proficiency and unemployment begins to emerge. It's been shown that the significance of the relationship between English proficiency and unemployment is inconsistent between two Melbourne suburbs. Further research has found a possible factor in this inconsistency, that is, the prevalence of languages other than English among local residents. In fact, the independent variable can be modified to 'local language proficiency', developing our hypothesis for further testing.

To do a comparison study you:

1 select variables relevant to the concepts under study
2 devise a way of measuring those variables
3 develop a data-recording device
4 measure the same variables in the same way in two or more entities at the same time (or 'practically' at the same time).

Such a study will enable you to determine whether there is any difference between the two groups.

For example, the OH&S officer concerned about workers' snack selections in the cafeteria might have been interested to find out whether there was any difference between machine operators on A-shift and those on other shifts. To make this comparison, the OH&S officer would have to observe and record the selections made by two groups of workers. It would be best if they could be observed at the same time (in this case, on their respective meal breaks on the same night). The data-recording sheet might look like that shown in Figure 6.9.

Let us say that Group A are the workers on A-shift and Group B the workers on other shifts. What could the OH&S officer conclude if the results looked like those in Figure 6.10? She could conclude that, of the workers

Figure 6.9 An observation recording form for a comparison study of snack selections made by two groups of machine operators

	Group A	Group B
Sweets		
Fruit		
Other		

observed, workers on A-shift on average selected fewer sweets and more fruit than did workers on other shifts. The OH&S officer might think that this difference was due to the nutrition education talk given to the workers on A-shift. However, there is no way of telling that from the above study. The study simply asks the question, 'Are these two groups of workers different?' From the results in Figure 6.10, the answer would be 'yes'.

Figure 6.10 Hypothetical results of a comparison study of workers' snack selections

	Machine operators on A-Shift	Machine operators on other shifts
Sweets	60%	70%
Fruit	30%	20%
Other	10%	10%

Information regarding the relationship between study and academic performance can be provided by a comparison study (see Figure 6.11). It may have

Figure 6.11 Data-recording form for a comparison study of the relationship between amount of study and marks by each class member in the subjects of history and maths

History class			Maths class		
Student	Study (hours)	1st semester exam mark (%)	Student	Study (hours)	1st semester exam mark (%)
Craig	5	90	Elise	3	90
Casey	4	80	Ben	1	80
Emma	3	70	Kim	5	70
Kathy	2	60	Tina	5	60
Eva	1	50	Nadine	4	50
etc.	etc.	etc.	etc.	etc.	etc.

occurred to you that the relationship between amount of study and mark on the history test held true for history but might not hold true for the maths class. You might ask the question, 'Is the relationship between study and academic performance the same in both the maths and the history class? One way to find out would be to compare the results of case studies of this relationship, conducted during the same period, for the maths and the history class.

The results of the two classes could be plotted on one graph, as in Figure 6.12.

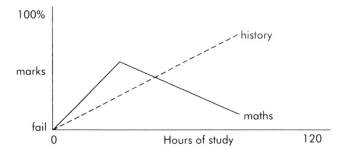

Figure 6.12 A sample graph of possible results from a comparison study

Figure 6.12 shows a clear and positive relationship between the number of hours spent studying and examination result in history. The same is not true for the maths class, for which there is no pattern between the variables. You would conclude that the relationship between the amount of time spent in revision and examination result differs between Groups A and B. Therefore, the relationship between study and results is different for Groups A and B and the hypothesis is supported in the history class but not the maths class. A and B are different.

What would be concluded if the results had been like those in Figure 6.13? Be careful in reading this graph.

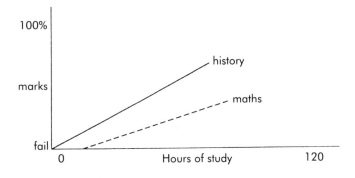

Figure 6.13 A sample graph of possible results from a comparison study

Given these results, you would conclude that in both the history and the maths classes, the amount of time spent in revision was positively related to examination results. The conclusion would be that Groups A and B were not different in terms of the relationship between hours of study and marks in history and maths.

4 The longitudinal comparison study

It was said earlier that the case study was in a sense the basic building block of research design. We have combined two case studies of the same group at two different times to produce a longitudinal study. Similarly, by combining two case studies, each one of a different group at the same time, we produced a comparison study. When the comparison and the longitudinal types are combined, the longitudinal comparison research design is produced. This type of research design asks the question, 'Have the differences between X and Y in entities A and B changed over time?'

A good example of this type of research would be a study of two groups of babies: one group bottlefed and the other breastfed. Each group would be measured at the same interval—weekly for eight weeks beginning one week after birth. The observation–recording device developed earlier would be used. We will assume that Group A is bottlefed and Group B is breastfed.

This study is longitudinal in that it involves a series of measures of the same variables in the same groups over time. It is also a comparison because it compares two separate groups. How might the data look? You have weight and length measures for each infant at weekly intervals. For the purpose of comparison between the two groups, assume that you report the average weight gain each week. The following table might be used to present the results:

Figure 6.14 A table of possible results from a longitudinal comparison study of two groups of babies

Average weight gain per week in grams

Week	1	2	3	4	5	6	7	8	Total
Group A	13	14	14	15	16	16	15	15	118
Group B	14	15	15	16	16	17	16	16	125

The research into the relationship between amount of study and academic performance can be done using a longitudinal comparison type of research design. We will retain the comparison between a history class and a maths class. We will also use the same data-recording form as before. In our last hypothetical research into this topic we discovered that there was a difference in the relationship between time spent in revision and examination result between maths and history. The question that can be asked is, 'Does this difference persist through time?' By asking the two classes to keep a record of the time spent revising each subject before two exams a few months apart, a longitudinal comparison is achieved. We will have two measures for each of two groups at two different times. A diagram of this research design might look like that shown in Figure 6.15.

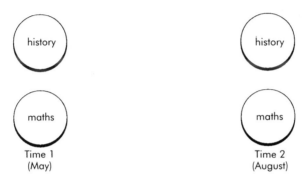

Figure 6.15 Diagram of a longitudinal comparison study of effect of amount of study on academic performance

You may recall that our first comparison study of history and maths results looked like Figure 6.16. A longitudinal comparison essentially involves doing a second comparison study using the same measures as the first one to see if there has been any change between the two groups.

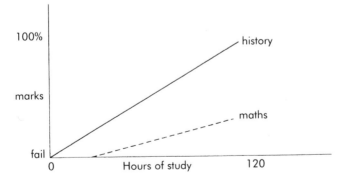

Figure 6.16 A sample graph of possible results from a longitudinal comparison study (first trial)

If the results of the second study were the same as the first, the conclusion would be that the difference between the two groups has persisted. On the other hand, the results of the second part of this longitudinal comparison study might have looked like Figure 6.17.

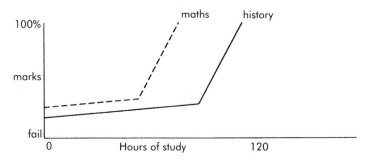

Figure 6.17 A sample graph of possible results from a longitudinal comparison study (second trial)

What conclusions could be drawn from these results? First, the differences between Groups A and B (history and maths in this study) have lessened. Second, the pattern for both subjects has changed. Have the students changed their study patterns? Were the examinations different? What has produced the change? That is still unknown. The longitudinal comparison research design can demonstrate changes in differences between groups over time, but it does not provide the tools to test hypotheses about factors that cause changes in differences.

This same problem arises in the case of the OH&S officer who is concerned about workers' snack selections. Let us say that the OH&S officer, after conducting the first comparison study between machine operators on A-shift and other machine operators, decided to put up posters in the cafeteria that promoted fruit as a healthy snack. After a few weeks she repeats the original comparison study. By being repeated, the original comparison study is transformed into a longitudinal comparison study.

What conclusions could the OH&S officer draw from the results shown in Figure 6.18? Both groups have changed. Both groups shifted 20 percentage points in the direction of the greater consumption of fruit. What is more significant, though, is that the difference between the two groups has persisted. The machine operators on A-shift are still more likely to select fruit than the machine operators on other shifts. However, it is impossible to conclude that the posters produced the change. It might have been something else, as suggested before. There might have been a change in the offerings at the cafeteria. There might have been a major television campaign at the same time. Other factors, not accounted for in this research, might have produced the result.

Figure 6.18 Hypothetical results of a longitudinal comparison study of workers' snack selections

	Machine operators on A-shift		Machine operators on other shifts	
	May	July	May	July
Sweets	60%	40%	70%	50%
Fruit	30%	50%	20%	40%
Other	10%	10%	10%	10%

To use a longitudinal comparison research design you must:

1 select variables relevant to the concepts under study
2 devise a way of measuring those variables
3 develop a data-recording device
4 measure the same variables in the same way in two (or more) entities at two (or more) different times.

Such a research design is diagrammed in Figure 6.19. A research design like this can answer the question 'Are entities A and B different through time?' It cannot, however, explain differences between variables in time, or test hypotheses about the causes of such differences.

Figure 6.19 Diagram of a longitudinal comparison study

5 The experiment

If the aim of your research is to determine the effect that a change in one variable has upon another, an experimental design is required. While the other research designs provide useful information, the experimental design provides the most rigorous test of a hypothesis that specifies that changes in variable X cause changes in variable Y. The fundamental requirement of an experimental design is that the researcher has some control over variation in the independent variable and can control the influence of other variables.

The ideal form of the experimental design can be set out as follows. Take the hypothesis that a talk on nutritious snacks will promote healthier snack selection by workers at the cafeteria. It can be diagrammed in this way:

In order to test this hypothesis using an experimental design the researcher must follow this procedure:

1 Select two groups of workers. These two groups must be as alike as possible on any variable that might affect the dependent variable or the relation between the independent variable and the dependent variable (e.g. age, same proportion of males to females).

2 Devise measures for the variables. The dependent variable will be measured by the workers' snack selections observation checklist we developed earlier. The independent variable is whether the worker was present at the talk on nutritious snacks ('yes' or 'no').

3 Select one of the two groups of workers to be the control group. The control group will not be given the talk on nutritious snacks; the other group will.

4 The dependent variable will be measured before and after the talk is given to A-shift.

5 The principle of experimental design is that since the groups are as alike as possible, except that one has been exposed to the talk on nutritious

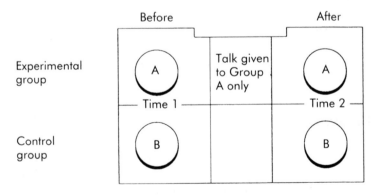

Figure 6.20 Diagram of experimental research design

snacks while the other has not, any difference between the two groups' snack selection behaviour can be attributed to the talk. The diagram of the experimental design is shown in Figure 6.20.

This research design asks the question, 'Is there a change in the difference between the experimental group and the control group following the manipulation of the independent variable?' Here the manipulation of the independent variable is the talk on nutritious snacks. Figures 6.21 and 6.22 provide two sets of hypothetical results. What would each set of results lead you to conclude?

Figure 6.21 Hypothetical results of an experimental study

Workers' snack selections at cafeteria 1 (in percentages)

	Before		After	
	A (Exp)	B (Control)	A (Exp)	B (Control)
Sweets	70	70	50	70
Fruit	20	20	40	20
Other	10	10	10	10

What do you conclude from this table of data? Did the talk have any impact on workers' snack selections?

Alternatively, what conclusion would you draw if the results were like those in Figure 6.22? Both groups changed but they changed by the same amount (A1 − A2 = B1 − B2). It would appear that the talk had no effect. Make additional tables of possible results and interpret them. It is good practice. First make one in which the control group changes but the experimental group stays the same. What would you conclude?

Figure 6.22 Hypothetical results of an experimental study

Workers' snack selections at cafeteria 2 (in percentages)

	Before		After	
	A1 (Exp)	B1 (Control)	A2 (Exp)	B2 (Control)
Sweets	70	70	60	60
Fruit	20	20	30	30
Other	10	10	10	10

How can an experimental research design test the hypothesis that changes in study cause changes in academic performance? Which is the independent variable? Which is the dependent variable? The operationalised form of this hypothesis has been diagrammed as follows:

In order to design an experiment, the researcher must be able to manipulate (change) the values of the independent variable. How can the researcher exercise control over the independent variable in this hypothesis? How can hours of study be manipulated?

The researcher selects two history classes that are the same in terms of variables considered critical to academic performance—age, past performance level, standard of teaching and lack of personal problems. For each class, the researcher distributes a reading and allows students 45 minutes to study it. She then administers a test on the reading. Later in the year, the researcher repeats this exercise with a reading of similar difficulty. For one class (the experimental group), she changes the amount of study time to 75 minutes. For the other class (the control group), she does not change the amount of study time. This class receives the same amount of time that was allocated in the original exercise—45 minutes. The researcher collates the results of each test for both classes and compares the results. This research would be diagrammed as shown in Figure 6.23.

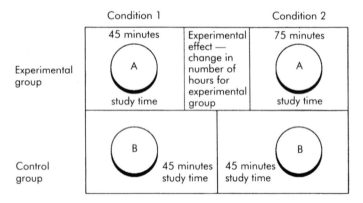

Figure 6.23 Diagram of experimental research design testing hypothesis on study time and academic performance

The independent variable 'time spent in study' is manipulated by the researcher in such a way that any time spent in study should be observable in the form of a change in the dependent variable, 'test marks'. The groups have been selected to be as alike as possible in all other respects. The results will be reported as average scores for each group since the researcher is interested in group performance rather than individual performance.

Figures 6.24, 6.25 and 6.26 depict possible results of such an experiment. Assume that the possible scores on the test ranged from 0 to 100. How would you interpret the results in Figure 6.24? Clearly, the results for the experimental group have improved and those of the control group have not. The results show that an increase in study has led to improved test results.

Figure 6.24 Hypothetical results of an experiment

Average results on comprehension tests for two classes 1

	Condition 1	Condition 2
Experimental group	60%	80%
Control group	60%	60%

The data in Figure 6.25 are inconclusive because results for both groups changed in the same direction by the same amount. The experimental group did better than the control group under both conditions but both groups improved from the first time to the second. It is not possible to conclude that an increase in study time contributed to the increase in results for the experimental group, because the control group increased by a similar amount.

Figure 6.25 Hypothetical results of an experiment

Average results on comprehension tests for two classes 2

	Condition 1	Condition 2
Experimental group	65%	70%
Control group	60%	65%

Look at Figure 6.26. What would you conclude from these results? They indicate that both groups improved but that the experimental group showed a much greater improvement. A likely conclusion would be that some of the improvement (that exhibited by both groups) was due to increased skill in doing this sort of examination due to the practice both groups received when writing the first test, but that the rest of the improvement (that shown only by the experimental group) was due to the increase in study time. Produce other hypothetical results in tables similar to these ones and practise interpreting them.

Figure 6.26 Hypothetical results of an experiment

Average results on comprehension tests for two classes 3

	Condition 1	Condition 2
Experimental group	65%	80%
Control group	60%	65%

In summary, an experimental research design is used to determine whether changes in the independent variable actually produce changes in the dependent variable. Does a change in X cause a change in Y? If you are planning to design an experiment consult the following checklist.

Checklist for designing an experiment

1 Are you able to manipulate the independent variable? Are you able to change the independent variable for the experimental group while holding it constant for the central group? Many independent variables cannot be manipulated satisfactorily. This may be due to our sense of what is ethical. For example, we do not arbitrarily move babies from one caregiver to another in order to assess the impact of the change.

2 Are you able to select two (or more) groups that are alike in all essential ways, one of which will become the control group and the other the experimental group (the group that gets the treatment)? Are you able to isolate the two groups so that the experimental group does not communicate with or otherwise affect the control group?

3 Are you able to measure the dependent variable for each group both before and after the change in the independent variable? An experiment requires before and after measures of the dependent variable for both the experimental and the control group.

4 Have you recorded your data and presented your findings in such a way that you can draw conclusions about the effect (or lack of effect) on the independent variable?

If you can answer 'yes' to all of these questions then you have designed an experimental study to test your hypothesis. You must be able to answer 'yes' to the first two questions in order to eliminate other possible explanations for the relationship between variables X and Y. By studying two groups as alike as possible, you eliminate the effects of outside variables. By manipulating the independent variable you come as close as possible to demonstrating that changes in variable X cause changes in variable Y.

How do you choose a research design?

Now that each type of research design has been described, you may be wondering how you choose between them. Remember that each design provides the answer to a particular kind of question. Hence, one of the first considerations in selecting a research design is 'What kind of question is being asked?' Figure 6.27 is a summary table of research designs and the questions each asks. Review it to refresh your memory of each design.

If the hypothesis you are testing asks, 'Does a change in the independent variable produce a change in the dependent variable?', then an experimental design is required. However, an experiment is not always possible. What can be done then? Use one of the other research designs, and mention in the limitations section of your research report that it is not the ideal design. Make sure that you draw only such conclusions as your data and research design permit.

Figure 6.27 The five basic types of research design

Type of design		Question asked
1 Simple case study (A)		What is happening?
2 Longitudinal study (A) (A) Time 1 Time 2		Has there been a change in A?
3 Comparison study (A) (B)		Are A and B different?
4 Longitudinal comparison study (A) (A) (B) (B) Time 1 Time 2		Are A and B different through time?
5 Experiment Experimental group (A) ↓ (A) Control group (B) (B) Time 1 Time 2		Is the difference between A and B due to a change (↓) in the independent variable?

Controlling the influence of other variables

At a number of points in this chapter we have referred to the possibility that other variables, not included in the study, might have been responsible for observed changes in the dependent variable. This is one of the greatest fears of a researcher—their results may be due to something not accounted for in the research design. For example, the improvement in students' exam performance might be due to increased skill in taking such exams and not to the increase in study time. For such reasons, it is important to control the influence of all other variables that might affect the variables under study.

How does the researcher control the influence of other variables? First, be aware of the fact that other variables may be influencing the data. As you design a piece of research, it is important to keep a list of other potentially influential variables. You may or may not eventually do anything about them, but it is important to be aware of such variables. All scientific conclusions are tentative, partly because of the impossibility of controlling everything. Thus, the first step is to be aware of the possible influence of other variables.

The second step is to take some of these variables into account when you design your study. You may wish to select people for your study who have the same characteristics, so the effects of outside variables will be the same for all people observed. If you were studying the relationship between age and smoking, you would have to control the effects of variables outside your research hypothesis, for example gender, social class, type of schooling, etc. Controlling the effects of these variables is a matter of keeping their effects constant for all people being studied—that way, differences in results cannot be caused by differences in the outside variables. For the study on smoking, you would ideally locate a sample of people whose attributes according to the outside variables are the same. The people would be of the same gender, social class and type of school. Then you could be confident that differences in the smoking behaviour of respondents of different ages are not caused by differences in the variables you have controlled, or kept constant.

The most important point about controls is to be aware of the possible influence of variables outside your hypothesis. Select groups in such a way as to eliminate the influence of as many outside variables as you can. Note the absence of controls for other outside variables in the limitations section of your report.

Questions for review

1   What basic question is answered by research design?
2   List the five types of research design. Diagram each design. What question does each ask?

SELECTING A RESEARCH DESIGN 111

3 Why is the case study said to be the basic building block of all research design?
4 What is required to do a longitudinal study?
5 What is required to do a comparison study?
6 What is required to do a longitudinal comparison study?
7 What are the key features of an experiment?
8 On what bases does a researcher choose a research design?
9 Why is it important to control for other variables?
10 How does one control for other variables?
11 What is done about variables over which the researcher has no control?

Suggestions for further reading

Blalock, H. M. Jr (1961), *Causal Inferences in Non-experimental Research*, University of North Carolina Press, Chapel Hill (a classic).

Campbell, D. T. and J. C. Stanley (1963), *Experimental and Quasi-experimental Designs for Research*, Rand McNally, Chicago (a classic treatment of research design).

de Vaus, D. A. (2002), *Surveys in Social Research*, 5th edn, Allen & Unwin, St Leonards, NSW, chapter 4.

Judd, C. M., E. R. Smith and L. H. Kidder (1991), *Research Methods in Social Relations*, Holt, Rinehart & Winston, Fort Worth, chapter 3.

Kumar, Ranjit (1999), *Research Methodology: A Step by Step Guide for Beginners*, Sage, London, chapters 7–8.

7

Selecting a sample

CHAPTER OUTLINE

To whom are you going to administer your questionnaire? Which history class will be the subject of your experiments? Which babies will be weighed and measured? Since it is impossible to weigh all babies, administer questionnaires to everyone and experiment on all history classes, researchers study a 'sample' of their subject populations. Indeed, it is often more desirable to study a sample than to try to study the whole population. A carefully drawn sample not only makes the task possible, it often produces more accurate results.

In everyday life we commonly use sampling to make judgments about facts and issues. If we want to check the seasoning of soup we stir it, take a sample and judge the seasoning level of the broth by tasting that sample. If we are buying a new car, we decide how the car can usually be expected to perform by taking it on a sample test drive. We make many judgments based on samples.

Care is taken to make sure the sample is an accurate reflection of the whole from which it is taken. In the case of soup, we stir so as to make sure the ingredients are as evenly distributed as possible, then we take a sample, taste it and draw a conclusion about—i.e. generalise the findings of our study to—the whole pot of soup. If we have heard that the car we are thinking of buying drives well on city roads but not on country roads, we would sample its performance on both types of road for an idea of how it handles in general.

Sampling is an important feature of all research. Part of the whole is studied and the results are taken to be an accurate reflection of the whole.

The most important point to remember about sampling is this:

The manner in which the sample is drawn determines to what extent we can generalise from the findings.

Only if the sample studied can be shown to represent a larger population can the results of a study of the sample be assumed to give reliable information about the larger population. If the sample studied is not representative, the conclusions drawn from the research must be limited to the sample studied.

For example, you might have developed a short questionnaire on attitudes toward nuclear weapons. If you had 20 of your friends, fellow students and relatives fill out your questionnaire, the results would be limited to that group of 20 people. On the other hand, if you had selected a sample of 20 people that accurately reflected the views of a larger group of 200 (for example, all the students enrolled in your course), you could draw conclusions about the 200 from the results of the sample of 20. In the first instance your findings were limited to the 20 people studied. In the second you could generalise the results to the larger population that your sample represented.

Although sampling soup is easy, sampling groups of people is rather more complicated. The basic problem is to select a sample that accurately reflects a specified larger group. Several techniques for drawing samples from groups of people have been devised by social scientists. The most basic and potentially useful of these techniques will be described in this chapter. The strengths and weaknesses of each will be discussed in order to help you select a technique appropriate to your research.

It should also be remembered that for some purposes sampling is not required. If the researcher is not interested in drawing conclusions for a larger population than that actually studied, sampling is not needed. For example, a psychologist might decide to study her baby's cognitive development. Only one baby (hers) is needed for the study. Why would she not be able to draw conclusions about all babies, or even other babies in her family? It is usually dangerous to rely on the observation of a single case to provide an accurate picture of a larger group. It would be like an American forming an opinion about all Australians after meeting one Australian. Depending upon which Australian was the basis of this 'case study', the most amazing and misleading impressions could be formed. In studies of single cases, generalisations cannot be safely drawn. There is no way of knowing whether the case studied will give an accurate impression of the whole.

The second situation in which sampling is not an issue occurs when the researcher can easily study the entire group about whom they wish to draw conclusions. If the interest is in the performance of one history class, or the comparison of two groups of workers, for example those who did and those who did not hear a speaker on nutrition, then sampling is not an issue. In these instances, the whole population is being studied. As long as the researcher is willing to limit the conclusions to the population they study, sampling is not an issue. If, however, the researcher wants to generalise—to draw conclusions about a large group on the basis of studying a few—then a sampling procedure must be selected.

Why do researchers sample? Samples are used to reduce the cost in time, energy and money of studying large populations. It is often simply not possible or desirable to study everyone. A sample is drawn from a large group in order to gain a reliable picture of that large group by studying a carefully selected smaller number of the population. The way in which the sample is selected determines whether reliable conclusions about the larger group can be drawn.

How to select a sample

What do you want to know? About whom do you want to know it? These are the questions to answer first. Given that it is impossible to know everything about everyone or all groups, selections must be made. First decide what you want to know. You did this when you formed a hypothesis, focused it and made it operational. You devised instruments and designed research. Once these things are done, attention is turned to the second question: about whom do you want to know?

The first step in sample selection is to identify the population about which you want to know something. Think back to your hypothesis. For example, the hypothesis about amount of study and academic performance relates to students. The largest possible population would be all students in the world at any time past, present and future. That would be an impossible population to sample. You may decide to limit your sample to students in Australian tertiary institutions. That is still a very large and diverse population. You might decide to limit your focus to students in your own institution. Finally, you might decide that making generalisations about all students everywhere is not so important and you are happy to settle for finding out what is happening in two history classes at your own institution.

Remember! It is perfectly legitimate to select any population as the object of your study.

The population about which you wish to generalise will affect your selection of a sampling procedure. Once you have decided whom you want to draw reliable conclusions about, you are ready to select a sampling procedure. What other practical factors might help you to decide which population you wish to be able to generalise about? Think about time and money.

Types of sampling procedure

There are two general types of sampling procedure: random and non-random. A random sampling procedure provides the greatest assurance that those selected are a representative sample of the larger group. If a non-random sampling procedure is used, the researcher can only hope that those selected for study bear some likeness to the larger group.

Non-random sampling procedures

Non-random sampling procedures include accidental sampling, accidental quota sampling, purposive sampling and systematic matching sampling. While useful for many studies, non-random sampling procedures provide only a weak basis for generalisation.

Accidental sampling

This sampling procedure involves using what is immediately available. A lecturer studies their own students; a psychologist studies their own children. A student studies the interaction patterns of the families of two friends and a cousin. These are all accidental samples. The persons, families and classes studied were selected because they were available, not because they were known to be representative of some larger group.

Some people confuse accidental sampling with random sampling. Persons met at random—that is, accidentally—do not comprise a random sample. Another difference with accidental samples is that the researcher does not know in what ways the sample is biased. How is the sample a misleading representative of the larger population about which information is desired? There is no way of checking this without doing a study of everyone, or a study of a properly drawn random sample.

The people on a given street at a given time will be a biased sample of residents of that suburb. Such an accidental sample will not give you reliable information about the residents of the suburb. A questionnaire on attitudes towards abortion given to every 10th person encountered at a suburban shopping centre will not provide a reliable indication of the opinions of residents of the suburb. It will only tell you the opinions of people who shop at that place at that hour on that day of the week. If you are interested in the opinions of the residents of the entire suburb, an accidental sample of Tuesday-morning shoppers will not provide the information.

Similarly, the families you know will be a biased sample of families in your city. They may be members of the same clubs, churches or political parties, or be at similar stages in the family life-cycle. In the same way, students enrolled in a particular subject or institution will be a biased sample of students. Think of ways in which the students enrolled in your subject would be a biased sample of students in your institution. This is why *the results of a study of an accidental sample apply only to the sample studied.*

An accidental sampling procedure is appropriate if you do not intend to draw conclusions about a larger group on the basis of the group you study. Accidental samples are handy, require little effort and are useful for many studies. The major disadvantage is that the findings of a study of an accidental sample are strictly limited to those studied because the researcher does not know in what ways the sample is biased. It is uncertain which aspects of the total population are included and which are not.

Accidental quota sampling

In an accidental quota sampling procedure, the researcher selects individuals or groups on the basis of set criteria. A researcher comparing the opinions of males and females might set a quota of 50 males and 50 females. This will ensure that the sample studied has both females and males. Another researcher, comparing the performance of history classes and English classes, might specify that the sample must contain the same number of students from each type of class. Someone interested in the difference between students of different universities, social classes, incomes or ethnic groups might specify in advance the number or proportion of each desired in the sample.

Perhaps a more developed example will help. Assume you are interested in comparing the attitudes towards university held by secondary school students from different ethnic groups. To make sure that the sample you study has students from each of the ethnic groups, you might set a quota of 10 students from each of the ethnic groups you wish to compare. By selecting 10 students from each ethnic group—that is, by filling your quota—you make sure that your sample includes people or groups with certain specified characteristics, in this instance ethnic background.

Quota sampling is useful when a particular group or characteristic is relatively rare in the population. By setting a quota and selecting people until the quota is filled, you ensure that the group or characteristics you want in the sample are adequately represented in the sample for the analyses you want to do.

Quota sampling, however, suffers most of the same defects as accidental sampling. Can you see why? Although the researcher is assured of the presence of certain categories in the sample, for example males and females, or Greek, Dutch, English and Vietnamese students, the representativeness of the sample is still not ensured. This is due to the fact that the individuals or groups are not selected randomly. The sample may have 50 males and 50 females, but of whom are these males and females representative? This is not known. The sample selected may have 10 Greek students, 10 Dutch students, 10 English students and 10 Vietnamese students. But it is not known whether the 10 Dutch students are an unbiased sample of Dutch students. It is not known whether a study of the 10 Greek students will provide reliable information about other Greek students. In other words, it is risky to draw conclusions about a larger group from an accidental quota sample of that group. Nonetheless, this sampling procedure is often used due to the pressures of time and budget. Conclusions drawn are strictly limited to the population actually studied. Tentative implications for others may be suggested.

Purposive sampling

Some researchers believe that they can, using their own judgment or intuition, select the best people or groups to be studied. The 'typical' rural school is selected and studied, and the results generalised to all rural schools. The 'typical' first-year sociology class is compared with the 'typical' first-year history class. How are these known to be typical? Unless objective criteria are set out beforehand and each group is shown to meet these criteria, there is no way of knowing. However, there are times when this is the only practical way to draw a sample. If a purposive sample is studied, only tentative generalisations may be made. The conclusions drawn from a comparison of a few 'typical' rural schools with a few 'typical' urban schools might be phrased in this way:

> The results of this study comparing three rural and three urban schools have revealed the following six major differences. While it is not strictly possible to generalise from this sample to all rural and urban schools, we think it is likely that these differences will be found in other instances.

The snowball technique

The snowball sampling technique is used when you need to gain access to certain types of people or to a particular group, but you know only a few people who fit the category and there is no publicly available listing. In this technique you gather your sample by first approaching those who are available and ask them to nominate others that they know, and then they nominate still others. In this way your sample grows like a snowball, the most recently formed layer providing the contact with those to be added next. For example, you may wish to interview practising shamans in order to understand some aspects of New Age religious practice. But you know only one shaman and the local listing of the Australian Shaman Network was not much help. You would ask the one you know to nominate others, who you then ask to nominate still others until you have a sample large enough for your purposes. The snowball technique is used a great deal in qualitative research into less well-organised aspects of social life. It can be seen as a variation of purposive sampling. The conclusion of your study of shamans might be phrased in this way:

This study of a sample of practising shamans reveals that people consult shamans for the following purposes and that the shamans interviewed provide the following services, have the following range of training, come from certain backgrounds and have been practising an average of X years. While these findings cannot be generalised to all practising shamans, the shamans interviewed represent 60 per cent of known shamans in Australia.

Systematic matching sampling

In this procedure, individual subjects or groups are systematically matched with others who are similar in all but one critical attribute. It can be effective in at least two situations.

First, it is useful for controlling the influence of variables outside the research hypothesis or research objective. Say you wish to sample Year 3 students in a large primary school, to find out if male and female students have reacted differently to a new method of teaching. The school has a great deal of ethnic diversity and you suspect that the new system will have different effects on students from different ethnic backgrounds. To control the variable 'ethnicity', you construct your sample by systematically matching males and females of the same ethnic background. You might arrive at a sample of 10 students, containing a male and female from five different ethnic groups, British–Australian, Vietnamese, Italian, Greek and Indian. You can now compare the differences between males and females for each ethnic 'pair' and summarise the general gender differences, noting any variations among the ethnic categories.

Second, a systematic matching sampling procedure is often appropriate when a researcher wants to compare two groups of very different sizes. A study might compare female and male politicians in terms of their goals for social reform. There are currently very few female politicians, so in sampling male politicians for comparison the researcher needs to be careful. The population of males in parliament is so much greater that they can be expected to be far more diverse than the females and many would be inappropriate for a gender-based comparison study. Some would have been in parliament much longer than any female politicians. Others might be from ethnic groups that are highly under-represented among the females. Also, many of the males would probably have less formal education than most female politicians. Therefore, it is important to 'match' the subjects in the sample. If the researcher doesn't, then their sample of females will be compared to males who are too different for a reasonable comparison.

We could select 10 female politicians (randomly or non-randomly) and systematically match them to 10 male politicians. Each male would be selected because they matched a female politician in certain features deemed to be important to the consideration of social reform. Examples of such matching features might be age, length of service in cabinet or the back bench, education, marital status, and sexuality. Though the claim to representativeness is weak, this sampling procedure is often a suitable compromise when comparing groups of extremely different size.

Summary of non-random sampling procedures

These examples of non-random sampling procedures are given because they are frequently used by researchers. If a non-random sampling procedure is used the researcher must be aware of the limitations to the conclusions drawn. Technically, the conclusions drawn from a study of a non-random sample are limited to that sample and cannot be used for further generalisations. Read through some research literature in your library. Can you find an example of non-random sampling being used?

Random sampling procedures

Random sampling procedures provide the greatest assurance that the sample accurately represents the population. There are four basic random sampling procedures: simple random sampling, systematic sampling, stratified random sampling and cluster sampling.

Simple random sampling

This is the ideal method of drawing a sample. It is, however, very difficult to do. A simple random sampling procedure guarantees that each element (person, group, university, etc.) in the population has an equal chance of being selected and that every possible combination of the specified number of elements has an equal chance of selection. The mathematics of such selection procedures is very complex and beyond the scope of this text.

In order to draw a simple random sample the researcher must:

1 identify the population from which the sample is to be drawn
2 enumerate and list each element (or persons, households, car owners, etc.) in the population
3 devise a method of selection that ensures that each element has the same probability of selection and that each combination of the total number of elements has the same probability of selection.

Given the virtual impossibility of meeting all these criteria, it is not surprising that a number of acceptable compromises have been devised. Essentially the task is to devise some form of lottery in which each combination of numbers has an equal chance of coming up.

The first set of 'compromise' random sampling procedures involves studies in which it is possible to identify and enumerate the total population. For example, while possible, it is usually too much work to identify and enumerate the total population of university students in a particular year. It would be possible to identify and enumerate the students enrolled in your course. Other populations that are relatively easy to enumerate are the members of a particular club, the students in a history class, the teachers in a school, the children in a particular day-care centre, people in a home for the elderly, people whose names are in a telephone directory on a voter registration roll, or all the state secondary schools in Queensland. The telephone directory may pose particular problems. If the city is large, do you enumerate all the subscribers? What about non-representativeness, since it only includes subscribers and usually only one name for each household? In what ways would a voter registration roll be biased? Once identified and enumerated (that is, numbered from beginning to end), a sample may be selected.

Here is an example. You want to study a simple random sample of the 250 first-year sociology students at a particular university. The first step is done. You have identified the population. The second step is to identify and enumerate each element in the population. In this instance the elements are the 250 students. The students will have to be listed and numbered from 1 to 250:

1   Jane Allsmith
2   Toula Papadopoulos
3   George Black
4   Amirah Mubavach
...
250 Mildred Zylstra

You have identified and enumerated the whole population to which you want to generalise the findings of your study. It is now possible to move to the next step—selecting the sample. We will deal with issues of sample size later in the chapter. Let us assume that you decided to draw a sample of 50 students from the larger population of 250 students.

The most acceptable way of selecting a sample from an enumerated population involves the use of a table of random numbers. Such a table appears in Appendix B of this book. A starting-point in the table is picked (usually by the accidental fall of the point of a pen) and those elements of the whole population whose numbers come up as you move down the column from the starting-point are selected for the sample. Do this until a sample of the required size is achieved.

To draw the sample of 50 students from 250 sociology students by this procedure you would do the following. Remember: each student has been given a number from 1 to 250. Figure 7.1 is a section from a table of random numbers. Because the numbers you need to select have between one and three digits (or are comprised of three digits, 001–250) you will use the first three digits of each number in the table. The next step is to select a starting-point.

This can be done by closing your eyes and pointing a pen at the table and starting there. It is permissible to move up or down the columns, as the numbers are random—that is, there is no pattern in the table. The numbers are in no particular order. Had your pen landed on a number for which the first three digits were outside the range 001–250, you would try again or move to the next number for which the first three digits were in this range.

Figure 7.1 Using a table of random numbers

28071	03528	89714
48210	48761	▷ 02365
83417	20219	82900
20531	43657	45100
94654	97801	01153
52839	42986	28100
74591	▷ 16100	91478
38921	56913	32675
40759	84027	52831
45980	70523	47985
52182	68194	62783
12890	59208	00691
08523	74312	13542

Assume your pen landed on number 161. If you decided to move down the columns the next number to be selected would be the next number in the range 001–250 that was not 161 (since 161 has already been selected). In this table it would be element (student) number 023. The next would be student 011, then 006, then 135. Then you would go on to the next column. You would continue this procedure until you had selected a total of 50 students. You would then have a simple random sample of 50 students, which is more likely to be representative of the population of 250 than a sample chosen non-randomly.

To give yourself practice start again at number 161, but move up the columns. Which numbers would then be selected? A different sample of 50 would be drawn, but because it was randomly selected the results of studying it would also be more likely to give reliable information about the whole group than the results of a non-random sample. Indeed, we would expect only the smallest difference between a study of the first sample and a study of the second.

Another acceptable form of selection is to put all the names or numbers in a hat and draw out the number required. To ensure that each element and combination of elements has the same probability of selection, each time a selection is made the name or number should be returned to the hat. If a number is drawn more than once it is again returned to the hat, but the number is not 'selected' twice.

The random selection of a sample of 50 students from 250 according to this method would require that all the students' names, or a set of numbers from 001 to 250, be put in a container. The container would be shaken before each draw. The first 50 students whose names (or numbers) were drawn would form the sample.

Although these techniques are somewhat laborious and time-consuming, they do provide the most reliable sampling procedures. The simple random sample is the ideal.

Systematic sampling

A systematic sampling procedure involves the selection of every n^{th} case in a list. Again, the population must be identified, but it is not necessary to enumerate the list. For example, if you had a list of 400 students in Communications 101 and you wanted a sample of 80, you might select every fifth name on the list. To draw a systematic sample you need to know the total number in the group and the number you want in the sample. By dividing the total number by the sample number you find the interval at which you will select people:

Total population   =   400
Sample desired   =   80
Interval   = $400 \div 80 = 5$

If the interval will be an uneven number, the nearest whole number is selected:

Total population   =   393
Sample desired   =   80
Interval   = $393 \div 80 = 4.9$ R 5

The critical step in systematic sampling is to select the first case randomly. To do this one of the first elements (names, groups, numbers or schools) in the long list must be selected. If the interval is five, one of the first five must be selected as the starting-point. If the interval is 10, then you must select one of the first 10 and so on. The easiest way to make a random selection is to put all the numbers (one to five, or to 10, or whatever) in a container, shake it and draw out a number. That number will be your starting-point. Or you could close your eyes and pick one of the elements in the first interval. The first element must be selected randomly. Once the first element is selected then each nth element (n = interval) thereafter is selected. In the example of the list of students doing Communications 101, the list had 400 names and the interval was five. Assume that the number four was drawn out of the container. Selection would start with the fourth student on the list. You then count down to the fifth next student on the list, E. Chatterly, and add them to your sample.

S. Aaron	D. Enticott
J. Adams	R. Farah
K. Adams	I. Grozdanovski
M. Belanti★	S. Harris★
A. Bordignon	T. Ho
P. Bourne	M. Todorovic
N. Bradley	E. Warnecke
L. Brookman	B. Wignell
E. Chatterly★	G. Yates
H. Donaldson	

If a selected student is unavailable, they are replaced by the preceding student on the list. If S. Harris were unavailable, then Grozdanovski would have been selected. When a selected student has dropped out of the subject, they are replaced by the next student on the list. If E. Chatterly had also dropped out, H. Donaldson would be the replacement. Another replacement strategy is to flip a coin (heads = name before, tails = name after). Note: names are replaced only if they are genuinely unavailable, not because the researcher might prefer someone else to be in the sample.

A systematic sampling procedure provides an acceptable approximation of the ideals of the simple random sampling procedure. It helps to overcome researcher bias in sample selection. Selection is done independently of the researcher's preferences and prejudices. As long as any biases in the ordering of the list do not occur at the same interval as the sampling interval, a reasonably reliable sample will be drawn by this procedure.

Stratified random sampling

This procedure is basically a type of quota sampling, where members of each 'quota group' within, or stratum of, the sample are selected randomly. You may wish to compare types of schools in terms of the overall performance of students. A simple random sample of schools might not provide enough cases in some of the categories of analysis you intend to use. You might classify the schools into urban, suburban and rural schools. Having done that, the schools in each group would be identified and enumerated and a random sample of each group identified.

For example, you might want to compare the attitudes toward nuclear disarmament held by university students studying maths and science with those held by humanities students. Rather than do a simple random sample of the students collectively enrolled in these faculties at a particular university, you would identify all students in each category, list them separately and draw a sample from each list using one of the random selection processes outlined above—using a table of random numbers, drawing names from a hat or using systematic sampling.

The criterion for identifying quota groups or strata will be suggested by your hypothesis. A hypothesis comparing males with females could be studied using a random sample with quotas of randomly selected males and females. Similarly, if the hypothesis compares high-income families with low-income families, it would be possible to use a random sample with quotas of randomly selected high-income and low-income families.

Cluster sampling

The fact that simple random sampling becomes tremendously complex and costly for large and scattered populations has led to the development of cluster sampling procedures. These usually involve several stages of random selections. Rather than enumerating the whole population, the population is divided into segments. Then several of the segments are chosen at random. Elements within each segment are then selected randomly following identification and enumeration. In this way, only the elements in the selected segment need to be identified and enumerated.

National samples are usually drawn on a multi-stage cluster sample procedure. So are samples of cities. For example, a sample of households in the Perth metropolitan area might be drawn by first dividing Perth into segments (these already exist for purposes of the census). A number of segments could be drawn at random. Within each segment, residential blocks would be identified and enumerated and a random selection of blocks drawn. Finally, the residences on each selected block would be identified and enumerated and a random sample of residences selected on the basis of an unbiased rule of selection. In this way, a random sample of Perth residences would be approximated. Cluster sampling procedures have been devised to provide a reliably random, and hence representative, sample of a large population without having to identify and enumerate the entire population at the outset. In this procedure, only smaller randomly selected segments (clusters) have to be identified and enumerated.

Choosing a sampling procedure

The essentials of the basic forms of sampling have been presented. How do you select a sampling procedure for your research? This depends largely on the population about which you wish to draw conclusions. If you are happy to limit your conclusion, for example, to the students in your tutorial group, that accidental sample will do perfectly well. If the demands of time and expense force you to examine a subgroup of a larger population, one of the random sampling procedures should be used. The extra effort pays great dividends in the value of your research conclusions. For a relatively small effort you can dramatically increase the representativeness of your findings and reduce the influence of any known or unknown biases.

Random sampling procedures are particularly important in research that aims to assess the attitudes, values or beliefs of a population. Public opinion polls usually use some form of random sampling. On the basis of their samples, such pollsters predict how people will vote, what brands of detergent they will buy and in what direction popular tastes are shifting.

Finally, it is impossible to generalise from most case studies. If a case study is conducted for the residents of a street, it cannot be stated that the street is representative of the suburb, the city or the state. Case studies only include observations of sections of larger populations and provide the researcher with no observations outside their boundaries.

Determining sample size

How large a sample do you need? What is the appropriate sample size for your project? These are very difficult questions to answer. Several basic issues need to be considered in determining sample size.

First, if statistics are going to be used in the analysis and interpretation of data there are usually requirements for sample size. We will not elaborate on these requirements since this text takes a non-statistical approach to the research process. Professional researchers must take these considerations into account.

Second, the more questions asked, the more variables controlled for and the more detailed the analysis of the data, the larger the sample will have to be to provide sufficient data for the analysis. In professional research, samples of hundreds or thousands will be drawn to accommodate this demand.

While large samples may seem more conclusive, it is how the sample is drawn that determines how representative it is. In general, large samples are not necessarily better than smaller ones. We do not have to drink a large amount of soup to determine whether it needs more salt—a taste will do. In addition, practical considerations of time, money and effort often combine to keep sample sizes relatively small.

Most of the research you will read about in journals or papers is based on large samples, but we have a few suggestions regarding sample size for student projects. Since the goal of such projects is to learn basic research skills rather than to produce results that are generalised to large populations, several basic compromises are possible. These suggestions for student projects take the form of two basic rules:

1 About 30 individual elements are required in order to provide a pool large enough for even simple kinds of analyses.

2 You need a sample large enough to ensure that it is theoretically possible for each cell in your analytical table to have five cases fall in it. A few examples will make this clear.

Remember the study of snack selection (in chapter 6). Workers' snack selections were categorised according to the table in Figure 7.2.

Figure 7.2 A dummy table for the categorization of workers' snack selections

Sweet	Fruit	Other
1	2	3

This is usually referred to as a 'dummy' table. It is a table prepared before the collection of data to help to focus the issues of the research, guide data collection and help determine sample size. In this case, the data-recording form, dummy table and final table for presentation of data take the same form. This dummy table has three cells. The minimum sample size for this study would be 3 x 5 = 15 (but it would still be preferable to have 30 because of the first basic rule regarding minimum sample size).

This example was also turned into a comparative study between food purchases by machine operators on A-shift and other shifts. The dummy table for such a study looked like Figure 7.3.

Figure 7.3 A dummy table comparing snack selections of machine operators on A-shift with machine operators on other shifts

Snack selected	Machine operators on A-shift	Machine operators on other shifts
Sweet	1	2
Fruit	3	4
Other	5	6

This dummy table has six cells; hence, the sample size required would be 6 x 5 = 30. Moreover, this study involves comparing two groups of machine operators. Since each group is accorded three cells in the table, each group requires a sample of 3 x 5 = 15. You might select an accidental quota, stratified random or cluster sampling procedure to draw a sample of at least 15 of each group of machine operators.

It is at this stage that you can best see the impact of adding variables to the analysis. It is always a temptation to add a variable. Indeed, you may have good reason to want to assess the impact of a number of variables. Professional research often analyses many variables. However, adding one variable will increase the sample size required and the complexity of analysing the data. Again, the use of dummy tables is very helpful in clarifying this for the researcher. By adding one variable to the analysis of workers' snack selections the sample size was doubled and the size of the dummy table doubled. If we were to add another variable, for example gender, we would require two tables like that in Figure 7.3, one for males and one for females. The sample size would be 12 x 5 = 60. A combined dummy table for such a study would look like Figure 7.4.

Figure 7.4 A dummy table for a study of workers' snack selections comparing males with females and machine operators on A-shift with machine operators on other shifts

Snack selection	Machine operators on A-shift		Machine operators on other shifts	
	Male	Female	Male	Female
Sweet	1	2	3	4
Fruit	5	6	7	8
Other	9	10	11	12

Adding another variable, such as 'marital status', would require yet another doubling of sample size and add further complexity to the data analysis.

What would a dummy table look like for a study of the impact of 'study time' on 'mark received in a history exam'? In our previous use of this example (in chapter 5), we used a line graph to present possible results. A second use of dummy tables can now be seen. They help to specify categories of analysis and data collection. The data–collection sheet suggested for this study (chapter 5, Figure 5.8) asked the student to keep track of the amount of time spent in revision and the mark received in a history examination. For each student the data-summarisation form (chapter 5, Figure 5.9) recorded total study time and mark. The number of students required for your sample depends on how you are going to analyse your data. A minimum of about 30 is required regardless of the form of analysis.

However, if you were planning to analyse the data by placing it in a table, the number of cells in the table would also play a role in determining sample size. It would be possible to have a very large table with a row for every mark from 1 to 100. That would require a sample of 500 if only one category of 'time spent studying' were used (1000 if two categories of 'time spent studying' were used, etc.). Needless to say, that is not suitable for our purposes. Hence a smaller number of categories for reporting and analysing both the dependent variable (marks) and the independent variable (time spent studying) must be found. The simplest categorisation for marks would be pass/fail, but that might not be satisfactory. You might prefer fail, 50–64, 65–74, 75+. That would be four categories of marks (see Figures 7.5 and 7.6).

Then there is the problem of finding categories for 'time spent studying'. This poses a different kind of problem. Again, you could have a row in your table for each possible value reported from 0 to perhaps 120 hours. This suffers from the same fault as does having a column for each possible mark. Such a table would require 100 x 120 x 5 = 60 000 students in the sample. How are numbers of hours to be categorised? You will not know the range of values until the data are collected. But you might decide to have two categories—high and low. When the data have been gathered you determine the average number of hours studied. All those above average are categorised 'high' and those below are categorised 'low'. Or you might decide to have three categories—high, moderate and low. In this case, you divide the sample into three even groups, those with the highest number of hours, a moderate number and the lowest number. It is best to work this out first because of the indications for your sample size. Figures 7.5 and 7.6 demonstrate this.

In Figure 7.5 two categories are used for the analysis of each variable. The sample required for such a study could be 4 x 5 = 20 (30 would be better). In Figure 7.6 four categories are used for the dependent variable and three for the independent variable. The sample size required is 4 x 3 x 5 = 60.

The role of dummy tables can now be seen. They focus the research. They help to determine the categories of data analysis. They help to determine

Figure 7.5 A dummy table for a study of the impact of number of hours spent in revision on examination results using two categories for each variable

Examination result	Number of hours spent in revision	
	High	Low
Pass		
Fail		

Figure 7.6 A dummy table for a study of the impact of number of hours spent in revision on examination results using four categories for the dependent variable and three for the independent variable

Examination result	Hours spent in revision		
	Low	Moderate	High
75+			
65–74			
50–64			
Fail			

sample size. By devising dummy tables before collecting data, the researcher will not collect more data than are actually going to be used. There is no point in collecting data that will not go into the tables. The researcher is also guided in sample selection by decisions about data analysis. In this way, neither too much nor too little data are collected for analysis.

A few more examples may help to clarify this important procedure. What samples are required for longitudinal or comparative studies? Take the example of a 'before and after' longitudinal study. In such a study, the same group is studied at two points in time. Hence the determination of sample size is made by only one of the tables.

Refer back to the example of a longitudinal study on nutrition in chapter 6. Because the same group is measured twice, there must be a sufficient sample of that group in each measurement. The before and after measures each have three categories, so the minimum sample would be 3 x 5 = 15.

Take the example of the questionnaire developed to assess attitudes toward the use of nuclear materials (chapter 5). Data produced by questionnaires have to be categorised just like test results or numbers of hours spent in revision. Like test results, scales on a questionnaire have a theoretical range. For the questionnaire on nuclear materials, the range was from a low of five (indicating agreement with anti-nuclear statements) to a high of 20 (indicating disagreement with such statements). It is unlikely that you would want a table with 16 columns for this dependent variable. It will have to be categorised. High versus low agreement, and high, medium and low agreement, are two possibilities. If you were comparing two groups, for example a sample from the local Returned Services League and a sample from the local Citizens for Peace, your dummy table might look like that in Figure 7.7. The sample for this study would comprise a minimum of 10 from each group. This might be achieved by a quota (accidental quota) or a stratified random (random quota) or cluster sampling procedure. Which would be best and why?

Figure 7.7 A dummy table for a study comparing the views of two groups on the use of nuclear material

Position on use of nuclear material	Returned Services League	Citizens for Peace
Agreement		
Disagreement		

The example of a study of sexist attitudes among males provides another opportunity to examine the utility of dummy tables. The questionnaire suggested for such a study is found in chapter 5. The hypothesis was this:

Males who have gone to single-sex schools are more sexist in their attitudes than males who have attended coeducational schools.

The independent variable is 'school social environment', single-sex vs coeducational. The dependent variable is 'sexist attitudes', as measured by responses to a five-item scale. The independent variable has two categories: single-sex and coeducational schooling (three if you include the 'mixed' category). Hence, the table for analysing the data will have two columns, one for each category (or three if the 'mixed' category is included).

How is the dependent variable to be categorised? Again it is unlikely that one row would be used for each of the 21 possible scores on the sexism scale. This would require a table with 21 rows. An alternative is to reduce the number of categories used to present and analyse the dependent variable. The way the scale was constructed, 'agreement' indicated a sexist orientation and 'disagreement' indicated a lack of sexism. The midpoint on this scale was 15. A score below 15 could be taken to indicate low sexism. A score of 15 or higher could be taken to indicate high sexism. This would give two categories for the dependent variable. The break-point in the categories is determined here by the nature of the scale. Since there are two categories for the dependent variable, the table for analysing data will have two rows.

Figure 7.8 A dummy table for a study of the impact of educational background on sexist attitudes among males

Sexism score	Educational background	
	Single-sex school	Coeducational school
High		
Low		

Figure 7.8 presents a dummy table for this study. The minimum sample for this study would be 20, 10 males from each educational context. If the researcher decided to use three categories for the sexism score, the minimum sample would be 30. If the researcher decided to include a category for mixed educational background as well, the sample size would have to increase to 45. Can you see why? To add a medium sexism category would add another row to the table, with the result that the table would have two columns and three rows, and thus six cells. Applying our guide rule of an average of five per cell, we would need a sample of 6 x 5 = 30. If the 'mixed' category were added to the education context categories as well, the table would have three rows and three columns, and thus nine cells: 9 x 5 = 45. Make up dummy tables for each of these proposed ways of analysing the data.

For practical purposes, the sample size of student projects can be guided by two basic rules. First, 30 is the minimum sample size for most studies. Second, if analysis is to be carried out using tables, the sample size must be five times the number of cells in the table. Students should remember that in professional research usually much larger samples are used. By limiting both the number of variables and the number of categories used to analyse each variable, smaller samples can be used. This will provide worthwhile experience in the research process.

Summary

The way in which the research sample is drawn determines the degree to which you can generalise from the findings of your study. Only randomly drawn samples ensure that the sample is likely to be representative of a larger population. Although other forms of sampling are used, the findings of such studies are limited to the samples studied. Dummy tables are helpful in determining sample size, focusing the questions to be asked in the research and preparing the way for the later analysis of the data.

Questions for review

1   Why do researchers use sampling procedures?
2   Why is it risky to rely on the observation of a single case in making generalisations about groups?
3   What are the two basic types of sampling procedure?
4   What are the advantages and disadvantages of each sampling procedure described?
5   What are the steps that must be taken in order to draw a truly random sample? Name two compromises with this ideal.
6   What are the critical issues in determining sample size?
7   While it is often necessary for researchers to study large samples in order to examine in detail the influence of many variables, what two basic rules can usefully guide student researchers in determining sample size?
8   Read several articles reporting research results that have been published in professional social and behavioural science journals. What sampling procedures were used?
9   Read an article, report or research published in a newspaper, then answer these questions. If you do not think the article contains enough information, say so. Then guess what might have been done.

a How was the sample for this study drawn?
b What type of sample would you say this was?
c What dummy tables might have been used for this study?
d What hypothesis might this study have been designed to test?
e What were the basic concepts in this study?
f What variables were selected to measure the concepts involved in this study?
g How were the data collected?
h What conclusions were reached?

Suggestions for further reading

Argyrous, George (2000), *Statistics for Social and Health Research*, Sage, London.

Babbie, E. R. (2003), *The Practice of Social Research*, 10th edn, Wadsworth Publishing, London, chapter 7.

de Vaus, D. A. (2002), *Surveys in Social Research*, 5th edn, Allen & Unwin, St Leonards, NSW, chapter 4.

Foddy, W. (1988), *Elementary Applied Statistics for the Social Sciences*, Harper & Row, Sydney, pp. 104–5, 223.

Judd, C. M., E. R. Smith and L. H. Kidder (1991), *Research Methods in Social Relations*, Holt, Rinehart & Winston, Fort Worth, chapters 6 & 9.

Kumar, Ranjit (1999), *Research Methodology: A Step by Step Guide for Beginners*, Sage, London, chapter 12.

Those interested might consult one of the following classic sources on sampling procedure:

Backstrom, C. and G. Hursh (1963), *Survey Research*, Northwestern University Press, Evanston, Chicago, pp. 23–66.

Festinger, L. and D. Katz (1953), *Research Methods in the Behavioural Sciences*, Holt, Rinehart & Winston, New York, pp. 173–240.

Goode, W. and P. Hatt (1952), *Methods in Social Research*, McGraw-Hill, New York, pp. 209–31.

Selltiz, E., M. Jahoda, M. Deutsch and S. Cook (1966), *Research Methods in Social Relations*, Holt, Rinehart & Winston, New York, pp. 509–45.

PHASE 2
Data Collection

8

Collecting data

CHAPTER OUTLINE

By now you should be well aware that doing research involves far more than data collection. The research process does not begin, nor does it end, with data collection. Before worthwhile data collection can be done the researcher must:

1 focus the problem
2 identify and define the basic concepts involved
3 select variables that relate to each of the concepts under study
4 devise ways of measuring each of the variables
5 select a research design that will provide the desired information about the relation between variables
6 decide on a sampling procedure
7 draw the sample.

Unless each of these essential first steps is completed, data collection will often be done in a wasteful, haphazard and unproductive way.

If preparatory steps are completed, data collection can proceed smoothly, efficiently and with little wasted time or effort on the part of either the researcher or the participants in the research. Time is a scarce resource for most researchers. Moreover, someone who is being interviewed has the right to expect the researcher to be organised, efficient and professional. More about this later.

There is a sense in which, having done all the preparation, all that is required of this chapter is to say: *Go to it!* While that is true, there are a few important issues to consider.

Attention to detail

While you are collecting and recording your data it is essential to pay careful attention to detail in observation. The loss of detail in data collection may make subsequent data analysis impossible. Here are some suggestions for attending to detail in the research process.

The following suggestions largely assume that records will be kept on sheets of paper or on cards. However, given developments in computer software, many who are computer-literate will record their bibliography on computer disks, keeping their notes in a program that allows them to recall notes on similar topics and will record their data for analysis. The logic of these activities remains the same. Certain records must be kept, and they must be kept clearly and in such a way that they can be retrieved easily. If you rely on computer storage and retrieval for your information, make sure you back it up frequently and print out hard copies from time to time to protect yourself against loss due to computer failure or human error.

Keep a research journal

A research journal is a good idea. Keep a record of the ideas you have considered. Record the decisions you make and the reasons for the decisions. It is amazing how much you forget in a short time. What decisions did you make as you narrowed the focus of your research project? What forms of the hypothesis and research question did you consider? Why did you select the one you did? Why did you select the variables you did? How did you develop the measure for your variables? What issues did you consider as you chose a sampling procedure and actually selected your sample? A few notes on these issues kept in a research journal (or logbook) will be very helpful when you write your report. They are also helpful in answering questions people may raise about the research.

Maintain a bibliography

Another useful tip is to keep a record of the material you have read or consulted in the course of your research. If you note the details when you consult the material you save yourself the effort of trying to find it again later. It is best to keep your bibliography and note cards separately. Then at the end you will have a complete bibliography in one place and your notes where you need them to write the text of your report. Both notes and bibliography records can be kept on cards or as electronic files. Remember to back up files to prevent accidental loss. Some examples follow.

Dixon, B. R. and G. D. Bouma (1981), *Human Development and Society*, Oxford University Press, Melbourne.

Figure 8.1 A sample bibliography card for a book

The information required for a book is author(s), date, title, publisher and place of publication.

Marks, Gary N., John S. Western and Mark C. Western (1989), 'Class and Income in Australia', *The Australian and New Zealand Journal of Sociology*, **25**, 3: 410–27.

Figure 8.2 A sample bibliography card for an article

The information required for an article is author(s), date, title, journal, volume number, issue number (if there is one) and page span.

Bouma, Gary D. (1991), 'By What Authority? An Analysis of the Locus of Ultimate Authority in Ecclesiastical Organisations', pp. 121–31 in A. Black (ed.), *Religion in Australia*, Allen & Unwin, Sydney.

Figure 8.3 A sample bibliography card for a chapter (or an article reprinted) in an edited book

The information required for a chapter in an edited book is author(s), date, title of chapter, page span of chapter, name of book editor, title of book, publisher and place of publication.

Rather than providing an example of every possible type of publication, the order of the information required is given below. In this way, if you encounter a type of publication you are not sure how to handle, you can work it out for yourself. If you are still confused, ask your tutor or lecturer. There is no single universally accepted format for referencing. This one is common in the social sciences. There are some very useful computer programs for storing useful bibliographic information.

1 **The author(s).** The authors are listed as they appear, in the order they appear, with initials or full names as you wish. If the author is a group or organisation, for example the National Health and Medical Research Council, it is listed as the author. If the author is unknown, put 'anon.' for anonymous instead of the author. If the author(s) is in fact the editor(s) of the book, place (ed.) or (eds) after the name of the author(s) as required.

2   **The date of publication.** This should be the date of the edition to which you are referring. Some people put the date of original publication in brackets after the publication date if the two dates are different. If one author has more than one publication in a year, they are listed in order of publication (to the best knowledge of the researcher) in the following manner:

Author (date a)

Author (date b)

3   **The title of the work cited.** If a book, it is underlined or put in italics. If a journal article or a chapter in a book, it may be enclosed in inverted commas.

   a   For journal articles, chapters in books and articles in newspapers, the title is followed by a statement of the larger source of which it is a part and the pages on which it is found. The form for an article and a chapter in an edited book is given in Figure 8.3.

   b   For books, government publications, newspapers (unless it is absolutely obvious), and encyclopaedias, the title is followed by the publisher and the place of publication.

The general rule is that a bibliographic reference must include all the information someone else would need to find the reference quickly and easily. One card is kept for each work consulted. When the time comes to do your bibliography or list of references, you need only put your cards in alphabetical order and type them up.

Recording notes

Note cards are useful for keeping track of ideas and information you read in the sources you consult. When it comes time to write your report you need merely consult your notes and you will have all the information you need for a proper quotation and reference. Begin a new note record for each work from which you take notes. Head the record with the name of the author and the date of publication. A sample record is depicted in Figure 8.4. It helps to relocate material if you keep both your bibliography cards and note records in alphabetical order.

Some computer software is designed for note-taking and retrieval, allowing you to 'scan' your notes using key concepts to locate relevant material when reading.

When taking notes, put inverted commas around direct quotations and note the page on the note record. If you are summarising the material in your own words, do not use inverted commas, but make a note of the page(s) on which the summarised material appeared in the source.

If you quote from a source when writing your report, you will have the information needed for a proper reference on the note card, from which you will draw the quotation. One convenient form of referencing, called the Harvard or scientific system, uses the following format. The author's name, the date

```
┌─────────────────────────────────────────────────────┐
│  Dixon and Bouma (1981)                             │
│                                                      │
│  p.        "  _____  │
│                                                      │
│            _____ │
│                                                      │
│            _____  "  │
│                     (direct quotation)              │
│                                                      │
│  p.        "  _____  │
│                                                      │
│            _____ │
│                                                      │
│            _____  "  │
│                     (direct quotation)              │
│                                                      │
│  p.           _____  │
│                                                      │
│               _____     │
│                                                      │
│               _____     │
│                  (paraphrase or summary)            │
└─────────────────────────────────────────────────────┘
```

Figure 8.4 Sample of note card

of publication and the page are given in the body of the text. In the bibliography at the end of the report the full information is listed. Readers wishing to find out more about a reference need only consult the bibliography under the relevant name and date. This reduces the clutter of bibliographic detail.

Dixon and Bouma (1981: 42) report that:

_____

_____

_____

If a direct quotation is used, the quotation is placed in inverted commas. The following forms are also used:

According to Dixon and Bouma (1981: 86–8):

' _____

_____

_____ '

or ' _____

_____ ' (Dixon and Bouma 1981: 92).

The decision about which form to use depends on the preference of the writer and the flow of the sentence. The reference is placed before the full stop, not after it. Long quotations are usually indented.

Data-collection sheets

Data collected for each 'unit of analysis' should be recorded separately. A unit of analysis can be any of the individual or collective elements of the entity being researched. You will need one data record for each unit of analysis, for example each person, group, or hour of television in your study. This is required for later analysis of the results. Therefore, you must keep separate the data collected on each entity studied, each person or group. For example, do not ask for the responses of more than one person on a single questionnaire form. It will be impossible to disentangle the results later.

To do this properly you must first ask what the unit of analysis in your research is. Is it the individual, the (university) class or the group? It is possible for the same hypothesis to be researched at different levels of analysis. For example, in studying the impact of the amount of time spent in revision on the result of a history examination, the unit of analysis was the student. Each student in each class filled out a questionnaire so the researcher had a record of hours spent in revision and exam result for each student. In contrast, the class was the unit of analysis in the experimental study of the relation between the amount of time a class had to read material and a test of the class's comprehension of that material. This study design is described in chapter 6. Classes were given different amounts of time to study the material and the average results for the classes were compared. In that case, a data sheet for each class was all that was required.

Similarly, in the study of workers' snack selections (in chapter 6), machine operators on A-shift were used as the unit of analysis. The proportions of the selections made by all A-shift machine operators of sweets, fruit and 'other' snacks was the datum collected. The machine operators on A-shift received the talk on nutritious snack selection and the results for the shift were recorded. One data-recording sheet for each shift, not each worker, was necessary.

By keeping separate records of each unit of analysis, you effectively manage data for both analysis and review. When conducting analysis, data for each unit can be easily recovered, allowing you to distinguish between cases that follow trends and those that do not. Further, if you suspect that some of your data is incorrect, you can review each unit individually.

In summary, be careful as you collect your data. Be careful and considerate of those you study. Be careful and meticulous to carry out your research with precision and to record your findings accurately.

Questions for review

1   What seven steps need to be taken before a researcher can collect data?
2   What information should researchers record in their journals?

3 What information should be kept on bibliography cards for:
   a a book?
   b an article?
   c a chapter in a book?
4 What is a 'unit of analysis'? Why is it important to know this in preparing data-collection sheets and data-recording sheets?

Suggestions for further reading

de Vaus, D. A. (2002), *Surveys in Social Research*, 5th edn, Allen & Unwin, St Leonards NSW, Part II.

Foddy, William (1993), *Constructing Questions for Interviews and Questionnaires: Theory and Practice in Social Research*, Cambridge University Press, Cambridge.

Minichiello, Victor, Rosalie Aroni, Eric Timewell and Loris Alexander (1995), *In-depth Interviewing: Principles, Techniques, Analysis*, 2nd edn, Longman Cheshire, Melbourne, chapters 10 and 11.

9

Summarising and presenting data

CHAPTER OUTLINE

You have collected your data. What are you going to do with the stacks of questionnaires, data sheets or completed interviews? You will have made some tentative decisions about this when you prepared dummy tables earlier. Nonetheless, when confronted with a pile of data, new problems emerge and further decisions will have to be made. Once data have been collected it is necessary to decide how they are to be summarised and presented.

Since this text presupposes no knowledge of statistics, some methods of data summarisation and presentation will not be covered. This book also assumes that the projects undertaken will be very limited in scale, so that computer analysis of data is not required. However, a standard 'common sense' approach to data summarisation and presentation is necessary in projects that involve both very simple and very sophisticated analysis. It is worth covering the basic rules of this approach to illustrate the common sense involved.

Summarising and organising your data involves three steps:

1 Categories must be selected in which the raw data can be summarised.
2 Once the categories are selected the data are coded, that is, they are sorted into the categories.
3 The data are presented in a form that helps you to draw conclusions.

Categories

Although data are collected in detail, they usually cannot be reported or presented at the same level of detail. In other words, it is unlikely that you will be able to report all of the data that you have collected. In order to summarise and present data, tables, graphs or charts are constructed; averages and percentages are calculated. To do this the data must first be categorised. We saw this earlier in the case of research into the effect of the amount of study time on academic performance. Assume that the data presented in Figure 9.1 were recorded on the data-summary sheet suggested in chapter 5 (Figure 5.9).

Figure 9.1 A completed data-summary form for a study of the relation between hours spent in revision and result on a history examination

Student number	Number of hours spent in revision		Examination result	
	Raw score	Code	Raw score	Code
1	30		98	
2	25		99	
3	10		50	
4	12		44	
5	20		65	
6	22		68	
7	25		80	
8	30		75	
9	30		80	
10	20		60	
11	24		65	
12	19		55	
13	18		54	
14	21		58	
15	22		60	
16	24		62	
17	28		70	
18	26		70	
19	27		65	
20	24		60	
21	18		58	

cont.

Figure 9.1 A completed data-summary form for a study of the relation between hours spent in revision and result on a history examination (continued)

Student number	Number of hours spent in revision		Examination result	
	Raw score	Code	Raw score	Code
22	19		57	
23	25		68	
24	20		65	
25	21		60	
26	14		45	
27	20		35	
28	22		50	
29	26		55	
30	10		40	

As it stands, no conclusions can be readily or reliably drawn from this data-summary form. No pattern emerges from a quick scan of the data. In this form, the data are too detailed. More inclusive categories are required for reporting both the amount of time spent in revision and its result on the examination. A possible starting-point for constructing categories is determining the extreme scores and the average scores.

What are the extremes:
• for amount of time spent in revision?
 most ___ least ___
• for result on examination?
 highest ___ lowest ___
Scan the list and record the results.
What is the average:
• for amount of time spent in revision?
• for result on examination?

An average, or the mean, is calculated by totalling the measures (number of hours or result on examination) and dividing by the number of measures (in this instance, students).

$$\text{Mean, or average, history result} \quad = \quad \frac{\text{Total number of history results}}{\text{Number of students}}$$

Several ways of categorising these data are now possible. The students could be classified into those who studied more than the average and those who studied less than the average. Similarly, the students could be classified into those whose results were above or below the average. Other ways of classification might include separating those who passed from those who did not. The results could be separated into high pass (65–100), pass (50–64) and fail (49 or less).

Once the categories are selected the data are coded. That is, the raw data are reclassified into the more inclusive categories. Let us say that you decided to use the categories of 'above average' and 'below average' for both number of hours spent in revision and for examination result. Go back to Figure 9.1 and codify the data—after each raw score indicate the category into which it fits. For example:

Figure 9.2 A completed and codified data-summary form

	Hours in revision		Result in examination	
	Raw score	*Code*	*Raw score*	*Code*
Student 1	30	AH	98	AR
Student 2	25	AH	99	AR
Student 3	10	BH	50	BR

AH = above-average hours   AR = above-average result
BH = below-average hours   BR = below-average result

In this way, the raw data are codified and can be more readily analysed.

If your calculations agree with mine, the average number of hours spent in revision was 652 ÷ 30, or 21.7 hours. Hence, students who studied more than 21.7 hours are coded as 'AH' (above average) and those who studied less are coded 'BH' (below average). How many students are there in each code?

Number coded AH = 16
Number coded BH = 14

How about the examination results? What was the average result? My calculations were 1871 ÷ 30, or 62.4. Students who scored over 62.4 were coded 'AR' and those who scored below 62.4 were coded 'BR'. How many students fell into each category?

Number coded AR = 13
Number coded BR = 17

You have codified your data and established the frequency of students appearing in each code. You are now ready to present your data in a form that will show the relationship between the two variables.

You can see that if you used different categories the coding would look different. To give yourself practice, copy out Figure 9.1 and codify the data results using high pass (65–100), pass (50–64) and fail (49 or less) as the categories. Whatever categories you choose, your aim is to reduce the raw data to a more manageable set of categories. Decide on the categories and then code the raw data into those categories.

The first two steps have been done. Categories have been selected and the data codified. How are they to be presented? The hypothesis guiding this research asserts that there is a relationship between the amount of time spent in revision and the result of an examination. This means that the way in which you present your data needs to show the strength of the relationship between the two variables. There are several ways to do this. These are presented in the following figures.

Tables

The most basic form of data presentation is 'tabular presentation'.

Figure 9.3 A table for presenting the data from a study of amount of time spent in revision and result on an examination

Result on history examination	Amount of time spent in revision	
	Above average	Below average
Above average		
Below average		

To come up with the numbers to put in the table in Figure 9.3 it is necessary to cross-tabulate your data. That is, you have to locate each case of data collected (in this case each student) in the appropriate box of the table. For this example, you would take each student listed on the data–summary sheet in Figure 9.1 and place a tick in the appropriate cell (blank square) of a table like that presented in Figure 9.3. Student 1 was categorised as 'above average'

Figure 9.4 The relationship between time spent in revision and result on a history examination (preliminary table)

Result on history examination	Amount of time spent in revision (number of students)	
	Above average	Below average
Above average	✓✓✓✓✓✓✓✓✓✓	✓✓
Below average	✓✓✓✓	✓✓✓✓✓✓✓✓✓✓✓

in both variables, so place a tick in the upper left-hand cell of the table. Student 2 was also categorised as 'above average' in both variables, so place another tick in the upper left-hand cell. Student 3 was categorised as 'below average' for both variables so place a tick in the lower right-hand cell of the table. When all the data have been cross-tabulated in this way, your preliminary table should look like Figure 9.4.

Next, add up the ticks in each cell and put that number in the cell. What do your results look like? They should look like those in the table in Figure 9.5. There were 11 students who were above average in both examination result and amount of time spent in revision. There were five who were below average in result but above average in study time. There were 12 students who were below average on both variables.

Figure 9.5 The presentation of the results tabulated in Figure 9.4

Examination result	Amount of time spent in revision (number of students)		
	Above average	Below average	Total
Above average	11	2	13
Below average	5	12	17
Total	16	14	30

The numbers at the side and bottom of the table in Figure 9.5 are called marginal totals. They are the same as the totals you calculated earlier for the frequencies of each variable. These serve as useful checks to make sure your coding and cross-tabulating were done accurately. It is amazing how many errors can creep in at this stage of the research process. The marginals must add to the total used for the construction of the table. They must also add correctly both across the rows and down the columns. It may seem tedious but it provides a critical check on accuracy.

How would you interpret the table in Figure 9.5? It shows a very clear relation between the two variables. It shows that the two variables are related in such a way that the more there is of one (study time), the more there is of the other (examination result), with few exceptions.

While interpreting Figure 9.5 is relatively straightforward, sometimes it is better to present the tabular results as percentages. There are two ways of doing this. Since each accurately reflects the data but does so in a slightly different way, the selection depends on which mode of presentation is easiest to interpret. Figure 9.6 presents the findings in Figure 9.5 as percentages of the total, 30. In all tables giving the results as percentages it is very important to indicate the total number upon which the table is based. That is why 'n = 30' (which means the total number is 30) is placed where it is. It is nearly a universal convention to use the lower-case 'n' to refer to the number of cases in a table or graph. Thirty is usually considered the minimum number of cases for the use of percentages in a 2 x 2 table like the one in Figure 9.6. The more cells a table has, the higher the number of cases should be.

Figure 9.6 The relationship between amount of time spent in revision and result on history examination

Result on history examination	Amount of time spent in revision	
	Above average	Below average
Above average	36.6	6.7
Below average	16.7	40.0

n = 30
100%

Figure 9.7 presents the findings in Figure 9.5 in column percentages—each of the columns adds to 100 per cent. When you set up a table like that shown in Figure 9.7, you show the impact of the column variable (in this instance, amount of time spent in revision) on the row variable (result in history examination). This is exactly what you wanted to do, because amount of time spent in revision was your independent variable and examination result the dependent variable. When you construct and interpret tables it is crucial to keep in mind which is the independent and which the dependent variable. Failing to do so can lead to nonsensical interpretations of data.

Figure 9.7 The percentage of students spending above- or below-average amounts of time in revision who scored above or below average on their history examination

Result on history examination	Amount of time spent in revision	
	Above average	Below average
Above average	68.7	14.3
Below average	31.3	85.7
	100%	100%
	n = 16	n = 14

How you read a table partly depends on which variable is the independent and which the dependent variable. In this example, 'time spent in revision' was the independent variable and 'examination result' the dependent variable. Figure 9.7 would be read in this way. Among those students who spent an above-average amount of time in revision, 68.7 per cent received above-average examination results and 31.3 per cent received below-average results. In contrast, among those students who spent a below-average amount of time in revising, 14.3 per cent received an above-average result in the examination and 85.7 per cent received a below-average result. We therefore conclude that the amount of time spent in revision had a definite and positive effect on the examination results of this group of history students; our hypothesis is confirmed or accepted.

As a general rule, if you are presenting your data in tables using percentages it is best to percentage the independent variable across the dependent variable (as in Figure 9.7). In this way you display the impact of the independent variable on the distribution of the dependent variable, which is of course what you are trying to show.

If you look back over Figures 9.4 to 9.7, it should become clear that the interpretation would be the same in each mode of tabular presentation of the data. Tabular presentation of data is very basic and very useful. To give yourself practice at tabular analysis take the data in Figure 9.1 and recode the exam result data into the three categories of high pass (65–100), pass (50–64) and fail (49 or less). Construct tables by cross-tabulating the data again. Present the tables numerically and as percentages of the whole, row percentages and column percentages.

There are other ways of presenting data as well. Remember, data are summarised and presented so as to clearly demonstrate the strength of the relationship between the variables under study. Other ways of summarising and presenting data include several kinds of graphs, the scattergram and the use of means (averages).

Graphs

Bar graphs

In order to prepare a graph it is necessary to perform Steps 1 (selecting categories) and 2 (coding the data) of data summarisation and presentation. It is also necessary to cross-tabulate the data in some way. Take, for instance, the bar graph or histogram. In both methods the amount of space given to each variable is proportional to that variable's portion of the sample. Figure 9.8 shows a bar graph presenting the data in Figure 9.5.

Essentially, this graph presents the information in the top two cells of the table in Figure 9.5. It shows a bar graph based on the frequency distribution of the data (the numbers falling into each category of analysis in the test). Figure 9.9 is a bar graph that gives all the data in Figure 9.5.

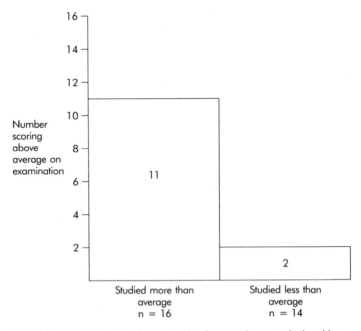

Figure 9.8 A bar graph showing the relationship between hours studied and history examination result

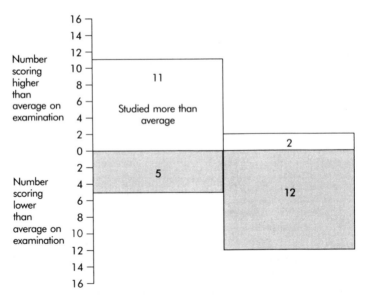

Figure 9.9 A bar graph showing the relationship between amount of time spent in revision and history examination result

Bar graphs can also be used to present percentage data. Figure 9.10 presents the data in Figure 9.7 in the form of a bar graph. In this instance, a table presented as column percentages is converted to a bar graph by making the space in the graph proportional to the percentage of each cell. The essential feature of a bar graph is that the size of the bar is proportional to the size of the variable. Again, it can be seen that different methods of presenting the same data, when used correctly, do not lead to different conclusions.

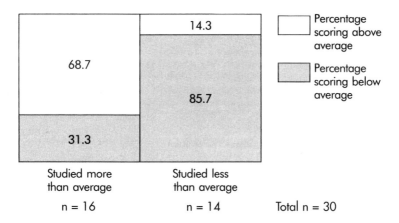

Figure 9.10 A bar graph depicting the relationship between the amount of time spent in revision and history examination result

Pie graphs

Pie graphs are appropriate when analysis examines the proportion of variable categories to all variable categories over the whole population. For example, we will construct a pie graph for the variable 'ethnicity' when it is measured for a class of students. The composition of each category of the variable might be as follows: Asian 10%, Greek 10%, Australian 60%, Italian 8%, Other 12%. Accordingly, the pie graph would look like Figure 9.11.

Each group occupies a 'wedge' proportion of the total area of the pie graph, equivalent to their proportion of the total class population. In Figure 9.11, the size of the wedge to represent the Asians must be 10 per cent of the circle area. This can be measured by calculating 10 per cent of 360 degrees (there are 360 degrees in a circle). Ten per cent of 360 degrees is 36 degrees. Using a protractor, count 36 degrees, place a dot at 0 and at 36 then draw lines to the centre of the circle and you have a wedge of the pie equal to 10 per cent of the circle. Repeat this for each group. The next group, the Greeks, would also require 36 degrees. Starting where you left off (at 36 degrees), count off 36, place a dot at 72 degrees and draw a line to the centre of the circle.

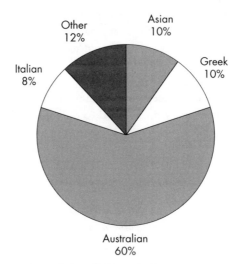

Figure 9.11 Ethnic makeup of class (fictitious data)

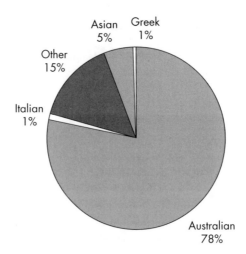

Figure 9.12 Ethnicity in Australia 2001 (Percentages rounded to nearest whole numbers)

This procedure may seem tedious, but there are now computer programs designed to produce accurate pie, bar and line graphs from data.

Figure 9.12 is a similar pie graph that could be constructed for the population of Australia. A comparison of the two graphs would show how the distribution of ethnic groups enrolled in your course compared with the distribution of such groups in Australia. The fact that the percentages are given as well as the visual impression of the different sizes of the various wedges helps us to interpret these graphs.

It should be noted that such differences are better displayed in simple tables, such as Figure 9.13.

Figure 9.13 A table comparing the percentages of several ethnic groups in two populations

	Percentage of students in your course	Percentage of Australian population in 2001*
Asian	10	5.2
Greek	10	0.6
Australian	60	78.2
Italian	8	1.2
Other	12	14.8
Total	100	100.0

Source: Census of Population and Housing, ABS cat. no. 2035.0

* These figures are from the Australian Bureau of Statistics and refer to birthplace of respondent

The pie graph is not particularly suited to presenting the type of data with which we have been dealing. Pie graphs in general are hard to construct accurately and very difficult to compare. They are usually used in journalistic reporting and for presenting financial data, such as government funding allocations, rather than in scientific reporting.

Scattergrams

The scattergram is another way in which data can be summarised and presented. A scattergram is produced by pinpointing each instance of measurement on a grid defined by the two axes of a graph. Figure 9.14 shows such a grid.

The two lines along which the units are marked are called axes and the space between them is defined by the grid formed by the intersecting lines drawn from each unit point along the two axes. The first step in constructing a scattergram is to decide on the scale of units to be used on each axis.

Data are not usually categorised and coded before constructing a scattergram. Instead, the scale of each axis is adjusted to accommodate the range of the variable being analysed. Remember we suggested that you analyse the data from the study of the impact of amount of time spent in revision on examination result. We asked you to identify the range of each variable by

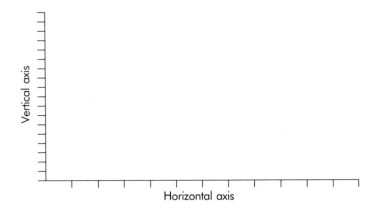

Figure 9.14 A scattergram grid showing horizontal and vertical axes

noting the extremes. This is a very important step if you wish to construct a scattergram. Re-examine the data presented in Figure 9.1:

• What is the range of the values recorded for the variable 'time spent in revision'?

Highest _____ ◄——————► _____ Lowest

• What is the range of the values recorded for the variable 'result on an examination'?

Highest _____ ◄——————► _____ Lowest

The scale of units along each axis of the scattergram must be able to sensibly record the full range of collected data. In this instance, the scale of the horizontal axis, the one used to indicate hours spent in revision, must range from 10 (the lowest reported) to 30 (the highest reported). The range for the vertical axis, the axis dealing with examination result, must go from 35 to 99. Figure 9.15 presents a grid upon which a scattergram for the data presented in Figure 9.1 could be constructed. The scattergram is constructed by putting a dot on the grid in the place defined by the two pieces of data for each student. Using graph paper makes this task much easier. The axes are drawn and units marked along them. Now a dot is placed on the grid for each student. Student number 1 studied 30 hours and received a 98, so place a dot at the intersection of a line drawn up from the 30 position on the horizontal axis with a line across from the 98 position on the vertical axis. The positions of students 1 to 5 are given as examples.

Using a sheet of graph paper, make a scattergram of all the data in Figure 9.1. Normally the intersecting lines are not drawn on the table. Rather, two rulers are used to indicate where the lines intersect and only the dot is placed on the grid. Place two dots close together where two data points are the same. The result is a pattern of dots. What does the pattern of 30 dots tell you?

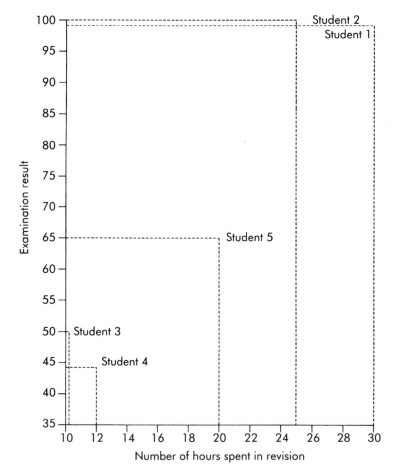

Figure 9.15 A grid for the construction of a scattergram for data on impact of amount of time spent in revision on examination result

Line graphs

A line graph is almost the same as a scattergram, except that consecutive points are joined by lines, making up one complete line joining all the data points.

The data tabled in Figure 9.16 can be presented by a line graph (as in Figure 9.17). The independent variable 'age of child' is placed on the horizontal axis. The dependent variable 'number of hours increased' is put along the vertical axis. The units are clearly marked along each axis. Then the data points are marked, as for a scattergram. The data points join by a line that begins at the first dot on the left and moves to the next dot to the right.

Figure 9.16 Number of additional hours spent on household activities by non-employed persons due to presence of child

Age of child	Number of additional hours
Less than 1 year	5.2
1 year	4.6
2–5 years	4.0
6–11 years	4.5
12–17 years	3.6

Source: Data from E. Walker and M. E. Woods (1976), *Time Use: A Measure of Household Production of Family Goods and Services*, Centre for the Family of the American Home Economics Association, Washington DC, pp. 50–1

As an exercise, convert your scattergram of the data on the relationship between 'number of hours spent in revision' and 'examination result' (refer back to Figure 9.1) to a line graph. To do so, start with the dot on the far left and move to the next dot on the right. You will encounter a problem. What do you do when there is more than one dot in a vertical line? Which is the 'next dot to

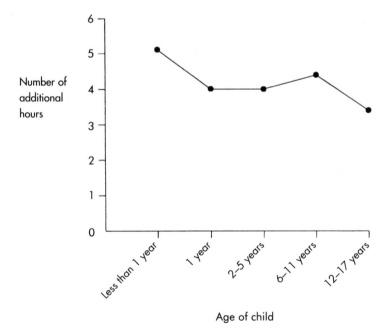

Figure 9.17 A line graph depicting increaed number of hours spent on housework due to presence of child at different ages

the right'? In such a case the average is calculated and the data point is put at the average position. For example, you will begin with a problem in the data in your scattergram when you find that there are two data points in the vertical line above 10 hours in revision. One received a result of 50, the other a result of 40. The data point for a line graph would be placed at 45. In this way a line graph 'smooths out' some of the detail of a scattergram. The advantage is that it makes the pattern clearer but the disadvantage is that it hides some of the variation.

There are several critical points to remember in constructing line graphs. First, the units of measure must be clearly specified, labelled and marked on each axis of the graph. In Figure 9.17 the vertical axis is marked in hours (0–6) and labelled 'Number of additional hours'.

Be aware that units of measure affect the appearance of line graphs and can make them misleading. Large units can underemphasise change in relative terms and small units can overstate the magnitude of change. The following example will demonstrate this. There is a lot of talk these days about divorce statistics in Australia. The data on divorce rates in Australia are presented in tabular form in Figure 9.18. The data given in this figure are from the Australian Bureau of Statistics.

Figure 9.18 Divorce rates per 1000 population

Year ended	Australia	NSW	Vic	SA	WA
1993	2.7	2.5	2.5	2.8	2.8
1994	2.7	2.3	2.5	2.9	3.0
1995	2.8	2.4	2.6	2.9	2.9
1996	2.9	2.6	2.7	3.0	2.8
1997	2.8	2.3	2.7	2.8	2.8
1998	2.7	2.4	2.6	2.8	2.9
1999	2.8	2.4	2.7	2.9	2.8
2000	2.6	2.3	2.6	2.7	2.8
2001	2.8	2.4	2.8	3.0	2.8

Source: Marriage and Divorces, ABS cat. no. 33110.0

First, Figure 9.19 presents all the data in a line graph.

Now let us assume that all the data we could find were the data for the last five years. Notice how two ways of presenting those data give very different impressions. Figures 9.20 and 9.21 show the same data recorded in line graphs using different scales of units. Do they look the same? They are both accurate but they give different impressions.

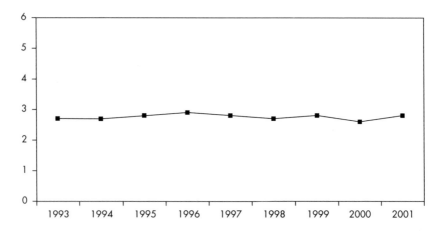

Figure 9.19 Line graph showing the Australian divorce rate from 1993 to 2001

Both Figures 9.20 and 9.21 are accurate. However, they express the data differently, due to the difference in measurement scale for the vertical axis. As an exercise, make line graphs for several states from the data presented in Figure 9.18. Use different scales to see what difference is made. Try using data from every second year, or even from every third year.

This effect can be particularly confusing in graphs that have two vertical axes with different scales. Although there are legitimate reasons for using this device, it can be very misleading. Figure 9.22 gives an obvious example. It shows line graphs of annual environmental spending by City A and City B. Say that both cities commenced allocating funds for the environment in

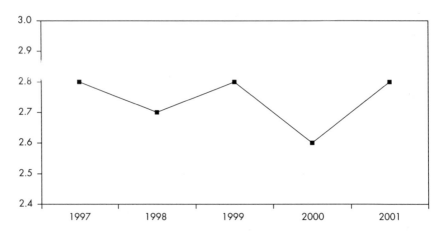

Figure 9.20 Australian divorce rate from 1997 to 2001—rising and falling (small scale)

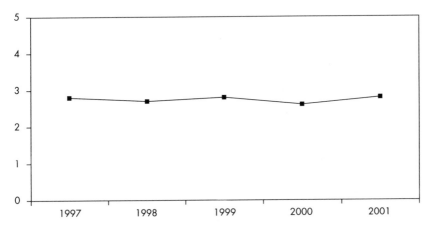

Figure 9.21 Australian divorce rate from 1997 to 2001—hardly changing (larger scale)

1987. The graph seems to show that City A has been increasing its spending on the environment at a much faster rate than City B. But is that correct? Read the graph carefully and keep in mind that the lines are drawn to axes of different scales, according to which spending for City A is expressed in smaller units ($100 000s) than data for City B ($millions). The same spending increases will appear to be more dramatic for City A than for City B.

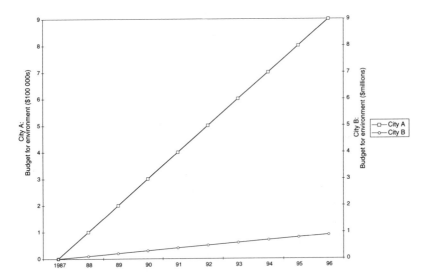

Figure 9.22 A misleading line graph using different units on two vertical axes to compare growth in environmental spending

With this in mind, an examination of the graph will show that the dollar amounts spent by the cities were the same each year. Spending in both cities increased by the same amount ($100 000 for City A, $0.1 million for City B) every year between 1987 and 1996. In 1996, both cities spent $900 000.

Spending on the environment was the same in both cities, despite the different appearances of the lines plotted against the different scales.

Finally, line graphs are very useful for comparing the trends or performance of several groups or persons. Figure 9.24 is a hypothetical line graph comparing the monthly phone calls received by three telephone counselling services in one year. The raw data are presented in Figure 9.23.

Figure 9.23 Phone calls received by three fictitious telephone counselling services

Month	Service A	Service B	Service C
January	205	920	860
February	255	750	620
March	300	605	275
April	350	410	350
May	520	300	360
June	620	275	380
July	880	275	400
August	925	275	450
September	620	290	350
October	540	420	300
November	480	590	580
December	320	830	690

These three services have different patterns of demand. The graph in Figure 9.24 shows these differences more clearly than the columns of numbers in Figure 9.23.

Service A receives more calls in winter than in summer. It may service an area with a tradition of loyalty to a local football team that is expressed in violence and alcohol abuse during the winter football season. Service B experiences a smooth pattern of demand, which begins at a relatively high level early in the year, 'bottoms' out mid-year and gradually increases as the end of the year approaches. The area covered by Service B might be a place where social problems change with the traditional holiday season. During the Christmas and New Year season social problems increase, perhaps due to shortages of money or increased spending on alcohol. The general 'mood' of the area calms after the New Year and the demand for counselling services decreases, remaining stable until September, when spending and alcohol use increase in anticipation of Christmas. Service C experiences increased demand in the summer months and a small upswing in the middle of the year. It may service a holiday region where social problems increase every summer and during a school holiday period, when tourists arrive. The minor increase in calls between March and August could be the result of seasonal unemployment, as the local tourist industry ceases to operate.

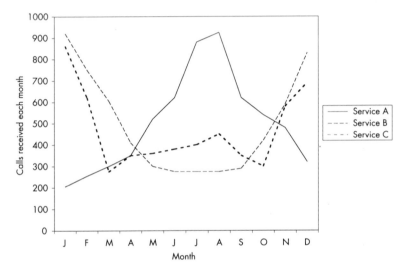

Figure 9.24 A line graph comparing the phone calls received by three fictitious Australian counselling services

The value of a line graph comparing the use of the three counselling services can be seen in Figure 9.24. Such presentation of data is very useful in policy analysis as it displays comparative information very clearly. What issues does Figure 9.24 suggest for a government administrator allocating funds between the three counselling services? Think about how you would allocate the funds and justify your decision based on the graph.

As a further exercise, construct a line graph comparing the divorce rates of New South Wales and South Australia (or any other state), using the data in Figure 9.18. By using a different style of line for each state, you can construct a graph that provides a good basis for drawing comparisons among the states on divorce rates. Make sure you get the data points in the right place before you connect the lines.

Scattergrams and line graphs can be very useful ways of summarising and interpreting data. They are frequently used in articles, books and research reports.

To construct a line graph you must:

1   select categories for your data
2   code the data into the categories
3   select a scale of units for each axis
4   plot the data points
5   link the data points with lines.

Means

Means, or averages, are often used to compare groups. Means are a useful way to summarise and present data. The average performance of groups, the average rates of consumption or the average incidence of a particular event may be compared.

To calculate an average, you add up the individual data and divide by the number of individuals. For example, earlier in this chapter you calculated the average number of hours spent in study and the average examination result.

Means could be used to summarise and present the data from our study of the impact of the number of hours spent in revision on examination results. The class could be divided into two groups, those who studied more than the average and those who studied less than the average. Once this is done, the average examination result for each group could be calculated. First, divide the students into two groups. Remember, the average time spent in revision was 21.7 hours.

The data in Figure 9.25 would simply be reported in this way. The group of students who studied more than the average received an average result of 70.3 and the group of students who studied less than the average received an average result of 53.3.

As an exercise, calculate the average number of hours spent in revision for each of two groups of students. First, do it for those who received above-average results and then do it for those who received below-average results.

We saw that the move from a scattergram to a line graph involved losing a certain level of detail in the presentation of the data. When groups are compared using means, all variation internal to each group is lost:

■   scattergram: presents most information
■   line graph, bar graph or pie graph: present less information
■   mean: presents least information.

Using the data in Figure 9.23, calculate the average monthly number of calls received by each counselling service. Service A's average monthly total was 501.25 calls, Service B's average was 495.0 calls and Service C's was 467.92 calls. This example shows one potential problem with an average. It does not show the variation in the measures. Although Services A and B aver-

Figure 9.25   The calculation of mean test scores for two groups of students

Group A Studied more than average		Group B Studied less than average	
Student	*Mark*	*Student*	*Mark*
1	98	3	50
2	99	4	44
6	68	5	65
7	80	10	60
8	75	12	55
9	80	13	54
11	65	14	58
15	60	21	58
16	62	22	57
17	70	24	65
18	70	25	60
19	65	26	45
20	60	27	35
23	68	30	40
28	50		
29	55		
16	1125	14	746
Group A average = 1125 ÷ 16 = 70.3		Group B average = 746 ÷ 14 = 53.3	

aged almost the same number of calls per month, they experienced different trends of monthly increases and decreases in calls.

While averages are very useful, they must be used and interpreted with care. The average tells us nothing for certain about an individual in a group. It is not legitimate to infer that the average for a group applies to an individual. For example, the average household income of residents in a particular suburb might be $100 000 per year. There are many combinations of household income which would lead to that average. For example, one household earning $910 000 and nine each of $10 000 would result in an average income of $100 000. Some averages can be almost meaningless.

On the other hand, we are often interested in group performance and not so interested in the outstanding cases. The average is a useful indication of a characteristic of a group. Trends in averages, like trends in percentages, are particularly useful. The local electricity supplier, in predicting energy supply requirements for the month of July, will rely on the trends in average energy consumption for the last 20 Julys. It will not be interested in the variations in individual household consumption.

Summary

Once your data are collected they are ready to be summarised and presented. To do this you must select categories in which to summarise your data. Although you did some preliminary thinking about this when you constructed your dummy tables, the final selection is done when your data are in hand. Once you have selected categories, the data are coded into the categories. Then the data are cross-tabulated in some way to show the relationship between the variables in question. We have looked at tables, graphs and means as the basic techniques for summarising and presenting your data.

Questions for review

1 What are the three steps involved in summarising and organising your data?
2 Why is it necessary to categorise your data?
3 Why is it important to remember which variable is the independent and which is the dependent when constructing tables for the presentation and interpretation of your data?
4 What does it mean to cross-tabulate your data?
5 Describe the difficulties associated with your graphs.
6 What is a scattergram?
7 What are the advantages of using means (or averages) rather than line graphs or scattergrams in presenting data?

Suggestions for further reading

Babbie, E. R. (2003), *The Practice of Social Research*, 10th edn, Wadsworth Publishing, London, chapter 15.

de Vaus, D. A. (2002), *Surveys in Social Research*, 5th edn, Allen & Unwin, St Leonards NSW, Parts III and IV.

Judd, C. M., E. R. Smith and L. H. Kidder (1991), *Research Methods in Social Relations*, Holt, Rinehart & Winston, Fort Worth, chapter 15.

Kumar, Ranjit (1999), *Research Methodology: A Step by Step Guide for Beginners*, Sage, London, chapters 15–16.

10

Doing qualitative research

CHAPTER OUTLINE

What is qualitative research?

Qualitative research sets out to provide an impression: to tell what kinds of 'something' there are; to tell what it is like to be, do or think something. Qualitative researchers exercise great discipline to find out 'What is going on here?' from the perspective of those who are in the situation being researched. By comparison, quantitative research sets out to give numerical results that can be reported in tables and graphs. It answers questions about situations in terms of 'How many?' or 'What proportion?' Drawing an absolute line between qualitative and quantitative research is never satisfactory as they have similarities, and researchers often combine the approaches.

For example, a few years ago I conducted a study (Bouma 1994) on the role of religion in the way Muslim migrants have settled in Australia. First I wanted to know how many Muslims there were in Australia, their education and employment levels and where they lived. This information could largely be gained from the census and other government statistics. However, I also wanted to find out 'what it is like' to be a Muslim living in Australia at the time. This could not be ascertained by reference to census data. To find out 'what it was like' to be a Muslim living in Australia, it was necessary to listen to Muslims describe their lives.

The fundamental disadvantage was that I could not assume that I perceived or appreciated the most outstanding issues in the lives of people with a different religious background from my own. If I had already known the dimensions of living as a member of a minority non-Christian religion in Australia, I might have been able to construct a questionnaire along the lines of those described in chapter 5. But I had no idea, and many of the issues that were important to me were not important to Muslims residing in Australia. If I had embarked on my research with preconceived ideas, I would not have found out what it is like to be a Muslim in Australia because I would have been appreciating their lives in the context of my own experience.

While it helps to declare preconceptions and biases at the start of a project, it also helps to share them with others in order to detect potential biases, of which you may be unaware. In designing this study I declared my biases, but I did so to a community liaison group, who then directed my attention to their concerns and their view of things.

I chose to use the qualitative technique of in-depth interviewing, so that the subjects of my research would be free to tell me what was important to them; free to tell me their stories, their perceptions, and their feelings. I did not attempt to take a random sample, nor would it have been relevant. Rather, people were selected as 'windows' into, or 'listening posts' on, some aspect of Muslim settlement in Australia. Male and female Muslims from a variety of national backgrounds (Islam is one of the most ethnically diverse religious groups in Australia), who had been in Australia a short time, a moderate length of time or a long time, were interviewed. The interviews, which each took about two hours, were conducted by interviewers who spoke the language of the interviewees. The interviews were guided by an interview schedule that essentially helped to produce a 'settlement biography' for each participant.

This research used both qualitative and quantitative research techniques because it was designed to answer both 'What is it like?' and 'How many?' questions. Once the data were collected, further questions of 'qualitative versus quantitative research' arose. The data could be analysed in a 'qualitative way' or a 'quantitative way'. It is important to remember this when discussing the differences between qualitative and quantitative research. These issues arise at each phase of the research process, and decisions are made at *each phase* about which to use. Sometimes quantitative options will be used at one phase and qualitative at another. It is possible to collect qualitative data and to subject them to quantitative analysis, just as it is possible to collect quantitative data in a way that can be analysed qualitatively.

When to use qualitative research

As with all decisions that arise during the research process, deciding whether to use qualitative or quantitative approaches depends on what the researcher wants to know—it depends on the questions they are asking. If you want to know how many Muslims live in certain suburbs of Melbourne, it will be necessary to do quantitative research. Counting households, citizens, adults, women, men and children and recording ages may be some of the tasks involved in the census required to answer 'How many?' That is why the census is conducted every five years in Australia. If there was no census, researchers would have to rely on sample surveys to estimate features of the population. Qualitative approaches will not answer questions such as 'How many?', 'How often?' or 'What proportion?' because qualitative research is not interested in these questions.

Qualitative approaches, such as visiting a suburb and looking it over, may give an impression, provoke a feeling about the place, or enable the researcher to describe the look of the suburb. For instance, if driving through certain commercial precincts in the Melbourne suburb of Richmond, a researcher will see many shops with Vietnamese signs offering foods from South-East Asia, and they may form the impression that this is a Vietnamese suburb. The shopping strip gives that impression, but it does not reveal how many Vietnamese live in that suburb, or what proportion of the businesses are owned or run by Vietnamese. But asking, 'What impression does a particular shopping precinct give?' is a perfectly valid research question. It may also be a very important question for market or ethnic-relations research. And that question cannot be answered by information on how many people of a particular ethnic background live in the suburb.

In addition to providing impressions and feelings about a particular situation, qualitative research often seeks to answer the question, 'What is going on here?' The aim of qualitative research is often to describe in detail what is happening in a group, in a conversation or in a community—who spoke to whom, with what message, with what feelings, with what effect?

Sometimes researchers apply qualitative methods as a preliminary to quantitative research. For example, you may want to know how many or what proportion of users of a particular service are satisfied with it. You could ask a simple 'yes/no' or 'much/some/little' question of each user over a few days. This would give a lot of quantitative information about levels of customer satisfaction, but this is probably not all you really want to know. You would soon become curious about the aspects of the service the users do and do not like, what users expect, and why they use this service. Unless you already know why people use the service and what their problems are, you will find that some qualitative research is required to answer your questions.

In this case, you may wish to interview a range of users to learn what they expect from the service and their range of perceptions of its performance. Having done that, you will know what using the service feels like, because respondents will have told you 'what is going on here'. Having listened to users of the service, you will be able to appreciate the range of reactions to the service, and you will have gained impressions about the users. You may even be able to identify types of responses to the service, themes in the comments, or other patterns in the users' responses. But you will not know how many or what proportion of users react in each way, or how many come away with certain types of feelings. In order to answer such questions, you will need to survey representative samples of the clients with a quantitative measure. Having already identified certain types of users and certain perceptions or themes in the users' responses in the qualitative research, the quantitative survey will enable you to discover the frequency with which these types or themes occur.

Often the best and most innovative research uses both qualitative and quantitative approaches. Well-executed qualitative research is often essential preparation for worthwhile quantitative research and vice versa. This does not mean that qualitative research should be regarded as secondary to quantitative research. In many cases, the relationship between the two is symbiotic. Quantitative research presumes that the researcher knows 'what is going on'. Having discovered the range of issues confronting certain people, it is often highly desirable to find out how these themes or issues are distributed among those people, demonstrating the close relationship that exists between quantitative and qualitative research techniques.

Which is better: qualitative or quantitative?

By now, it should be clear that the difference between qualitative and quantitative research is not one of 'better' or 'worse' but rather one of appropriateness to the question. However, since the mid-1960s, when the importance and value of qualitative research became an issue in the conduct of social science, some people have taken staunch ideological positions on the relative merits of quantitative and qualitative research. This has resulted in an artificial and politicised conflict between those who claim to practice one method and those who subscribe to the other. Fortunately, this conflict is subsiding as it becomes increasingly obvious that this polarised view does not coincide with what researchers are actually doing. However, some traces of the conflict persist, and there are people who still resolutely claim to be on one side or the other.

For example, some argue that each individual, family or situation is so unique that it is impossible, indeed immoral, to group them for purposes of analysis and generalisation. To do so, they contend, is to fly in the face of reality.

For them, the only valid research is individual case studies, in which the uniqueness of each subject or group is appreciated. This is a difficult position to maintain because someone will eventually begin to identify patterns within and between groups: the stories of women share certain themes; villagers recount different experiences from those of urban dwellers; as do people with a common lifestyle and those of particular age groups. The original careful attention to the details of individual stories is valuable in itself, and with these details it may be possible to begin to see patterns that could be tested by more quantitative approaches, demonstrating again the necessity for both qualitative and quantitative research methods.

Both qualitative and quantitative approaches are absolutely essential to the research process in social sciences. They require some common and some different skills. Neither approach sets the standards for the other, as each has its own rules of practice and requires various disciplines of the researcher. Neither is easier than the other, nor is one approach more creative than the other.

The qualitative research process

Qualitative research has its own demands and integrity. Some of its similarities with quantitative research were discussed in chapters 3 to 5 in the discussion of research guided by a research objective. While the qualitative approach shares some requirements with quantitative research, there are subtle and not-so-subtle differences in the way the research issue is conceived, the data collected, analysed and reported.

One of the major differences between quantitative and qualitative research is that, once the basic decisions are made in quantitative research, there is little opportunity to alter them in the light of early findings. Once a questionnaire is designed and sent, it is out of the researcher's hands. Once an experiment has been carried out, it is over. However, qualitative research allows more continuous reflection on the research in progress and more interaction with the participants in the research, and there is usually more room for ongoing alteration as the research proceeds. For example, if early observations or interviews reveal that one approach is not working or that additional issues need to be considered, later interviews and observations can be adjusted accordingly. One way of expressing this is to say that in qualitative research the researcher is more interactive with the data-generating process than in quantitative research, where, once set up, the research proceeds more according to a predetermined plan.

The general process model developed for the description of quantitative research will be used to describe qualitative research, because the underlying logic of the research process applies to both approaches.

Phase one: essential first steps

Selecting a problem

As with the research procedures outlined in earlier chapters, selecting a research problem is the first stage. Each of the examples in chapter 3 could have led to a qualitative research project, and the ways they were developed usually presumed that qualitative approaches to the issue had been taken to some extent. Take the first example of family decision-making. The prompting situation was this:

> **An important family decision**
> The Wright family has to decide whether to send their daughter to a state school or to a private school.

There are many research focuses that this situation might stimulate. What is the nature of family decision-making? What kinds of issues arise? Whose arguments carry more weight—males' or females'? Young people's or older people's? Or you might focus on the differences associated with attending a state or a private school. You could select a more quantitative approach by asking questions such as, 'What proportion of girls attending state schools, as opposed to private schools, go on to university?' Or you could ask a more qualitative question like, 'What is it like to attend a state school or a private school?'

As with all research, it is necessary to focus when doing qualitative research. It is not possible to answer all the questions. If you focus on the nature of family decision-making, you might go to the library and look up information on various databases. In doing this you will, in part, be checking to see if much is known about family decision-making. You will also assess the nature of the research already done, which may lead you to do some basic qualitative research to find out the themes and issues in family decision-making. Or you may feel that previous research has focused on different groups from those they had in mind—for example, Americans in 1980 rather than Australians in the 2000s. The literature search will help focus the research.

On completing the background reading, you may be ready to state the goal, objective or central question of the research. This will play the same guiding role as the hypothesis in quantitative research. It states your aim, goal or focus. For example, you might express your goal as one of the following research objectives:

> **Objective**
> To ascertain the themes that emerge in family decision-making about a daughter's education.

Objective
To describe the way the Wright family decided where to send their daughter, Amy, to school.

Objective
To find out what it is like to be the subject of family decision-making about one's education.

There are other ways to state a research objective about family decision-making, but each of these provides a sharper focus and describes a qualitative approach to the general issue raised in the above area of 'family decision-making'.

Sampling in qualitative research

Qualitative research is usually less interested in generalisation to large populations than in understanding what is going on in specific settings. However, you must not forget that the findings of any research project are limited by the nature of the sampling procedure. Sampling issues in qualitative research involve the selection of subjects, locations, groups and situations to be observed or interviewed. Sampling issues therefore focus on how well the subjects and situations provide 'windows' on social processes. Qualitative research will not be able to tell what proportion of women managers feel a certain way about their work environments, but it will be able to present in detail what it is like for women to work in selected types of managerial environments.

Sampling will also be an issue in the selection of locations, timeframes and points of orientation for observational research. Each of these selections will affect what is observed, so they must be made intentionally and described in the report so readers will understand the nature of the observations upon which the research is based.

Phase two: collecting, summarising and organising data

At this stage some key differences between quantitative and qualitative research become apparent. One is the degree of focus on the topic and the degree of commitment to the given research method before gathering data. In quantitative research much effort goes into preparing questionnaires, setting up experiments or selecting groups for comparisons. This is done to ensure comparability of data and to make data summarisation more efficient. Also, such preparation lowers the chance that collection will encounter problems after it starts. Quantitative researchers must know the research topic very well to foresee problems.

At the outset, qualitative research is usually less focused. One of the key aims of qualitative research is to provide the maximum opportunity for the researcher to learn from the participants. This requires data collection to be flexible. Quantitative research produces a relatively small amount of data focused on predetermined issues or variables. Qualitative research tends to produce large amounts of information that can only be focused after data collection. Generally, quantitative research progresses through a series of distinct stages—problem-focusing, choice of measurements, design of data-collection instruments, and data collection. By comparison, in qualitative research these stages blend together and may be repeated or conducted at the same time, depending on the researcher's discretion. Qualitative researchers progress back and forth, through the stages, sensitising themselves to the situation, so they can eventually give a fuller description of 'what is going on'.

Data collection

Qualitative research usually involves one or more of the following data-gathering techniques: observation—including *participant* and *non-participant* observation—in-depth interviewing, focus groups and the use of textual material.

Observation

Observation is a basic qualitative research technique that requires discipline, planning and alertness. There are two basic forms of observation: *non-participant* and *participant*. Three general focuses of observation are relevant to both forms:

1   the whole situation—e.g. the 'whole situation' of a committee meeting can be aggressive, conciliatory or defensive
2   the participants in the situation—e.g. at a committee meeting there will be people from different factions, expressing different points of view, and expressing different interests
3   what the researcher perceives given their own preconceptions and values —e.g. personal 'surprise' when a committee conducts itself in an un-expected way. It is important that you be aware of how you perceive and appreciate events. Later, when reviewing observations, you will be able to distinguish your opinions about events from the events themselves.

In *non-participant observation*, the researcher stands back from the situation and observes. An example would be when a researcher sits in a corner, at a committee meeting, to find out how the committee arrives at decisions.

As an example, say you were doing a project for which the research goal was to find out what it is like to be Muslim in Australia. Part of this project could be an observational study of a section of Melbourne's CBD when Muslims walk in *hijab* (female head covering) or the *qamis* (male smock). Your purpose is to observe the social situation when Muslims are present in tradi-tional Islamic dress. This will hopefully give some indication of the social situation Muslims face every day. You stand on a corner in the CBD during lunchtime, knowing that Muslims often walk there at this time because a mosque is nearby.

One of your tasks is to observe the 'whole situation'—that is, the whole social situation on the corner, which includes every person: Muslim and non-Muslim. The whole situation might contain 'social tension' or 'social harmony'; it might be 'loud', 'quiet', 'energetic' or 'subdued'. The environment may seem very 'multicultural' because it contains people of a range of races and ethic dress codes. You should be alert for changes, particularly if they occur when Muslims enter the area.

Second, you must observe the participants, who in this case are the Muslims and everybody else. There are two things to observe: how participants act and how these actions express intentions, group feelings or states of social relations. When observing how participants act, the researcher may see some women in *hijab* walk with other women not in *hijab*. The men in *qamis* may often speak among themselves about football. Some groups of non-Muslims may stare at Muslims or pay them no special attention. You should interpret these actions. If Muslims often smile warmly and make way when their paths cross with non-Muslims, you may discern that the Muslims have a genuine friendliness toward others. If non-Muslims often gaze directly at the Muslims' *hijabs* and *qamis*, you might take such action to indicate curiosity about Islamic lifestyle.

Last, it is also important to observe and record how you personally react to the situation and the participants. Entries about 'how I felt', 'what I thought', 'what I was reminded of' provide a vivid recording of the observation experience. Self-observation can also make you aware of biases or wrong preconceptions. If you felt surprised to see a female Muslim student with textbooks from a 'male' discipline like engineering, you should consider why this seemed unusual. It may signal that you have misconceptions about Muslims, which, if not corrected, could lead to misinterpretations of other events and actions.

It is also necessary to find a suitable observation point. This would be a place from where you can observe things critical to the research objective without disturbing participants. If observing a section of the Melbourne CBD when Muslims are present, you would need a place where you could discretely observe facial expressions and body language. This will allow you to appreciate how Muslims and non-Muslims react to the presence of each other. A seat on the footpath is suitable. Then again, if people see you watching them and taking notes, they might feel self-conscious and not act in their usual manner. There might be a more discrete observation point such as a table inside a cafe where you can observe through a window.

Even while observing from a discrete point, participants may notice you watching and taking notes and ask about your activity. Your Human Research Ethics Committee (HREC) is likely to ask that you prepare printed information for such enquiries. This might be a one-page summary of the project including the title, project number, your student number, date of HREC approval, project description, supervisor's contact details and complaints instructions. Such a document can quickly inform others of the purpose of the project and demonstrate its legitimacy.

Participant observation is where the researcher becomes a participant. The difference between researcher and participant blurs, as the researcher not only observes what is going on among the regular participants but also their own reactions as a participant. In effect, the researcher shares some aspects of the standpoint of regular participants.

If researching Muslims in Australia, you may become a participant by wearing the *hijab* or the *qamis* while walking through the Melbourne CBD. You would observe not just other people—Muslim and non-Muslim—but also your own participant actions and reactions. You may feel physically uncomfortable, very self-conscious, intimidated by unwanted attention or hardly different at all. Such data would directly inform you about one aspect of what is like to be a Muslim in Australia.

Participant observation has three possible disadvantages. First, your presence may affect the situation and cause other participants to feel self-conscious or even 'trespassed' upon. People sometimes become upset if others pretend to be like them. Second, the researcher might be unable to observe much of the situation while participating. For example, while wearing a *hijab*, it may not be possible or practical to look around very much. Last, certain forms of participant observation are likely to be subject to scrutiny by an HREC. The issues are considered further below.

What are some of the issues to consider when choosing between participant and non-participant observation? Some argue that participant observation is far superior and that the only way to get to know what something is like is to be 'part of the action'. However, as shown above, researching 'what it is like to be a Muslim in Melbourne' raised several issues.

First, you could be a non-participant observer, taking stationary positions and watching the reactions of non-Muslims to Muslims in *hijab* and *qamis*. You might also walk a few paces behind some Muslim men, or watch service employees deal with Muslim women at a bank, supermarket or government office. Alternatively, you could be a participant observer and wear the *hijab* or *qamis* in public for a while and note how others relate to you and how you feel.

What level of participation is possible or desirable in observational data collection? The possibilities range from absolute non-participation (such as observation from a distance with a concealed video camera) to fully involved participant observation.

First, the research goal can determine what level of participation is appropriate. If you wish to research how charity collectors gain donations, you can make an informative range of observations by not participating and simply watching and listening as collectors solicit donations. If however, your goal is to find out what it is like to be a charity collector, then participation would be appropriate, and you could expect to gather more relevant data by working as a collector.

Second, the research setting may lend itself more to either participation or non-participation. When for example researching the society of a prison, there would be little advantage in doing participant observation. Unless you work undercover—which would be dangerous—other inmates and prison staff would never treat you as 'one of the regular prisoners' and you would never observe from the prisoners' viewpoint. However, through non-participant observation, you and prisoners could interact without encroaching on each other's social space. You would also be free to interact with prison staff to appreciate how they affect the society of the prison.

Conversely, there are situations where participation is the only option. If you wish to observe the crowd at a Mardi-Gras ball, you are unlikely to gain entry without wearing an appropriate costume. You would have no choice but to participate.

The last issue is the policy on participation of your Human Research Ethics Committee (HREC). HRECs are likely to delay projects involving unacceptable types of participation. For example, HRECs are not likely to approve participation in dangerous activities. If you proposed to hang out with a violent street gang or take part in illegal drag-racing, your HREC would almost certainly refuse the project because these activities are not safe. HRECs will also oppose participation that may offend people as being culturally insensitive. The wearing of a *hijab* or *qamis* by a non-Muslim may upset some Muslims and most HRECs would ask for reassurance that such a form of participation would cause Muslims no offence. Participation is also unacceptable for HRECs when the researcher is likely to obstruct people in regular roles and duties. Should you propose to participate in lifesaver activities, your HREC would certainly delay the project, because without training you would be likely to hinder the group's regular activity of saving lives.

Similarly, HRECs are likely to be negative about non-participation that leads to possible identification or the recording of personal information without participants' consent. For example, for many HRECs the observation of people via hidden cameras is unacceptable, because participants can be identified and they have no chance to consent or refuse.

Data recording

The most basic technique for gathering data in either type of observation is note taking. There are three issues to consider in note taking: first, the separation of observations and personal reactions; second, how to divide attention between observing and note taking; and last, notation.

It is easy to get events and personal reactions to events confused and then take notes that do not separate the two types of observations. Therefore you should note events and your reactions to them separately. For example, while observing a group of Muslims in the Melbourne CBD, you may see a non-Muslim collide with a Muslim. Following is an inaccurate way to record the incident:

At this point a non-Muslim man bumped into one of the Muslim men. This deliberate act was the first example of unfriendliness today.

Such an observation is a mixture of objective fact and reaction. A collision took place, as someone else could verify, but you do not know for sure that it was the outcome of a deliberate and unfriendly act. Unless you separate your interpretations and observations, your notes will indicate that the collision was indisputably deliberate.

A simple way to keep observations and reactions separate is to divide pages as in Figure 10.1. On notepaper, rule a vertical line about one-third of the way from the right side. Use the 'two-thirds' column to record observations and the 'one-third' column to record personal reactions such as opinions and emotional reactions. In this way, records of events show observations and feelings separately, but on the same page.

What you observe	Your reactions/thoughts

Figure 10.1 Data-recording sheet for recording observations

Second, you should not allow note taking to distract you from the important task of observing. This can happen if you decide to take notes about everything you experience and feel. You may try to write too much and be distracted from the observation situation while frantically creating volumes of notes. Hence, it is better to spend most of your energy observing while taking notes on the things that seem most significant at the time. Your close observation will provide comprehensive memories of the situation and you will be able to write up other details immediately after.

Last, you should feel free to use any style of notation that is comfortable. You might use long hand, short hand, abbreviations, diagrams or symbols or foreign words. As long as the act of note taking is not a distraction from the situation, and your notes are legible, you should feel free to take notes however you wish.

During participant observation, it may not be practical to write down or record data, so a good memory is the most important data-collection tool. It may be necessary to schedule a time, such as lunch break, to rapidly write notes from memory.

A popular set of tools for gathering observational data are audio and visual recording devices such as cameras and tape recorders. These provide comprehensive records of situations and can be reviewed many times. Tapes also allow you to re-observe a situation to refocus on events that had seemed unimportant.

While making recordings you should also take notes to document the experience of observing the situation as it happened. It is also important to observe or listen to recordings with discipline. Recordings do not observe for you, they do not distinguish between significant and insignificant events, nor do they record your perceptions. Last, be aware that under current principles of research ethics in Australia, it is only appropriate to make recordings when participants give permission (see chapter 11).

In-depth interviewing

In-depth interviews provide the best opportunity to find out what someone else thinks or feels. The idea of in-depth interviewing is to get a 'window' on reality from the point of view of a participant and to allow them to tell their story as they wish, identifying the issues that are important to them. The common approach is to ask only very general questions so as to encourage participants to 'open up' and lead the interview and give their perspectives with as little influence from the researcher as possible. Usually researchers have a list of general topics but are ready to discuss others the participant identifies as important.

Another feature of in-depth interviews is that they often take several hours and may extend for more than one session. This allows participants to talk as exhaustively as they wish. Hence, some people call them 'extended interviews'.

In-depth interviews are usually more productive if you gain some rapport, or mutual sense of comfort, with participants. You should conduct in-depth interviews in places that are safe and comfortable for yourself and participants. It is important to be discerning in your style of language and careful not to use words that might cause participants to feel offended or patronised. Similarly, you should select your dress carefully, wearing clothes that do not cause offence. Ties or suits, for example, may cause factory workers to see you as a member of the same social class as their employers.

Also, it is important not to ignore participants' cultural practices. In some cultures, for example, women do not shake hands or remain alone with males who are not family members. Being aware of such practices not only avoids offence, but also demonstrates respect that participants are likely to return.

Two problems often occur during in-depth interviews. First, as participants have a lot of freedom in how they respond to general questions, they often drift to topics unrelated to the research. Some idle talk is polite and also productive, particularly when it generates rapport. However, it is important to be able to redirect discussion back to a research topic; otherwise you will collect very little data.

One strategy is to show interest in the participant's discussion before redirecting them back to the research topic. For example, you might be interviewing Muslims about their lives in Australia. One male participant begins talking about what it is like to go shopping while wearing a *qamis* but drifts into a discussion of a car he saw on a recent trip to the supermarket. You might get the discussion back on track with the following:

> That's interesting, it sounds like some car. I'd like to know more about that car when we finish. Just getting back to what we were discussing before, I'd like to hear you talk a bit more about what it's like to wear the *qamis* while shopping in that centre.

Communicate to the participant that you respect them enough to engage in friendly conversation and then gently restate the original question. Note that if you ever indicate that you will chat about other subjects later, it is respectful and considerate to do so. For their time, participants usually ask for nothing, and you can show some appreciation by sharing some friendly talk.

A second common problem is the tendency of some participants to provide only brief answers. Some people just tend to answer 'Yes', 'No' or 'Maybe' without elaborating, thus rendering little data. Such responses often occur when questions do not invite participants to talk at length or reflect on personal experience. Take the following question that might be asked in an interview with Muslim women:

> What is it like to wear the *hijab* in the city?

It would not be surprising for participants to give short replies like 'All right' or 'Don't even think about it.' A short answer is sufficient given the form of the question and, further, the question contains no explicit request for the participant to reflect on their experience. The question stands a better chance of gaining an extended answer if it requests participants to tell a story about themselves. For example:

Can you tell me about your personal experience of wearing the *hijab* while in Melbourne?

Could you describe what it's been like for you to wear the *hijab* in Melbourne since you first came here to live?

Before conducting interviews, researchers should consider whether their questions invite short or extended answers and make appropriate changes.

Sometimes you will have no success regardless of how you prompt a participant as they may be a person of few words or they may find the question sensitive. Once you realise that you will not get an elaboration, move to the next question. You must respect the right of participants to answer questions as they wish. Participants are not obliged to answer questions and may complain to HRECs if they feel pressured. Also, a general tendency of participants to give only short answers to a particular question may be informative. It could indicate that the question touches on a subject that is sensitive.

One way of documenting an interview is to take notes of the participant's dialogue and then do a 'write-up' immediately after the interview is finished. It must be stressed that any delay undermines the record's accuracy and reliability, so 'write-ups' should be done immediately.

Another common method is to tape record interviews and then create a transcription. This allows a thorough collection of the interview data, which you can review as many times as you wish. However, transcriptions do not record gestures and body language. It is valuable then to take notes while recording an interview to document a participant's physical reactions. Transcribing interviews is a time-consuming task. It is reasonable for an hour-long interview to require between four and five hours of transcribing. While it may be possible to hire transcribers, this is very expensive, particularly if a project has a large number of interviews.

Rather than doing in-depth interviews, it is sometimes preferable to issue questionnaires containing 'open-ended' questions, that is, questions that request extended responses. If participants are literate and accustomed to expressing themselves in writing, it may be practical to ask for written answers. For example, a recent study of clergy asked, 'Please tell us about your accomplishments and successes in your ministry.' Such 'open-ended' questions (that is, without references to specific aspects of a 'successful ministry') gave respondents the freedom to discuss those things they perceived as important (Bouma et al. 1996).

Life narratives

A modification of the in-depth interview is to ask people to write or record their life stories. In the field of oral history, a disciplined expertise has been developed in using this technique to gather material about what life was like in various places and times by asking people to narrate their life stories and recollections of significant events. Researchers can audio record the narrations and produce written reports of life stories in the participant's narrative voice, like a piece of autobiographical writing.

The main purpose of collecting life narratives is to give the participant the opportunity to tell their own story, their way. It is therefore critical not to impose your own viewpoints on the data. You may do this by omitting events that are unimportant for you but important for the participant. It is also possible to misrepresent the participant by emphasising events that are consistent with your own political, social and moral concerns. It is important to be aware of these possibilities, particularly if you and participants have different political, social class, cultural, ethnic or educational backgrounds. Therefore participants should view and appraise your edited versions of their life stories. They can comment, suggest changes and verify that the report is representative of how they remember and feel about events.

Focus groups

Focus groups combine the strengths of in-depth interviewing and observation in a group context. In a focus group, a small number of people, such as between six and twelve, agree to meet for collective discussion with the researcher, who acts as facilitator.

Focus groups are used increasingly as a way of learning about public opinion on a variety of issues. It would be possible to recruit a focus group of Muslims to talk about wearing *hijabs* and *qamis* in public and ask them to discuss issues they perceive as important. Other types of people may also attend, such as Muslims who prefer not to wear *hijab* or *qamis*, or non-Muslims. This would generate data on a cross-section of views and provide observations of different parties reacting to each other's ideas.

Note taking can be very difficult when administering focus groups, simply because so much is usually going on. The best way to collect data is to make a video recording with a camera mounted in a non-intrusive place. The recording should capture the dialogue of individual participants and their interactions. Video recordings also document body language and gestures, which can also be valuable data.

Textual material

The use of textual material, including records, is described at length in chapter 5 with respect to a quantitative form of research, content analysis. Here the researcher counts frequencies of themes, phrases or ideas. However, texts can also be a source of data in qualitative research, where, rather than just counting the number of times themes occur, researchers use the themes to construct a picture of what it is like to experience a given situation.

For example, documents can be used to answer the question, 'What was happening in this time and place to these people?' Letters, diaries and minutes of meetings are useful sources of data about what it is like to experience particular situations. When using documents, it is important to keep in mind the identities of the people who wrote them, who was to receive them, and for what purpose they were written. Such information specifies the perspectives of those who participated in the creation of the text.

Organising and summarising qualitative data

Once you have made your observations, recorded or written up your interviews or focus group interactions, or collected your open-ended questionnaires, what do you do with the data? Qualitative research tends to produce vast amounts of information, which you must first organise and summarise.

Organising data

As in content research, qualitative researchers look through interviews, textual data and observational data for recurring 'themes' or issues. They identify themes and organise them into systems of categories, a practice called 'coding'. Following is a simple example of coding. When asked a question on the topic of employment, 'Why don't you work?', a Muslim woman might answer:

> Employers say the *hijab* is a safety hazard and refuse to hire women who wear it.

There are two dimensions to the thematic content of the sentence, the topic and the issue. The topic is 'employment', as given by the question. In response, the participant raised the issue of 'cultural discrimination', the non-hiring of Muslim women because they wear the *hijab*.

The next task is to 'code' the theme, that is, apply a label designating the topic and the issues. A simple way to code the above statement is therefore:

1.1 Employment: Cultural discrimination

The word or phrase before the colon identifies the topic, the following words or phrases identify the issues. The code also receives a number, for easy indexing, in this case 1.1. In this example, 'Employment' is Topic 1 and 'Cultural Discrimination' is Issue 1 for the topic; hence the full code is '1.1'. There are many ways to code themes and you should devise or borrow ways that make greatest sense for you.

As you read interviews and create new codes, write the code numbers on the pages of the interview transcripts where they occur. While doing this, also write a 'codebook'—that is, a list of codes, indexed to the interviews in which you identified them (see Figure 10.2). When finished, the code book will be a useful tool for analysis. As a list of codes, it will give a structural overview of how you have perceived the data. The codebook will also indicate how often codes occur, thereby showing their relative importance according to your own reading of the data. Lastly, the index of interviews and page numbers will allow you to quickly review and extract coded text.

It is valuable to review a coding scheme at least once. This leads to a refinement of the coding and greater familiarity with the data. If possible, another researcher should review the coding to assess its coherence and depth of understanding of the data.

You can create a codebook on computer with a simple spreadsheet or word processing program. There are a number of software packages designed specially for coding and analysing textual data. Students should gain some skills with these if they intend to pursue research as a career.

Figure 10.2 Code Book: Muslim Settlement

Topics: issues	Interviews: page numbers				Total
1. Employment					
1 Cultural discrimination	Int 1; page 3	Int 2: page 6	Int 4: page 8	Int 5: page 5	4
2 Lack of training	Int 1: page 4	Int 3: page 5			2
3 Language problems	Int 2 page 7	Int 4: page 6	Int 5: page 5		3
2. Social life					
1 Events arranged by Islamic society	Int 1 page 4	Int 3: page 6			2
2 Activities for children	Int 3 page 3	Int 5: page 7	Int 6: page 8		3
etc.					

Phase three: analysing data

Having organised your data, how do you analyse or 'make sense of it', so you can write about 'what is going on' with the benefit of an informed understanding? Most importantly, you have to develop your sense of having 'been there' or having 'been close' to the situation, so you can look at the data with the sensitivity of someone who knows the situation personally. When a person has visited a remote place, they can describe it with reference to personal experience—the sights, sounds, smells, social values and customs. The visitor is 'sensitised' to the place and can analyse its social situation by referring to their first-hand knowledge of 'what it was like' to be there. Similarly, you have to develop the same type of sensitivity to the situations you research.

If you have done participant research for an extended period, your sensitivity may be adequate. Then again, if you have used less intimate methodologies like non-participant observation or interviews, you may need to develop extra sensitivity through immersion in the data. Read and re-read interview transcripts and notes, review and re-review sound or visual recordings and photographs and continue to revise the coding.

As your sensitivity increases, take notes of your changing impressions. The notes will eventually expose 'forms' in the data. Patterns and relationships between actions and social structures will become perceptible, allowing you to explain 'what is going on' or 'what it is like' in the situation. For example, after a thorough reading of interviews with Muslims living in Australia, you may 'see' systems of support within the Muslim communities that participants never describe explicitly but take for granted. Their dialogues could contain assumptions of reciprocal duties of support to certain people—family, clergy, friends, school teachers—but participants may never make direct references to these duties. You may also perceive social problems to which most participants refer only in their jokes. Participants may 'send themselves up' because they cannot get work in Australia that is appropriate to their qualifications. These jokes, however, may indicate a general problem for Muslims in the labour market.

Fundamentally you should approach all qualitative analysis with a view of developing sensitivity to the data. This way, you can discuss 'what is going on' or 'what it is like' to be in a situation just like you have been inside it—or as close to it as possible. In addition to developing sensitivity, you can employ a number of frameworks to make sense of data from particular analytical perspectives. Descriptions of two appear below, the 'action/cultural' and the 'typical actions' frameworks.

Action/cultural framework

The action/cultural framework makes reference to cultural or social facts in understanding social actions. It often requires extra data about the culture of the people within the research situation. Therefore it may be necessary to consult historical books, religious texts or company mission statements.

For example, if you are a non-Muslim researching Muslims in Australia, you may want to understand why Muslim women wear the *hijab* and Muslim men wear the *qamis* in a predominately non-Muslim country like Australia. The immediate answer, as you would be told in interviews, is that they wish to neutralise unwanted attention of the opposite gender. This answer only provides a superficial understanding and raises the further question, 'Why do Muslims wish to neutralise attentions of the opposite gender?' If you look more closely at the culture and social norms of Islam, you will find that a neutralisation of interest from the opposite gender is a religious requirement (Eposito 2002: 95) stated in two verses of the *Holy Koran* (Surah 24: Verses 30–31). The advantage of following this requirement is made clear, as believers are reminded that those who 'turn to God in penitence' will 'prosper' (Surah 24: Verse 31). Therefore, you can explain the wearing of *hijab* and *qamis* as a response to a command in the *Holy Koran* that makes Muslims eligible for God's favour.

Typical actions framework

This analytic approach considers how people construct their social lives. It examines what actions are generally understood as 'typical actions', which make social life possible. Typical actions by which Muslims recognise other Muslims are attendance at the Friday prayer; abstinence from pork; wearing the *qamis* or *hijab*; and the standard greeting of 'Asalaam amalykum'. These are typical actions that for Muslims signify qualities of Islamic identity. Muslims recognise each other through these actions and have socially defined interpretations of meaning behind each.

In a study of Australian Muslims, a significant issue among participants could be their relations with non-Muslims. In analysing any friction between the communities, the researcher might search interviews for Muslims' negative interpretations of the 'typical' actions of non-Muslims. The participants may note that many non-Muslims stare at their *hijabs* and *qamis*, assume that all Islamic marriages are 'arranged', express a lack of understanding of abstinence from alcohol, and that some non-Muslims attempt to stop the building of mosques in their suburbs. Likewise, the interviews may indicate typical actions that Muslims interpret as friendly. Interviews may contain several references to participants' feelings of solidarity with non-Muslims at work or to the prayer facilities for their children in state schools. Repeated references to such types of social actions indicate what it is like to be a Muslim in Australia and how Muslims construct the social actions of others. The recognition of both negative and positive interpretations of typical actions by non-Muslims would be the basis for a rich description and set of explanations of 'what it is like' to be a Muslim living in Australia.

Reporting on qualitative research

Qualitative research does not always lead to clear conclusions. Therefore, it is important that when writing up results you remind yourself of the question or research objective that guided the research. It is that question that you must now answer, that research objective about which you must now conclude. If you asked, 'What is it like to be a Muslim in Australia?', your conclusion, based on your data, will express a response to this question. If the research objective was 'to describe how the Wright family made an important decision', then you will summarise the findings and observations in terms of themes, interaction patterns, sequence of argumentation, patterns of power and submission, or whatever you found. This will allow you to describe what is involved in the situation and to interpret this for readers.

Reporting on qualitative research involves careful description of what was observed and heard, 'what it was like', and how people felt, reacted and behaved. This may involve data summarisation and categorisation into themes or patterns, or it may involve description and interpretation of observations. Here are some examples.

Princess Diana's meanings for women: results of a focus group study

Elizabeth Black and Philip Smith
Anthropology and Sociology
University of Queensland

Abstract

The death of Princess Diana set in train a series of official and popular responses, which are broadly consistent with Durkheimian ideas of civic ritual. Mass media accounts of Princess Diana's purportedly extraordinary appeal are speculative, lack methodological foundation, and fail to give adequate consideration to potential variability in responses to her life and death. In order to explore popular understandings of Diana, focus groups were conducted in Australia with Anglo-Celtic women of different ages within three weeks of her death and funeral. The women professed a diversity of orientations and experiences towards Diana. Significant barriers to identification with Diana included a wealth gap between her and the participants in the study, the routine nature of charity work and suffering for many ordinary people, the irresponsible circumstances of her death and reflexivity about the media as a source of information. Sources of identification included her physical and character attributes, the mothering role and the universal tragedy of death. There was no support in the transcripts for the view that women identified with Diana as a feminist heroine. Caution is expressed about both the generalisability of the results of the study to other groups of women and also the comparability of the study with data collected at other points in time.

Journal of Sociology, Volume 35, No. 3, November 1999

Marital conflict and men's leisure: how women negotiate male power in a small mining community

Marion Collis
Humanities and Social Sciences
Monash University

Abstract

Against a background of unequal power relationships between men and women, and utilising Lukes' three dimensions of power, this paper examines how the wives of shift workers in a small mining town deal with the conflicts that arise over their male partners' use of leisure time. It looks at the range of influence strategies women use to actively nego-tiate men's manifest power and the coping strategies/forms of resistance which they fall back on when these strategies fail, or when men's latent or hidden power prevents any overt challenge. The data suggest that women not only use a wide range of influence strategies with varying degrees of success, but they are creative and resilient in finding alterna-tive ways to resist the structures of male power. However, the outcomes of their agency at an individual level are limited by the social, economic and ideological structures of male power at the community level.

Journal of Sociology, Volume 35, No. 1, March 1999

Questions for review

1   How do the questions asked in qualitative research differ from those asked in quantitative research?

2   Why is it not helpful to ask whether quantitative or qualitative research is better, or which is more important? What question should be asked?

3   What are the basic data-gathering techniques in qualitative research? What are the advantages and disadvantages of each?

4   What is involved in the summarisation of qualitative data?

5   In qualitative research the subject of the research participates more in the project than in quantitative research. Discuss.

Suggestions for further reading

Babbie, E. R. (2003), *The Practice of Social Research*, 10th edn, Wadsworth Publishing, London, chapters 10, 11 and 13.

Berger, Peter L. and Thomas Luckmann (1966), *The Social Construction of Reality: A Treatise on the Sociology of Knowledge*, Doubleday, Garden City, New York.

Bouma, Gary D. (1994), *Mosques and Muslim Settlement in Australia*, Australian Government Publishing Service, Canberra. This research was supported by a grant from the Bureau of Immigration and Population Research and conducted under the auspices of the World Council on Religion and Peace.

Bouma, Gary D. (ed.) (1997), *Many Religions, All Australian*, Christian Research Association, Melbourne.

Bouma, Gary D., Patricia Bouma, Kristin Diemer, Anne Edwards and Peter Hiller (1996), *Commencing Clergy Careers: Gender Differences Among Anglican Priests and Deacons*, Report to The General Synod of the Anglican Church of Australia, Women's Commission.

Buckner, H. Taylor (1970), 'Transformations of reality in the legal process', *Social Research*, 37 (1): 88–101.

Denzin, Norman and Yvonna Lincoln (eds) (2000), *Handbook of Qualitative Research*, 2nd edn, Sage, London.

Eliaeson, Sven (2002), *Max Weber's Methodologies*, Polity Press, Cambridge, pp. 41–4.

Eldridge, J. E. T. (ed.) (1971), *Max Weber: The Interpretation of Social Reality*, Thomas Nelson and Sons Ltd, London, pp. 92–102.

Esposito, John L. (2002), *What Everyone Needs to Know about Islam*, Oxford University Press, Oxford.

Gilcun, Jane F. (ed.) (1992), *Qualitative Methods in Family Research*, Sage, New York.

Holmes David, Kate Hughes and Julian Roberta (2003), *Australian Sociology: A Changing Society*, Pearson Education, Frenchs Forest, NSW, chapter 15.

Judd, C. M., E. R. Smith and L. H. Kidder (1991), *Research Methods in Social Relations*, Holt, Rinehart & Winston, Fort Worth, chapters 11–13.

Kellehear, Allan (1993), *The Unobtrusive Researcher: A Guide to Methods*, Allen & Unwin, Sydney.

Kreuger, Richard A. (1994), *Focus Groups: A Practical Guide for Applied Research*, Sage, New York.

Larson, Colleen L. (1997), 'Representing the subject: problems in personal narrative enquiry', *Qualitative Studies in Education*, 10(4), pp. 455–70.

Minichiello, Victor, Rosalie Aroni, Eric Timewell and Loris Alexander (1995), *In-depth Interviewing: Principles, Techniques, Analysis*, 2nd edn, Longman, Melbourne.

Silverman, David (1999), *Doing Quantitative Research: A Practical Handbook*, Sage, London.

Taylor, Steven J. & Robert Bogdan (1998), *Introduction to Qualitative Research Methods: A Guidebook and Resource*, 3rd edn, John Wiley & Sons Inc, New York.

Ethics in human research

CHAPTER OUTLINE

The key to identifying ethical issues in research is to take the position of a participant. How would you feel if you were asked certain questions or observed doing certain things, or if your records and papers were examined for research purposes? How would you want researchers to handle and report on the information they have about you? The ethical issues involved in doing research on humans are very much the same for both quantitative and qualitative research.

Staff of Australian universities, many research organisations and members of most professional organisations are now formally required to conduct their research according to stated ethical principles and to demonstrate this to Human Research Ethics Committees (HRECs). These ethical principles basically require that participants in the research must be able to give informed consent to being part of the research, the identity of informants must be protected unless they give written permission to be identified in stored data and research reports, researchers must not coerce participants into participating or divulging information, and researchers must keep data for five years to protect themselves against charges of 'forging' data.

The ethics of research

Research in the social sciences usually involves dealing with people, organisations and groups. Unless you are only dealing with data that have already been collected, public records (such as census data) or public documents, you will be asking people questions, observing their behaviour, or collecting other information about them. All our dealings with other people raise ethical issues. We are familiar with the ethical issues relating to our personal lives—issues of loyalty, honesty, integrity, and others. Lately, businesses and corporations are beginning to ask questions about the ethics of economic life. So, too, are there ethical issues in research that need to be addressed.

As with many ethical issues in other areas of life, being thoughtful and considerate of the needs and feelings of others goes a long way towards guiding the researcher. How would you react if you were in the place of the person or group you intend to study? Would you respond well to the questions you intend to ask, or the procedures you intend to employ?

Be considerate. You are asking people to do you a favour. You are appealing to their generosity to help you with your work. Not everyone will share your view of the importance of your research. This is true even if you are asking friends, family, or students you know. It is even more true if you are going into the community to do your research. You have a responsibility to the participants in your research to be considerate and not to waste their time. Moreover, you have a responsibility to researchers who will come after you not to irritate and alienate the community. By being inconsiderate or poorly prepared you let yourself down, waste the time and effort of others, and jeopardise future research.

Part of being considerate is being prepared. Another part is to take up only as much time as is essential. Not only does an unnecessarily long questionnaire waste your time but it also wastes the time of those to whom it is administered. Ask yourself 'Is this question necessary? Do I really need to know how many children the respondent has?' If the study is about sharing tasks between husband and wife, then yes, you probably do want to ask that question. But if you are inquiring about past achievement in maths, you may decide to eliminate the question. Does each question really relate to the hypothesis? Or, is it really personal curiosity? Interviews and questionnaires with a clear focus not only produce better data, but they are also less disruptive and wasteful.

You should also be considerate of participants because you are to some extent invading their privacy. If respondents sense that you are being intrusive or asking inappropriate questions, they may refuse to cooperate, or may sabotage the research by giving misleading information. Your manner and the nature of your research should be carefully designed so as not to offend, embarrass or annoy those you are studying. They are doing you a favour.

Part of being a considerate researcher is being careful about the way you seek permission from those you wish to study. While it is appropriate to tell people why you are doing the research, it is usually not wise to tell them what you hope to find as this may bias the information they provide. At the completion of their projects, many researchers offer to tell participants what they found and their conclusions. This often provides interesting feedback for the researcher and those studied.

It is usually a good idea to have a letter of introduction signed by yourself and/or your lecturer or head of department. This will help to identify you and to secure the cooperation of those you wish to be part of your study. Such a letter should describe who you are (e.g. a student at a specified university), how you accessed the person's name, why you are doing your

---

Figure 11.1 Sample letter of introduction

An Australian University

1 May 200x

Dear Resident of Ashwood,

I am a student at An Australian University and am conducting research on who performs which duties in the home as part of my course of studies toward a BA. I would appreciate your help in my research.

Your name was drawn randomly from the electoral role (or from the white pages of the telephone book, or supplied by a specified organisation, person or agency).

The research involves a one-hour interview, which I will conduct with you in your home, or some other place that you nominate. The interview will involve questions related to the way you and your partner organise to do household tasks. The interview will be taped. You will be free not to answer any question and you may terminate the interview at any time you wish.

I will telephone you some time next week in order to make an appointment if you agree to be interviewed. At the time of the interview I will ask you to sign a form consenting to be taped and explain what will happen to the tapes in the course of my research. I will also discuss your rights to the material on the tapes.

I assure you that your privacy and anonymity will be respected and protected by our procedures; no real names or identifiable places will be included in data anr¹   and research reports.

When I have finished the research I will send to you a summary copy of the results of the research.

Should you at any time have any complaint about this project (No. 568/2001) please feel free to call or write to The Secretary, Human Ethics Committee, Research Division, An Australian University (telephone, fax and email details provided).

Sincerely yours,

Student's name

Lecturer's name

research (e.g. for a degree, a thesis or a class project) and what the research will require from the person whose permission you are seeking (e.g. filling in a questionnaire that will take 10 minutes, an interview lasting an hour, a group interview lasting 15 minutes, or participating in an experiment that will involve watching and assessing some videos for half an hour). Providing this information makes it possible for the potential participant to make an informed decision about whether to participate. The letter of introduction, or 'Plain Language Statement', about the research is essential to ensuring that 'informed consent' has been given.

A letter of invitation to participate in research usually concludes with information about what the participant should do if they have any complaint about the research. This complaints clause usually directs the participant to the HREC of the university, hospital or organisation responsible for the research. One regularly used complaints clause is found in the sample letter in Figure 11.1. Preparing a letter of introduction is a good exercise to test whether you have thoroughly thought through your research plan. It will give your lecturer an opportunity to advise you about what you are doing. When students do research as part of their course, their lecturer is responsible for them and for the conduct of the research. Hence it is in the interest of all for students and lecturers to confer carefully about each research project.

A personal card issued by your institution, stating your position (e.g. PhD student) and contact details is an effective introduction to participants (see Figure 11.2). By giving these cards to people, they see that you are being honest about your identity and purpose and that you are willing to allow others to verify who you are. This action, which shows prospective participants that you wish to act ethically and do the right thing by them usually wins their attention and co-operation quickly. Further information, such as a complaints clause, can also be placed on the reverse side of the card.

Australian University	If you dislike anything about this study you can complain to the Secretary of the Human Ethics Committee. Quote the number of this project, 2004/### when contacting the secretary at:
Reece Urcher PhD Student (Student No. #######) School of Social Inquiry Australian University, Vic. 3000 City Campus Mobile Telephone: #### #### Facsimile: +61 3 9905 2410 Email: ###@Ausuni.edu.au	Telephone: +61 # #### ### Email: SCERH@adm.Ausuni.edu.au Address postal complaints to: The Secretary Standing Committee on Ethics in Research Involving Humans

Figure 11.2 A sample card

Formal ethical review of research

Simply being considerate is not enough. The ethics of all research involving human participants has become a major area of discussion and policy review. Most professional associations, like the Australian Sociological Association and the Australian Association of Social Workers, have devised codes of ethics to guide their members. Find out whether the professional association related to your intended occupation has a code of ethics. Get a copy and read it. Your lecturer may have a copy.

Following a number of excesses perpetrated by some over-zealous or unscrupulous researchers in various fields, procedures have been instituted in all tertiary institutions for the careful ethical scrutiny of research proposals by Human Research Ethics Committees (HRECs) prior to the commencement of the research and before funding is approved or passed on to the researchers. First instituted to guide medical research, ethical review is now required for all research involving human participants. The fundamental principles are stated in a document called *National Statement on Ethical Conduct in Research Involving Humans* (*National Statement*), prepared by National Health and Medical Research Council (NHMRC) in 1999. This document states the current thinking on ethics for Australian research involving humans. HRECs use the principles in this statement to guide their consideration of research proposals. Most universities now require all research involving humans, including most sociological, psychological, business management, marketing, science, education and oral history research, to be scrutinised by an ethics committee.

Basic principles of research ethics

The following principles of research ethics summarise the concerns most HRECs focus on in evaluating research proposals.

Principle 1: Researchers must treat with dignity and respect the persons, groups and organizations who participate in their research.
People have feelings, orientations, cultures, rights to privacy, and rights to control their lives and information about themselves. The rights of people are greater than the researcher's 'need to know'. However important you think your research is, you must place participants' well-being first. Referring to participants as 'participants' rather than 'subjects' and remembering that you are dealing with people not objects helps to retain the levels of respect and concern appropriate to humans.

Sensitivity to others is very important, but especially in social science research, where it is precisely that sensitivity that may open new insights into the nature of social situations. You are asking people 'What is it like to be you? What is your perspective on this? How do you respond to this or that situation?' In order to 'hear' their responses you need to both ask sensitive questions and listen very sensitively to their responses.

Following current discussion of ethics in human research, we will refer to people who consent to be researched as 'participants', rather than 'subjects', for several reasons. First, being a participant infers a degree of cooperative activity on the part of those we study. Participants are not passive subjects but cooperate with us in our research. It is important to remember that without the cooperation of participants we will not get our data. This helps to remind us of our dependency on them and to enhance our respect for them.

'Participants' is also a useful term as it includes groups, corporations, organisations, and neighbourhoods as well as persons. All participants have rights, needs for privacy, and a claim on our respect.

The respect accorded participants extends to treating the information they provide with great care and not violating their privacy. One way of protecting your informants is to mask their identity by never recording names, changing the names on your files and using fictitious names in your reports, assigning numerical codes, and referring only to grouped data (that is, not individually to Tom Brown's score but to the average score of 'young males' in response to a particular question). You can mask the locality of your research by not naming the suburb or organisation in which the research was done.

If you are promising participants that you will protect their identities, your HREC will wish to know how you will accomplish this (e.g. de-identifying records and reports of information with codes, keeping records locked in a secure place).

After gaining permission, you must retain sufficient information, including letters of invitation, consent forms and data to prove that you actually did what you proposed to do and were given ethical clearance to do so. This is necessary to defend yourself against the possible charge of forging your data and to be prepared for an audit by your HREC.

Personal information and privacy
In most social science research there is no need to collect information that identifies individual participants. Researchers seldom need facts that can identify individual participants to others. However, if you plan to gather and publish such information, you must know the relevant law regarding privacy. The Commonwealth and most states and territories have 'privacy principles', which bind researchers to protect their participants' 'personal information'. Section 6 of the *Privacy Act 1988 (Cth)* describes personal information as 'information or an opinion...whether true or not, and whether recorded in a material form or not,

about an individual whose identity is apparent, or can reasonably be ascertained, from the information or opinion'. 'Personal information' identifies individuals.

Depending on the relevant privacy principles, there can be additional restrictions on the collection, use and disclosure of a type of personal information—'sensitive information'. According to section 6 of the *Privacy Act*, this includes information or an opinion about an individual's race, ethnicity, political opinions, memberships of political parties, trade unions, and professional associations, sexual preference, criminal record, religious beliefs and affiliations, philosophical beliefs and their health information. 'Health information' also has a definition in section 6 of the *Privacy Act*. It is information or an opinion about an individual's health or disabilities; their health service usage or intended use; personal information they give to health services; and personal information they give when organising the donation of their body parts.

Before gathering personal information, always consult an expert in privacy regulations. If you research within a government department or private firm, talk to the privacy officer. If you research as a consultant or with a volunteer organisation, seek advice from a lawyer. Find out which privacy principles—Commonwealth, state or territory—apply to your research. Otherwise, you may compromise participants' rights and break the law.

The following list contains some of the Commonwealth *Information Privacy Principles* (IPPs), from the Privacy Act 1988 (Cth) (Part III, Division 2). It is an introduction to the types of obligations that researchers encounter, when the Commonwealth *Privacy Act* is relevant.

- **Informed collection:** researchers must inform participants of the purposes for which they are collecting personal information, and the identities of other people who will have access. (IPP 2)
- **Relevant collection:** researchers can only collect personal information relevant to their research. (IPP 3(c))
- **Relevant use:** researchers can only use personal information in ways relevant to their research. (IPP 9)
- **Accuracy of information:** before using personal information, researchers must take reasonable steps to ensure the information is up-to-date and accurate. (IPP 8)
- **Storage of information:** researchers must ensure that personal information is protected by reasonable security to prevent loss or unauthorised access. (IPP 4)
- **Openness:** unless authorised to refuse, researchers should be open with any person about the nature of personal information they hold and the purposes for which they hold it. (IPP 5 (b))
- **Limits on use:** researchers may only use personal information for purposes which participants give consent. Exceptions apply in some other circumstances, such as when other uses will save lives. (IPP10)

- **Limits on disclosure:** researchers may only disclose personal information to others for whom participants give consent. Exceptions apply when further disclosure will save lives or the law requires further disclosure or when non-disclosure is a threat to the health of people. When a participant consents to the disclosure of their personal information to others, the receiver may only use the information for the consented purposes. (IPP 11)

Principle 2: Research must be based on knowledge of the work of others in the area and be conducted and/or supervised by persons qualified to do the work who have the necessary facilities to ensure the safety of participants.
It is unethical to rush into the field to collect data before doing a literature review to learn about what has been done before, what is known and what questions remain in the field of study you propose. It is also usually a great help to see how others have tackled the problem you propose to study. It is unethical to carry out poorly designed research, since, at the very least, people's time is wasted and, at worst, misleading results might be declared. It is likely that any research you do as a student will need to be cleared by an HREC.

While many of the skills required for social science research are ordinary skills of human interaction, their use in research requires careful supervision, particularly when students are learning how to research. In my nearly 20 years' experience on an HREC the most hair-raising research proposals have come from students who were being inducted into the skills of social science research. Students require close assistance from their supervisors, who should not allow students to choose sensitive topics that are more appropriate for experienced researchers.

Supervision is also required because in the process of interviewing someone you may uncover problems that are beyond your ability to resolve—a difficult domestic situation, a deeply troubled person, or some other circumstance. You are probably not trained as a counsellor, as a family therapist, or in other helping skills, and hence you have no business trying to solve these problems. You should carry the name of a social worker, counsellor, or medical practitioner to whom you can refer people in need. You may have to report a particularly serious situation to the police or a social worker. However, you are only there to collect information relevant to your research project; you are not a helping agent. Your abilities and responsibilities are quite limited. Discuss these issues with the person responsible for your research, your lecturer or supervisor.

Principle 3: The potential benefits of a research project must substantially outweigh the potential harm to participants.
Again, discuss these issues with the person responsible for your research, your lecturer or supervisor. Your HREC will also provide input on these issues.

HRECs are called on to weigh the promised benefits of a project against its potential to harm participants and also to ensure the collection of relevant data. While researchers have a responsibility to minimise harm, the role of the researcher is different from the role of the therapist or helper. Confusion of therapy and research often leads to serious ethical dilemmas.

Principle 4: Participants in research must be able to make a voluntary, informed decision to participate.

Informed consent. The decision to participate must be based on knowledge of what will be involved; what will be demanded in terms of time, activity, and topics covered; what risks are likely; and where to lodge a complaint should that become necessary. This information is usually provided by means of a letter like the sample in Figure 11.1, otherwise referred to as a 'Plain Language Statement'. Potential participants must understand such information. This may require translation, careful wording in everyday language and avoiding the disciplinary jargon that researchers use for efficient communication with each other but that leaves the layperson bewildered.

While the ideal is written (informed) consent, there are many circumstances in social science research where this is not needed or may even be unhelpful. Questionnaires are often returned anonymously, and the very act of completing and returning them is an indication of consent. There are times when the last thing a researcher wants is the identity of the person, or when the formality of written consent would violate the research context or the nature of the relationship between researcher and participant.

Usually the risks and discomforts involved in social science research are minimal. However, there are risks that need to be carefully examined. The most important issue here is the risk of the disclosure of information, which might be damaging to a person. It is not possible for you to promise confidentiality to the people you interview. You could be subpoenaed for results if they have a bearing on a court case. Your files are open to searches under the freedom of information legislation current in your state. Before embarking on a project where this might happen, ask yourself 'How would I deal with this?'

Gaining informed consent poses particular problems for social research. Much of what is studied is public behaviour. This does not usually require consent. Some research is little more than having a conversation with someone. However, that conversation may have proceeded differently if the participant in the research had known the intent of the conversation. In such a case it would be ethically correct to inform the participant, but such information might destroy the validity of the research. HRECs now assist researchers to resolve some of these ethical issues.

Another issue related to discomfort and risk relates to asking questions about sensitive areas. Topics may be sensitive because they are public issues, politically sensitive or personally painful. For example, to interview parents a few months after the death of their child through Sudden Infant Death Syndrome ('cot death') may be important in understanding the grief process following such a death, but it may be too disruptive to the parents and in fact affect (positively or negatively) the very process you intended to study. Students are usually encouraged to avoid such sensitive areas while they are learning to do research.

Voluntariness. While rarely an issue in social science research, it is important not to coerce compliance by offering overly enticing rewards for participation such as large sums of money or holidays in the sun. At most, participants may receive reimbursement for expenses, or given some small compensation for the time they give.

In some cases of social science research the investigator may be in a position of power over the participant (parent/child, lecturer/student, employer/employee, supervisor/supervisee, parole officer/parolee). When this is the case, particular care must be taken in securing consent. In some cases it may be impossible to get free consent and the research may have to be abandoned. In other cases a neutral person may be able to secure the consent. An interviewer wearing a lab coat, or a clerical collar, while conducting an interview may be playing on a symbol of authority in order to gain the participant's acquiescence. The style of clothing to wear while conducting an interview needs to be considered in terms of the power relations between interviewer and interviewee.

However, in most social science research the most powerful figure is likely to be the participant, who can just walk away, refuse to answer, or give a 'safe' or misleading answer.

Freedom to withdraw. Participants in your research must not only be free to consent to participating at the outset; they must also be reminded that they are free to withdraw at any time without penalty. This can be very frustrating to researchers, but it is not ethical to pressure participants to complete interviews and questionnaires, or to stay for the completion of the experiment. This may be very frustrating, but to do otherwise violates the rights and freedom of the participant. Arguing or pleading with a participant that their withdrawal will waste your time, threaten your grade in a subject, hold up your degree, necessitate another interview with someone else, or render invalid the questionnaire constitutes pressure and is therefore unethical. Students should bear this in mind when constructing questionnaires. Keep them short, so that people will complete them.

Principle 5: Research is a public activity, conducted openly and accountably to both the researcher's community and to the participants in the research.
Research is a public activity conducted to increase our knowledge of some aspect of the universe. Its very public nature is one of the strengths of

knowledge generated by research. Recall the definition of science in chapter 1. This public nature of research also helps to keep researchers honest and affords a level of protection to participants.

This applies to research teams and covers the rights of co-researchers and assistants. It is important that all involved are as fully informed as possible so that they know what they are part of, what their role in the project is, what the overall goal is and which procedures are involved. Keeping co-workers and subordinates in the dark is dangerous, inconsiderate, a waste of their input and unethical. Imagine how you would feel if after working on some aspect of a project you discovered that its overall goal or basic technique violated your sense of right and wrong.

Most tertiary institutions have Human Research Ethics Committees with representatives from a variety of disciplines—from medicine, law and religion—and from the wider community to provide a public forum for assessing the ethical considerations in specific research projects. All research involving humans, organisations and corporations requires the scrutiny and approval of an HREC. For much of social science research this does not raise life and death issues; however, many proposals require important advice, caution or redesign to protect either the researcher or participants.

Ethical issues in qualitative research

Qualitative research often brings researchers and participants into close contact and creates a need for the interests of both to be balanced. Researchers can improve the lives of participants if they can access such data and need support in their efforts. Since participants provide researchers with personal data they need to be protected from infringements on their privacy. Human Research Ethics Committees (HRECs) consider a number of issues as they seek to support the interests of both participants and researchers.

First, the close and sometimes extended contact between researchers and participants can change researcher/participant relationships and compromise the original conditions under which studies receive ethics approval. HRECs require formal relationships between researchers and participants based on clear explanations by researchers and the official consent of participants. During in-depth interviews and participant observation, you and your participants develop a rapport and personal trust and the relationship can become less formal and more personal. Eventually, participants may reveal personal secrets, trusting you to remain silent. Such confidences are often of little consequence, but participants may confide personal information that will force you to make difficult choices. They may reveal facts that you as a researcher are obliged to report—that they are victims of abuse or the perpetrators of crimes. In such situations, you would be faced with a conflict of trust. Either you betray the trust of your participant or your professional and ethical obligations.

Similarly, in-depth interviews about sensitive issues may stimulate memories that participants find upsetting. HRECs often require that researchers make provisions for referring participants to counselling agencies in the event they have such problems. It is not ethical for you to conduct an interview or series of interviews that leave respondents upset and with nothing in place to meet this need.

Given the personal nature of much qualitative data, HRECs seek to protect participants' privacy. You must obtain permission from participants if you wish to quote them in reports. If participants prefer to remain anonymous, your HREC will require that you refrain from producing their names and refer to them by pseudonyms instead. Researchers must also take steps to de-identify data—that is, you must remove all references to the identities of participants from tapes and transcripts, such as names and unique characteristics. Lastly, HRECs oblige researchers to keep data in secure places such as deposit boxes that only and their supervisors can access. You must have such places ready before collecting data and should officially notify participants in your explanatory statement that you have made such an arrangement to protect their data.

HRECs also have concerns about observational studies. University and TAFE students must obtain permission from their HRECs for all observational research. This includes observations of public events such as church services and concerts. In addition, where observation focuses on specific organisations, groups or individuals, HRECs may require that researchers gain permission from the intended participants. Therefore, if you wish to observe a local political group, an order of nuns or a touring soccer team, your HREC may not give approval until the potential participants supply their written permission. If researchers plan to conduct observation studies on premises that are privately owned or have restricted entry, researchers are obliged by their HRECs to gain permission to enter the premises from owners or caretakers. Hence, if you wish to enter factories to observe workers; convention centres to observe visitors; or nightclubs to observe patrons, your HREC will require letters of permission from owners or managers. Most research done in shopping centres also requires permission from the manager of the complex.

Regarding covert observation, there are a number of conditions in section 17 of the *National Statement* (NHMRC 1999: 51) that HRECs use in considering research proposals. Generally covertness in all research is unethical unless it is necessary for the research to have scientific validity; the researchers are able to accurately define the extent of the covertness; no alternatives exist; participants are not exposed to any increased harm by the covertness of the project; researchers make immediate disclosures to participants; participants are able to withdraw their data; and the research will not bring notoriety to the research community.

If you intend to audio or video record people in any situation, you must show your HREC that you will take steps to gain the consent of participants. Moreover, your HREC will require that you tell potential participants about what you intend to do with their taped material and undertake not to use it otherwise.

In the event that you wish to access archives, your HREC will require that you gain permission from legal custodians. You would also be obligated to inform the custodians of how you intend to use the material and not use it for any other purpose.

Aboriginal and Torres Strait Islander Research

The National Health and Medical Research Council (NHMRC), the Australian Institute of Aboriginal and Torres Strait Islander Studies (AIATSIS) and the Aboriginal and Torres Strait Islander Commission (ATSIC) have developed ethics guidelines for research about Aboriginals and Torres Strait Islanders. The NHMRC have published the most recent guidelines in its report *Values and Ethics: Guidelines for Ethical Conduct in Aboriginal and Torres Strait Islander Health Research* (2003). This report states six guidelines for ethical research with Aboriginal and Torres Strait Islander people. Note that these guidelines have some conceptual overlaps.

1 **Respect:** researchers must respect cultural differences between themselves and participants, taking care to avoid disrespect by ignorance. Also, researchers must consider how their work will affect participants, being sensitive to the possibility that participants may suffer harm.

2 **Reciprocity:** researchers must engage with participants in a spirit of reciprocal respect, recognising that participants also have the right to expect benefits from the relationship.

3 **Equality:** researchers must consider participants as equal partners. Therefore, researchers should recognise participants' equal rights to practise their culture; participants' knowledge as being of at least equal value to their own; and that benefits of research should be shared equally.

4 **Responsibility**: researchers must take care to avoid doing harm to participants. This requires schemes of accountability that allow researchers to show their level of care.

5 **Survival and protection:** researchers must be conscious of the survival and protection of Aboriginal and Torres Strait Islander people, particularly with respect to their cultures and social solidarity. Therefore, researchers must take care not to encroach upon participants' values and respect the social bonds in their communities. Researchers must not diminish participants' opportunities to assert their cultural distinctiveness.

6 **Spirit and integrity:** researchers must respect Aboriginal and Torres Strait Islanders' cultural and spiritual links to 'past, current and future generations' (NHMRC 2003: 19).

Researchers must always exercise integrity in adhering to the above guidelines. These guidelines already have practical support in protocols developed by AIATSIS and ATSIC with respect to research with Aboriginal and Torres Strait Islander communities. The first protocol requires researchers to engage with Aboriginal and Torres Strait Islander communities as 'collectivities', that is, as entities representing their members. It is always necessary to negotiate formal participation and consent with Aboriginal and Torres Strait Islander communities through their representative bodies. As when engaging with individual participants, researchers must obtain written consent. Human Research Ethics Committees usually require that negotiations occur in face-to-face situations. By doing so, researchers observe the guideline of equality. Researchers must also respect the power of Aboriginal and Torres Strait Islander communities to refuse their approaches.

When participation and consent are agreed, a second protocol requires that researchers accept the role of 'guest' to their 'host' Aboriginal and Torres Strait Islander communities, thereby observing the guidelines of respect and reciprocity. Aboriginal and Torres Strait Islander communities must make final decisions about the design and conduct of all stages of research. Communities are then able to retain project ownership, ensure their receipt of benefits, protect themselves against exploitation and preserve their voices and cultural viewpoints in findings.

For example, communities and researchers must collaborate in the first stage—the formulation of research goals. Communities can then ensure that goals are relevant to their needs and hence that projects lead to benefits for them. In the past, researchers have built careers studying Aboriginal and Torres Strait Islanders, who in return have received little benefit. Such exploitation is no longer acceptable and researchers must negotiate topics pertinent to communities' needs. Researchers must also present frequent progress reports in formats and language that host communities deem appropriate. This responsibility upholds partnership and ensures that projects remain true to agreements.

Communities should also participate in decisions about methodology, particularly with respect to issues of cultural sensitivity. For example, a community can advise that questionnaires be written in its first language or that the researcher should not interview members of their opposite gender.

Also, communities may impose guidelines on the administration of research. A community may ask a researcher to only recruit assistants from among its members. It may also require a researcher to respect the secrecy of certain knowledge. A community may also stipulate that findings be presented in its own language and only in the context of its anticipated benefits.

A third protocol requires researchers to respect the knowledge of Aboriginal and Torres Strait Islander people—that is, their interpretations and viewpoints of the world. Aboriginal and Torres Strait Islander knowledge always takes prominence over that of other cultures and researchers must acknowledge this in analysis and reporting. If a community attaches special meaning to certain wildlife on their land, researchers must respect this knowledge, and, if the community consents, make it a context of their findings. This protocol supports the guideline of equality.

A fourth protocol requires researchers to enter legal contracts with communities who have legal corporate status, thereby formalising researcher–community relationships. In doing so, researchers observe the guidelines of responsibility and equality. Such contracts should contain clauses on administrative matters. These may include project timetables; principles for project evaluation; methods of obtaining consent from individual members; ways of negotiating changes to research; payments to communities; and procedures for resolving disputes between communities and researchers.

Contracts should also have clauses regarding cultural sensitivities. These may formalise agreement on a researcher's access to culturally sensitive materials, information and places; the production of images in reports; and appropriate forms of interactions between the researcher and individuals.

Clauses should also appear on matters of cultural and intellectual property. The *United Nations Draft Declaration on the Rights of Aboriginal and Torres Strait Peoples* (1992) recognises Aboriginal and Torres Strait Islander peoples' ownership of their cultural practices, artefacts and knowledge. For research that incorporates these possessions, communities have legal claims to intellectual property like final reports, books, cinema and sound recordings.

This is only a general description of the ethics of researching among Aboriginal and Torres Strait Islander communities. You are advised to look at the official documents on research ethics published by your university or major Aboriginal and Torres Strait Islander organisations (AIATIS 2000; ATSIC 1997; NRMHC 2003).

Summary

For social scientists the major ethical issues centre on gaining an appropriate form of informed consent, respecting individual privacy and confidentiality, being aware of the power dimension of the relationship between the researcher and the participants in research, and ensuring that the research procedures (variables selected, measurement used, sample selected, and design employed) are adequate to answer the questions being asked. Confidentiality is a particular problem since it is necessary to keep original data in a readily retrievable form in order to prove that they really were collected, not faked. Further, your files can be subpoenaed if they are relevant to legal proceedings and you would be liable for charges of withholding evidence if you refused to hand them over, or to charges of destroying evidence if you obliterated your files. Therefore, it is not possible to guarantee absolute confidentiality to participants. You can promise to protect the privacy of participants and interviewees by assigning case numbers, changing names, and dealing with group-level data, but there are limits to all undertakings of confidentiality and anonymity.

It is essential that you be aware that there are always ethical issues involved in doing research. Sometimes it is necessary to discuss proposed research with others, who are not as close to the research as we are, in order to become aware of these issues and to help find a way to solve the problems. Some think that only medical or biological research poses ethical issues. This would be true if social research were inconsequential, if it had no effect. Emphatically, though, most social research is consequential and thus does pose ethical issues regarding its consequences for those who participate in the research.

The responsible researcher is considerate, does nothing to injure, harm or disturb the participants in research, keeps data collected on individuals and groups secure, accurately records information and reports the findings of the research in a public manner.

Questions for review

1   Why is the ethical review of research necessary? Why is this something with which researchers need outside help in the form of a Human Research Ethics Committee?

2   List some of the ethical issues involved in social research. Read research reported in journals or newspapers and discuss with other students the issues you see. For example, would you like to have been a participant in the research? Is it ethical to waste other people's time? Is it ethical to conduct poorly designed research? Is it ethical to conduct research in such a way that those following you find it harder to gain access to people for research?

3   Find out the procedures in your university, TAFE or other institution for the ethical review of research. Try filling out the required form for a piece of research you are considering.

4   Does your professional association have a code of ethics? If so, read it and compare it with the codes of two other professions.

Suggestions for further reading

Babbie, E. R. (2003), *The Practice of Social Research*, 10th edn, Wadsworth Publishing, London, chapter 17.

For various documents on research ethics regulation in Australia consult the website of the National Health and Medical Research Council: <http://www.nhmrc.gov.au/issues/researchethics.htm>.

National Statement on Ethical Conduct in Research Involving Humans (1999), Government Publishers, Canberra <http://www.nhmrc.gov.au/publications/pdf/e35.pdf>. (See Appendix 2 'Information Privacy Principles'.)

National Health and Medical Research Council (2001), *Human Research Ethics Handbook* <http://www.nhmrc.gov.au/hrecbook/misc/prelims.htm#top>.

The Commonwealth *Privacy Act 1988* and other useful documents and links on privacy in Australia are available on the website of the Office of the Federal Privacy Commissioner: <http://www.privacy.gov.au/act/privacyact/index.html>.

The Centre for Human Bioethics at Monash University publishes a journal called *Monash Bioethics Review* that has many articles relevant to social science research.

The codes of ethics published by various professional bodies such as the Australian Sociological Society, the Australian Association of Social Workers, The Australian Association of Psychologists and others.

For information and advice on the ethics of conducting research among Aboriginal and Torres Strait Islanders' communities:

Aboriginal and Torres Strait Islander Commission (1997), *Protocols for Undertaking Research Relating to, Involving and About Aboriginal and Torres Strait Islander Peoples*, ATSIC, Canberra.

Australian Institute of Aboriginal and Torres Strait Islander Studies (2000), *Guidelines for Ethical Research in Indigenous Studies* <http://www.aiatsis.gov.au/corp/docs/EthicsGuideA4.pdf>.

McAulley, Daniel, Robert Griew, and Ian Anderson (2002), *The Ethics of Aboriginal Health Research: An Annotated Bibliography*, VicHealth Koori Health Research & Community Development Unit Discussion Paper No. 5, University of Melbourne, Parkville, Victoria.

National Board of Employment, Education and Training (1999), *Research of Interest to Aboriginal and Torres Strait Islander Peoples*, Commissioned Report No. 59, Commonwealth of Australia, Canberra.

National Health and Medical Research Council (2003), *Values and Ethics: Guidelines for Ethical Conduct in Aboriginal and Torres Strait Islander Health Research*, <http://www.nhmrc.gov.au/publications/synopses/e52syn.htm>.

Smith, Arthur (1997), 'Indigenous research ethics: policy, protocol and practice', *Australian Journal of Indigenous Education*, 25 (1): 23–9.

United Nations Draft Declaration (1992), *The United Nations Draft Declaration on the Rights of Indigenous Peoples* (Plain Language Version), <http://www.atsic.gov.au/issues/Indigenous_Rights/International/Draft_Declaration/Plain_Version/default.asp>.

World Health Organisation (2003), *Indigenous Peoples & Participatory Health Research*, World Health Organisation, Geneva.

PHASE 3
Analysis and Interpretation

Drawing conclusions

CHAPTER OUTLINE

You have now reached the point where you analyse and interpret the findings of your research. You have clarified your thinking, formed a hypothesis and gathered data. Now what? Essentially, it is time to draw conclusions about your hypothesis on the basis of the evidence you have collected.

A proper conclusion is grounded on careful analysis and interpretation of data gathered in the light of the basic question being researched. Data have been collected and presented but they still require evaluation and analysis. Four basic questions guide the activities of data analysis and interpretation:

1 What did you ask?
2 What did you find?
3 What do you conclude?
4 To whom do your conclusions apply?

What did you ask?

The first step in drawing conclusions is to remember what it was you asked. It is surprising how easy it is to lose sight of the purpose of a piece of research. Before leaping to conclusions, it is useful to remind yourself about the questions that originally motivated you to do the research. You may have made many interesting discoveries as you gathered data or prepared your data for presentation. But what was the central issue?

Do you remember the questions that you first asked? If you kept a research journal, you should look back to remind yourself of your original questions. Some will seem very broad and unfocused now. You may be able to see how in the process of clarifying your thinking and narrowing the focus of the research you tackled a manageable part of a much larger issue. Try to clarify now how you see both the larger issue and the role your research plays in that larger issue.

The clearest statement of what you are asking is your hypothesis or your research objective. Recall the process by which you narrowed the focus of your project and formed the hypothesis or objective. Now look at your hypothesis again. How does your hypothesis relate to the larger issues? Take as examples the hypotheses we have used in this book.

We have spent a lot of time on research involving hours spent in study and exam results. The hypothesis stated:

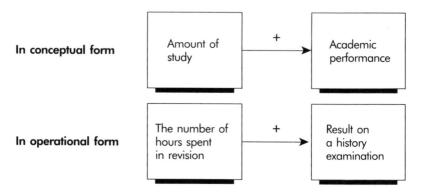

What was the background of this hypothesis? In chapter 3 it was observed that some students get better marks than others. This prompted a series of clarifying questions. Refer back to chapter 3 to remind yourself of the other possible explanations that were put forward. It should become clear that your hypothesis and hence your research will tell you something, but not every-thing, about the general issue. There were other factors, which were not explored. Hence, any conclusions you draw will be limited to the factor you examined. Your research pertains to the general area but deals specifically with one isolated factor. When asked, 'Why do some students get better marks than others?' you cannot conclude, 'because some study more than oth-ers do'. You know there are many possible factors. Your research deals with only one. You could conclude that 'amount of time spent in revision seems to be a factor in examination results'. Your research deals with one aspect of the overall issue. Be careful to ensure that in drawing a conclusion you draw attention to the general issue and the way your research relates to it.

The first step in drawing a conclusion is to restate the general issue and the hypothesis, showing how the hypothesis relates to the general issue.

Another hypothesis used as an example throughout this book concerns the relationship between a talk on 'healthy snack selection' and the selections that workers actually make in the cafeteria. Reread the sections of chapter 6 in which this example is first developed. Then answer these questions:

1 What is the general area of concern?
2 What is the conceptual hypothesis?
3 What is the operational form of the hypothesis?
4 How does the hypothesis relate to the general area of concern?

Here again you see the importance of stating conclusions in a way that clearly relates to both the specific hypothesis and to the general issue. There are many ways that the nutritional status of workers could be studied. In this case, snack selection in the cafeteria was chosen as the focus. First, a general observation study was done to discover the patterns of selection. Then an experiment was conducted to ascertain whether a talk on healthy snack selection would change workers' snack selection patterns. The conclusions of such research would relate to the general areas of worker nutrition, cafeteria operation, and nutrition education. How does the specific hypothesis tested relate to each of these areas? In this way, the conclusions of a small study are related to larger issues.

The first step in drawing conclusions is to clarify the way your research relates both to the hypothesis and to the larger issue. You did not start collecting data on the number of motorists who had run red lights for no reason. What were the reasons? How does your research relate to these reasons? If you did research comparing the degree of sexism among different groups of males, why did you do so? To simply conclude that levels of sexism among males who had attended coeducational schools were higher or lower or the same as those among males who had attended single-sex schools may be correct, but too limited. Relate the findings of your small study to the larger context of which it is a part.

What did you find?

Once you have reminded yourself what it was you were asking and how your hypothesis or research objective related to that general area of interest, you can ask, 'What did I find?' Yes, the data your study produced are by now displayed in tables or graphs or expressed as averages. But what do you think they say? They do not analyse or interpret themselves.

There are several basic aspects to answering the question, 'What did you find?' First, the data need to be interpreted. Second, the data must be related to the hypothesis or research objective. Third, you need to evaluate the data. We will discuss each of these aspects.

First, what do your data, as presented, say? This involves expressing in words what the tables, graphs or averages say. We spent some time on this in chapter 9. Look again at Figure 9.7. It is followed by a simple statement expressing in words the relationships between the data in the table. That is an example of interpretation.

Now turn to Figure 9.8. What does it 'say'? The interpretation of this table might be written in this way:

> Among those 16 students who studied more than the average amount of time, 11 (or 68.7 per cent) received an above-average result on the history examination, while among those 14 students who studied less than the average amount of time, two (or 14.3 per cent) received an above-average result.

Interpreting your data means restating the relationships depicted in your tables, graphs, or calculations of averages as clearly as possible in words.

How would you interpret the data presented in Figure 9.13 comparing the ethnic composition of one course with the ethnic composition of the Australian population? The interpretation of these data depends on the question being asked. Let us assume that the question was this:

> How does the ethnic composition of Course X compare with that of the Australian population?

An interpretation of the data in Figure 9.13 might be as follows:

> The data shows that the ethnic composition of the class enrolled in Course X is different to that of the general Australian population. The ethnic composition of Course X shows more students from Asian, Greek and Italian backgrounds and fewer Australian students than the ethnic composition of the population of Australia.

When you interpret the data, you simply restate in words what is presented and summarised in the table, graph or averages. You do not try to explain the data, nor do you draw conclusions from them. If the results are unclear, you report that the data are unclear.

As an exercise, try to interpret the data presented in Figure 9.16. Remember, interpreting the data means restating in words the relationship between the variables presented in the table, graph, or average. Finally, interpret the data presented in Figure 9.18.

Once you have interpreted the data, you are ready to relate your findings to the hypothesis or research objective. That is, 'What do these data tell you about your hypothesis?' Is the evidence 'for' or 'against' the hypothesis?

What are the implications of the findings for the narrowly defined research question?

This is usually straightforward. Problems emerge if the data are unclear, when there is no strong trend one way or the other. If this is the case, your analysis should state that the implications of the data for the question, or the hypothesis, are unclear.

It is best at this stage to report the implications of the data without discussion or comment. Either the hypothesis is supported or it is not. Ambiguous findings cannot be taken as support. It is important to remember that a hypothesis is never proven to be absolutely correct. Rather, a hypothesis is tentatively accepted or likely to be correct given the evidence, or it is not accepted given the lack of evidence.

Once the findings are stated and related to the hypothesis or research objective it is time to evaluate the data and to acknowledge the limitations of your study. General issues are critical here. First, the operationalisation of the variables would doubtless have not entirely satisfied you. Again, if you kept a research journal, you would have noted limitations in it. These limitations can be noted at this point in the report or earlier in the discussion of variable selection, decisions regarding research design, sample selection, and data collection. You may have questions about the instrument (questionnaire) or the interviewers. The limitations of your sample are to be noted.

The most important limitations involve the possible influence of those variables you are unable to control or measure. Possible alternative explanations for the relationship between the independent and dependent variables need to be noted. You may have suggestions for future research. It may be that your findings were not clear, and you suspect the interference of some variable. It is useful to note this.

Your findings may have come out in an unexpected fashion. It is here that you can comment on this and suggest explanations. Your findings may conflict with the findings of others. This can be discussed.

Whatever they are, acknowledge the limitations of the study. This shows that you know what you might have done if you had more time, money or other resources. It also shows that you know your conclusions are made tentatively in the light of the limitations of your research.

What exactly do you conclude?

A good conclusion has two levels. First, it clearly states in simple terms what the data reveal. Second, it relates this simple statement to the larger issues. This can be seen as the reverse of the process by which you narrowed your attention in the first stage of the research process.

Here is a sample conclusion for the study of revision time and marks:

Conclusion

A study of 30 students in a history class in a university in X revealed that those who spent more than the average time in revision tended to receive above-average results in a history exam. While there were some exceptions, the data as presented in Figure 9.7 show a clear trend in this direction. It is safe to conclude that these data provide evidence that support the hypothesis.

Thus it is likely that amount of time spent on revision is one among other factors that affect academic performance. Other factors such as IQ, social life, nutritional status, and specific study habits may account for some of the exceptions in this study. Further research is required to establish how widely this finding applies. Further research should compare students at other universities, the effect of time spent in studying on the examination results in other subjects, and on the results of other methods of examination.

This conclusion clearly states the relationship demonstrated by the data. It supports this statement with references to the data summaries and graphs. Next, it states the implications of the data for the larger issue and future research. The first part of the conclusion restates what the data reveal about the operational form of the hypothesis. Data do not interpret themselves; you have to interpret them. Do the data support the hypothesis? Do they reject the hypothesis? Or is the situation unclear? Then the implications of the findings are drawn for the conceptual form of the hypothesis and, finally, the larger issue. The role of a conclusion is to restate the findings of the study and then to state the implications of the findings for both the hypothesis and the larger issue.

Take the example of the study comparing sexist attitudes among males. The hypothesis (see chapter 5) was as follows:

Males who have gone to single-sex schools are more sexist in their attitudes than males who have attended coeducational schools.

The dummy table suggested for this study is found in Figure 7.8. Let us assume that Figure 12.1 presents the data from a study of 60 males. Thirty had attended single-sex schools and 30 had attended coeducational schools.

Given the data in Figure 12.1, what would you conclude about your hypothesis? Is it supported or rejected, or are the results unclear? The data in Figure 12.1 do not immediately present a clear picture. They are not compelling. There is too little difference. A conclusion drawn from a study based on these data might read as follows.

Figure 12.1 Findings from a hypothetical study of sexism among males

| | Educational background | |
Sexism score	Single-sex school	Coeducational school
High	24 (80%)	20 (67%)
Low	6 (20%)	10 (33%)
Total	30 (100%)	30 (100%)

Conclusion

In an attempt to determine whether educational background played a role in the development of sexist attitudes among males, a questionnaire was administered to two groups of males. One group had attended single-sex schools for all of their schooling, the other group had attended coeducational schools. Does an educational context in which males have to interact with females regularly produce lower levels of sexist attitudes?

The results of our research indicate that males from both educational contexts show high levels of sexist attitudes as measured by the sexist-attitude scale used in the study. Males from single-sex schools are slightly more likely to have highly sexist attitudes. The differences between these two groups of males are not sufficiently large to conclude that the hypothesis is clearly supported. While the data are in the hypothesised direction, the relationship is too weak to draw any firm conclusions.

While educational context may well have an effect on the development of sexist attitudes among males it cannot be concluded that this is so on the basis of this research. Additional research is required to ascertain whether this relationship is stronger or weaker in other schools. It may well be that the general level of sexism in our society is such that educational context has little effect on the development of sexist attitudes among males. Again, the role of the conclusion can be seen. It relates the specific findings back to the hypothesis and then to the general issue.

As an exercise write a conclusion for this research given the findings in Figure 12.2. In writing your conclusion be sure to:
1 restate the general aim of the research
2 restate the finding of the research
3 indicate whether the hypothesis is supported or rejected or if the result is unclear
4 explain the implications for the larger issue
5 make suggestions for future research.

Figure 12.2 Findings from another hypothetical study of sexist attitudes among males in two educational contexts

Sexism score	Educational background	
	Single-sex school	Coeducational school
High	14	5
Moderate	10	10
Low	6	15
Total	30	30

In the conclusion, you state what the data as summarised and presented in your tables, graphs or averages tell you about the hypothesis you formulated. The implications are then drawn for the larger issue. This is also true for a research objective. However, research objectives are not accepted or rejected. The data are simply summarised in words and a conclusion drawn.

Take the example of the simple observation study of one baby's growth. Once the data have been collected and recorded, the simplest conclusion would be that the baby had grown by the addition of X cm and Y g. But there is a background to this study. You could look up the average growth rates for infants and compare this baby's growth record with that standard. Then a conclusion about one baby's growth in comparison with the average could be made.

Since no specific comparisons are being made, and neither are data on other factors kept, no other conclusions can be drawn. If the purpose of the study had been to compare the growth rates of different infants, for example one group that had been breastfed with another that had been bottlefed, then the study would have had a hypothesis about which conclusions could be drawn.

An appropriate conclusion for a study of infant growth guided by a research objective might take the following form:

Conclusion

The purpose of this study was to observe the growth of one infant over a period of eight weeks in order to see, in a specific infant, the general patterns of growth as described in the textbooks. The specific measures were of growth in length and weight. Other aspects of growth and development were observed but not systematically recorded.

The baby I observed grew by X cm and Y g during the eight-week period of observation. The baby was eight weeks old at the beginning and 16 weeks old at the end. A growth of X cm and Y g is well within the bounds of normal growth for infants of this age.

This observation has also made me aware of the complexity of observing infant growth and development. I would suggest that in future observations of this type the following be considered ...

Although a conclusion about a hypothesis is not drawn, the conclusion of a study guided by a research objective may well make suggestions for future research. For example, take an observation study guided by the following research objective:

To discover what factors are considered by the person(s) in charge of meal planning in the selection and preparation of food.

The researcher might conclude at the end of the research as follows:

Conclusion

An observation study conducted in a single household revealed that the following factors were taken into consideration in the selection and preparation of food:

- cost
- preferences of family members
- availability
- preparation time required
- preparation skills required
- nutritional quality
- balance and diversity in foods
- kilojoule content of foods.

While in the single case-study household cost was the predominant factor, closely followed by preference of family members, this may well vary from household to household. Future research into the factors shaping household decision making about food should ascertain how the importance of these factors varies among households.

While we interviewed each member of the household, we discovered that in this household one person is responsible for meal planning and preparation. Given our experience in this household we suspect that this person is not always 'the mother'. This means that future research can focus on one member of each household but that care is required in selecting which member to interview. We also suspect that a questionnaire could be devised to measure the relative importance of various factors ...

The researcher here used the observations of a single case study as the basis for many suggestions for the next stage of research on this issue. She could well have made other comments. Further observations regarding the amount of time spent in meal preparation, meal planning and shopping might also have been made. The researcher might have commented on the accuracy of the information available to the participant and the suitability of the meals planned to the purposes outlined by the participant.

Thus, although research guided by a research objective does not lead to conclusions about hypotheses, the results are summarised and related to the general issues behind the research. Suggestions for future research may also be made.

This introduction to the research process has deliberately avoided the introduction of more mathematical forms of analysis, so that you can become familiar with the essential logic and flow of doing research. There is not space here to discuss the application of statistical analysis to data. However, conclusions that are drawn using non-statistical techniques are often very limited. There are now a number of computer programs that allow quite complex statistical analyses to be made by students, even those who consider themselves to be weak in mathematics. Consult your lecturer to determine whether your data are suitable for statistical analysis and for advice on what programs are available.

To whom do your conclusions apply?

The question 'To whom do your conclusions apply?' can be answered in a narrow sense and in a broader sense. On the one hand, your conclusions are limited to the sample studied and to the population of which it is representative. This is the narrow interpretation of a conclusion.

If you studied a representative sample of history students in your university, your conclusions are limited to history students in your university. If you observed one family, your conclusions are limited to that family.

The narrow interpretation of the applicability of conclusions is based on the limitations imposed by the sampling procedure selected. This narrow interpretation refers to the data, to the 'facts' produced by the research. Take the example of the study of sexist attitudes among males. The data in Figure 12.1 relate to two groups of 30 males. The groups had different educational backgrounds. The specific findings are limited to those males. That is, the finding that two-thirds (67 per cent) of males from coeducational schools scored high on sexist attitude, while four-fifths (80 per cent) of males from single-sex schools did so, is limited to those males. If those males were a representative sample of a larger population, then that finding applies to that larger population. It is not permissible to conclude that, in general, 67 per cent of males from coeducational backgrounds and 80 per cent of males from single-sex schools will score high.

The conclusions regarding the data apply to those from whom the data were collected, or to the larger population of which they are a representative sample. On the other hand, research is done to gain some understanding about larger issues. Some of the conclusions refer to the implications of the research findings for those larger issues. This is the broader sense of the applicability of the conclusion. In drawing conclusions, the researcher moves from the narrow conclusions about the findings of the study to the implications of those findings for the larger issues. It is in this sense that conclusions have a broader applicability.

Again, take the example of the study of sexist attitudes among males. The data in Figure 12.1 were too close to conclude that educational context made much difference between those two groups. Then the example conclusion discussed the implications of the findings for the larger issue. When drawing the implications, a much more tentative style of expression is adopted: 'It may well be that ...', 'Additional research is required ...'.

The sample conclusion for a study of 30 history students demonstrates the shift between the narrow conclusion and the drawing of implications. First it summarises the empirical findings (the data), then it continues, 'Thus it is likely that amount of time spent on revision is one, among others, of the factors ...'.

Thus, in drawing conclusions, the first step is to restate the empirical findings. This part of the conclusion applies narrowly and strictly to those studied or the population of which they are a representative sample. Then the implications of the empirical findings for the more general issues are discussed. In this, the findings are related to a broader context and made more generally relevant. However, the discussion of implications is done tentatively. In this way, the conclusion can be seen to have a narrow aspect (the summary statement of the empirical findings) and a broader aspect (the discussion of the implications of those findings).

Questions for review

1   What four basic questions guide the activities of data analysis and interpretation?

2   Interpret in words the data on the effect of age on Australian religiosity presented in Figures 12.3 to 12.6. Note that your task is simply to restate in words what is presented in the graph. Do not try to explain, moralise or draw conclusions. Simply state what each graph 'says'.

3   Why is it important to acknowledge the limitations of a study?

4   How does the sampling procedure you choose influence the conclusion you draw?

Figure 12.3 Age differences in church attendance

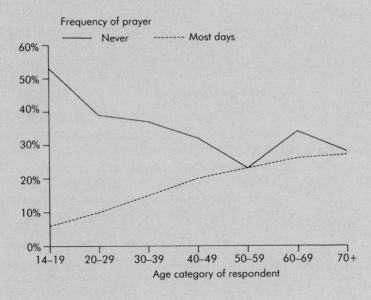

Figure 12.4 Age differences in praying

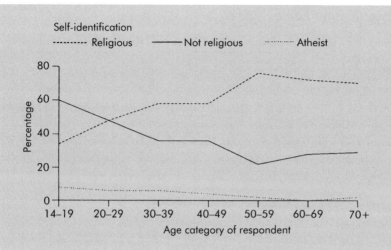

Figure 12.5 Age differences in religious self-identification

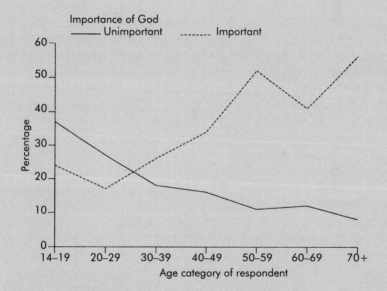

Figure 12.6 Age differences in importance of God.

Source: These tables, sourced from the Australia Values System Study 1983, are from Bouma, G. D. (1992), *Religion: Meaning, Transcendence and Community in Australia*, Longman Cheshire, Melbourne, pp. 126–7.

Suggestions for further reading

Babbie, E. R. (2003), *The Practice of Social Research*, 10th edn, Wadsworth Publishing, London.

Betts, K. and A. Seitz (1994), *Writing Essays and Research Reports in the Social Sciences*, Thomas Nelson, Melbourne.

Judd, C. M., E. R. Smith and L. H. Kidder (1991), *Research Methods in Social Relations*, Holt, Rinehart & Winston, Fort Worth, chapter 19.

Minichiello, Victor, Rosalie Aroni, Eric Timewell and Loris Alexander (1995), *In-depth Interviewing: Principles, Techniques, Analysis*, 2nd edn, Longman Cheshire, Melbourne, chapter 11.

Reporting your research

CHAPTER OUTLINE

By now you have focused on a research issue, identified and measured variables, drawn samples, selected research designs, collected data, summarised and presented data, drawn conclusions and discussed implications. You are now ready to write the research report. If you have kept a research journal you will probably have a mountain of notes and records. These will be valuable to you in writing the report.

We have not said anything about the research report until this time because it is the last activity in one cycle of the research process. The research process does not begin with a report. The research process consists of a series of activities that are completed and then reported. Although your assignment might be to write a research report, that task occurs once the research is complete. Not everything that is done during the research is reported in the research report. The research report summarises the activities so that they are clear to the reader and so that the reader could repeat the research.

What is worth reporting?

What should go into your report? How much is worth telling? The research report communicates your research to others. This is as true of your report as it is of articles published in research journals and books that report research. In order to communicate your research, it is necessary to make clear what you did, why you did it, what you found and what you concluded from your findings. Readers must be able to tell what you did and understand why you did it the way you did. Readers can then decide whether they would draw the same conclusions given the data you present. They could also conduct the research again to see if the same results were found.

A general outline

The research report should take the following general outline:
1 statement of problem
2 review of relevant literature
3 statement of hypothesis or research objective
4 selection and operationalisation of variables
5 description of research design
6 description of sample selection procedure
7 description of how data were collected
8 data presented and summarised in words
9 conclusion, limitations and implications
10 bibliography or references
11 appendices.

A research report need not be very long. One paragraph should be adequate to introduce the problem. A brief statement of what the literature review revealed about the problem is all that is required. References to the material reviewed should be included.

Below is an outline of a possible research report. The important thing to remember is the form and what is covered. The length and degree of detail in the report depend on the size of the research project and the requirements of the assignment.

The problem

State succinctly the question or problem your research deals with. Some call this 'the human problem', that is, the ordinary daily, policy, or intellectual issue that inspired you. Youth homelessness, marital breakdown, how to care for the elderly, the impact of legislation to prevent sexual harassment, and how people who live in Canberra are different from people who live in Darwin are examples of such issues. They are unformed, large, wide-ranging issues, the sort of concerns that awareness of everyday life brings to the minds of social scientists.

The review of relevant literature

The literature review section of a research report takes the ordinary human issue and locates it in a body of theory and previous research. This helps to transform the human issue into a researchable question or hypothesis. For example, reviewing past work on youth homelessness will tell you what is already known, what questions are current in the field and what research approaches have been tried and with what results. Your readers deserve to know that you have consulted the literature in the field, what your conclusions about the field on the basis of your reading are, and how you see your research contributing to the field and the understanding of or knowledge about the issue.

Statement of hypothesis or research question

At the end of the literature review section, it is possible to state your hypothesis or research question. In so doing you transform the human issue into a limited, researchable issue. The human issue concerning youth homelessness becomes 'What is the incidence of youth homelessness in St Kilda during February?', 'How many housing enquiries are made each night at a youth drop-in centre?' or 'Has there been an increase in the incidence of youth homelessness as a result of the deepening of the recession?' The human issue concerning marital breakdown could be transformed into such hypotheses as 'Similarity of religious background and commitment is negatively related to marital breakdown', 'Strength of religious commitment is negatively related to marital breakdown' or 'Degree of financial stress is positively related to marital breakdown'.

The hypothesis or research question is a restatement of the human issue in the form of a researchable issue.

Methodology

In this section, you describe and give reasons for your choices in the selection and operationalisation of variables, research design and sampling. The discussion of methodology must appear at this stage. It cannot appear earlier, because it will only make sense if the research problem and the hypothesis have already been explained. It cannot appear later because the next section, 'Description and presentation of data', will not make sense unless it is preceded by an explanation of the methodology.

Description and presentation of data

Here you briefly describe how the data were collected and present your findings. It is important to stick very closely to a simple description of the data, leaving speculation and discussion for the next section. This section, like the last, is guided by your hypothesis or research question. Here you present the data that are relevant to the issues you raised and clarified before. It is important to present the findings that are relevant to the hypothesis or question guiding your research in a consistent and clear manner. This section presents the results of your research into the researchable question.

Conclusion and discussion

In the conclusion, you return to the 'human issue' with which you began and relate the findings of your research to this issue. You state your conclusions clearly, then discuss the implications for this issue. The conclusion may include speculation on possible future research, plus discussion of some of the limitations of your research and its possible policy implications.

Bibliography

In this section, you list all the references you consulted while doing your research. Use a bibliographic format that is currently used in one of the major journals in your field. Pay careful attention to the information required for books, chapters in books, and articles. Some forms of material, such as documents, may have to be codified and listed separately. Consult with your lecturer about the format required.

Appendices

Appendices are convenient places to put material that is relevant to your report but that would interrupt the flow or take too much space in the body of the report. This may include copies of questionnaires or other research instruments, letters written seeking permission to conduct the research, more detailed reports of data collected or supporting documents.

Your research report should tell a story, or have a logical flow, so that the reader progresses from issue to issue and is always aware of how each section of the material relates to the rest. This 'storyline' or logical flow is not always clear until the end of the project. If your report does not read well think it through again, reminding yourself of the issues raised at each stage and how these issues are related to the overall flow of your argument.

The length of a research report depends on various factors. Your lecturer may set a word limit. You may wish to publish your report in a journal that has expectations about the size and style of articles it publishes. MA and PhD theses have book-length word limits. Appendix A presents a full article-length research report. It is a good example of a report that does not require advanced statistical analysis, yet says something significant about an area of social life. Below are some very brief research reports called 'abstracts'. A well-written abstract, in a paragraph, provides a great deal of information about a research project.

Men getting real? A study of relationship change in two men's groups

Andrew Singleton
School of Political and Social Inquiry
Monash University

Abstract

Questions about men's capacity to change the ways they relate to one another have informed recent scholarly and popular discussions about men's relationships. One social context which consistently produces anecdotal claims about changes in men's relationships is dedicated men's groups. This article presents the findings from a qualitative study conducted with participants in two relationally centred men's groups. It discusses the type and quality of relationship change experienced by the participants in both groups and identifies the socio-cultural factors which appear to have facilitated this change. According to the inform- ants, group involvement enabled them to transcend traditional masculine modes of relating and form intimate and trusting relation- ships with other participants. The interviews indicate that this change is attributable to various immediate contextual factors related to the group itself, rather than to a strident commitment to challenging tra- ditional masculine codes of behaviour.

Journal of Sociology, Vol. 39, No. 2, June 2003

'That's my Australian side': The ethnicity, gender and sexuality of young Australian women of South and Central American origin

Zuleyka Zevallos
School of Social and Behavioural Sciences
Swinburne University of Technology; Victoria

Abstract

Through an analysis of qualitative interviews, this article explores the ethnic identities of Australian women aged 17–25 years of South and Central American backgrounds. The interviews show that expressions of Latin ethnicity are constructed around four 'emblems' symbolizing Latin 'culture'—food, language, music and dancing, and festivity. Adopting a social constructionist perspective, this article details the respondents' agency in the reconstruction of Latin ethnicity, and the consequences of the racial categorisations of 'Australian-ness' encountered by the participants. Their emphatic rejection of an Australian identity arises from their experiences growing up in Australia, where they are not 'seen' as Australian, highlighting that Australian identity continues to be regarded as synonymous with an Anglo-Celtic appearance. Nevertheless the respondents acknowledge Australian values of egalitarianism as significant when negotiating gender and sexuality. This 'paradox' of ethnic identity in the context of this study is best exemplified by the recurring comment, 'That's my Australian side', and will be investigated through a critique on the limitations of 'multicultural' ideology and its lived experience.

Journal of Sociology, Vol. 39, No. 1, March 2002

Questions for review

1 Why do professional researchers publish their findings? When they do, what information must the report include? Why?
2 What information must your research reports include? Why?

Suggestions for further reading

Babbie, E. R. (2003), *The Practice of Social Research*, 10th edn, Wadsworth Publishing, London.

Betts, K. and A. Seitz (1994), *Writing Essays and Research Reports in the Social Sciences*, Thomas Nelson, Melbourne.

Judd, C. M., E. R. Smith and L. H. Kidder (1991), *Research Methods in Social Relations*, Holt, Rinehart & Winston, Fort Worth, chapter 19.

Kumar, Ranjit (1999) *Research Methodology: A Step by Step Guide for Beginners*, Sage, London, chapter 17.

Minichiello, Victor, Rosalie Aroni, Eric Timewell and Loris Alexander (1995), *In-depth Interviewing: Principles, Techniques, Analysis*, 2nd edn, Longman Cheshire, Melbourne.

Appendix A: Autowork in Australia: Human Resource Development on the Factory Floor

Rod Ling
Monash University

Abstract

Early images of work in the automotive industry, or autowork, are commonly interpreted as negative descriptions of employment in mass production. The ubiquitous assembly line symbolises monotonous, repetitive work and the basic tasks suppress the development of human potential. This paper considers the experience of autowork now, in the early twenty first century. The data is from interviews with nine Australian autoworkers on an engine assembly line who spoke with the researcher in early 2003. Participants' tasks were very similar to those of early autoworkers. The line was very labour intensive, as the autoworkers assembled engines with their hands and airguns. However, the conditions under which the participants worked were certainly different. Both they and their firm looked at their employment as 'long term', participants undertook training, they worked in teams, contributed to production decisions and some became team leaders having responsibilities similar to those of foreman. This limited empowerment is a local version of an international best practice called 'lean production'. The study concludes that lean production has provided autoworkers with opportunities to develop and use new skills. It has also encouraged autoworkers to seek further opportunities for development and promotion that the current authority structure of their firm frustrates.

Statement of problem

Films, photographs and descriptions of early automobile factories contain despondent imagery of working life. 'Autoworkers'—the unskilled workers on the shop floor—repeat small tasks, tightening single nuts, perhaps all day, every day for any number of weeks, months or years (Ford 1922: 105; Meyer 1989: 81). To the outsider, the activity seems monotonous and boring, developing no skills or knowledge.

This image of autowork is associated with the plants of Detroit between about 1910 and 1930. But what is autowork like now? Are autoworkers, still doing simple, repetitive work that is unlikely to develop their knowledge and capabilities?

Today, the Australian industry follows Japan in using the 'best practice' form of automobile production, 'lean production'. Australia's adoption of lean production is associated with three factors. The first is the Federal Government's elimination of trade protection to force the industry to be efficient and competitive with overseas producers. Second, the presence of Japanese car makers in the Australian industry and market. Last, the embrace of lean production by US parent companies of local firms, Ford and Holden (Deyo 1996: 3–4; Williams et al. 1994: 108; Ingrassia and White 1994: 414–33). The change to lean production has had significant consequences for labour organisation and human resource policies. As will be shown below, workers now receive training, autonomy and recognition of their knowledge and experience.

Review of literature

Following is a very general description of lean production that will serve as a literature review. The review draws mainly from Ohno (1988), Womack et al. (1991), Fucini and Fucini (1990), Garrahan and Stewart (1992), Graham (1995), Adler (1995), Ingrassia and White (1994), Rinehart (1996), Parker and Slaughter (1995) and Babson (1995).

The development of lean production is usually associated with the Toyota Motor Company. Conceptually, it is a self-regulating form of organisation that continually improves the productivity of its resources by constantly seeking and eliminating waste. Lean production has three fundamental principles: *kaizen*, 'just-in-time' materials flow and 'autonomation'.

Kaizen means continuous improvement (Adler 1995: 209) or continuous waste reduction. Here 'waste' refers to excess costs, overcapacities and underutilisation of resources. Waste is a 'thing' that all employees (Berggren 1992: 31), including autoworkers, are empowered to continually seek and eliminate (Rinehart 1996: 179). As *kaizen* extends to autoworkers, it recognises that autoworkers have special knowledge and can therefore make special contributions to production decisions (Rinehart et al 1997: 132–3).

With 'just-in-time' (JIT), the final assembly line regulates the flow of parts and materials through the plant. The line 'pulls' work-in-process towards itself, only in the amounts it requires and accepts deliveries just as it needs them. As an example of a just-in-time approach for front seat delivery, assume that a plant handles and assembles parts one pallet at a time. Also the production of front seats starts with the manufacture of parts and materials by a supplier. This firm delivers its stock directly to the Front Seat Assembly Department (FSAD), who assemble seats for Final Assembly.

As Final Assembly fit the last front seat from their current pallet, a full pallet arrives just in time from FSAD. Final Assembly give FSAD the empty pallet to fill with the next delivery, which will also be 'just in time'. FSAD have the same relationship with the parts and materials supplier. As FSAD was running out of parts and materials, the supplier arrived 'just-in-time' with a full pallet and work on the next delivery of seats was able to begin. The supplier, who is probably located a few streets away, takes the empty pallet, and goes back to their plant or warehouse to prepare another delivery. Hence, Final Assembly, FSAD and the supplier are synchronised in their operations, receiving and delivering along the 'stream' of production at about the same time. Similarly, other zones of Final Assembly—windows, breaks, transmissions, engine, axles—receive their components from subassembly areas, 'just in time'. The subassembly areas also receive materials from suppliers, 'just in time'. Hence with JIT, Final Assembly sets the timing of production throughout the entire plant (Japan Management Association 1989: 67).

JIT has two main production consequences. First, there are no inventories between departments because they start and finish their production runs together. Lean producers consider that inventories are harmful because they obscure problems and wastes (Ohno 1988: 15). Should, for example, Final Assembly hold a three day inventory of windscreens, and the Windscreen Department begin making defects, the problem may not be exposed until the defects reach the top of the inventory three days later. Second, changes in any department affect others. Notably if one department stops or slows, so do the rest. Or, if one department makes undetected defects they travel through the rest of the process and cause the end product to also be defective.

The immediate human resource effect of just-in-time is stress, which may be positive or negative depending on the levels of stress that workers consider acceptable. Workers have to meet deadlines regularly at least once a shift and they have to deal with problems immediately because they have no inventories to compensate for lost production. Hence they must be reliable and able to solve problems fast. This requires confidence, the ability to think and willingness to accumulate knowledge from experience.

To streamline JIT lean producers organise workplaces into formal teams around departments or sub-departments. The basic function of formal work teams is to synchronise the process, not just between departments but, *within* departments or sub-departments. While departments might perform to the speed of Final Assembly by meeting their quotas and deadlines, they may be 'out of sync' internally and require conscious reorganisation through *kaizen*.

For example, some individuals within a department may work very slowly, forcing others to compensate by working faster. In a lean system this would be wasteful, because the slow worker represents an overcapacity of labour— they are doing less than they are capable of doing while others are working at the appropriate rate, which is at their fastest. The formalisation of teams focuses team members' attention on internal processes. With the practice of *kaizen*, teams are obliged to improve their internal flow of work-in-process, to make it constant and consistent with the flow between departments. Hence JIT requires that autoworkers be able to work in teams, rather than simply by themselves.

The third principle is 'autonomation' which refers to self-regulation through system intelligence. Autonomation operates in machines that shut down immediately after completing quotas of parts. The just-in-time system is autonomatic because it regulates the flow of materials between departments according to the needs of the final assembly line (Williams et al. 1994: 111), avoiding inventories and overproduction. Lean producers recognise that autoworkers can make plants more autonomatic if they are able to do a range of tasks, can solve problems and have the autonomy to correct problems immediately. Hence, autoworkers receive training in a number of production tasks, problem solving and personnel skills (Graham 1995: 50–8). Autoworkers can then relieve each other when there are staff shortages and they have tools for confronting production and personnel problems. Also, given that lean production is fragile, with its lack of safety nets like inventory and surplus labour, autoworkers are likely to encounter problems often. As they solve problems they learn, and make the system more intelligent and less fragile. The system becomes 'smarter' thanks to the workers.

This is only a general conceptual view of lean production, which in practice is more complicated.

Goal of research

The goal of this paper is to describe 'what is it like' to be an autoworker in Australia today and consider how local autoworkers perceive their opportunities for human resource development, i.e. to acquire knowledge, skills, recognised experience and possible promotions. The study attempts to answer this question from the viewpoint of autoworkers.

Research design

This paper is a case study of nine autoworkers from an engine assembly line owned by an Australian automotive firm. For privacy reasons the firm will be referred to as 'Engine Makers'.

Sample selection procedure

The sample was the only one available, hence, it is a 'convenience sample'. The foreman approached line workers during work time and requested their cooperation. Those who accepted met the researcher in an office. The researcher explained the nature of the project, his ethics obligations and their rights and asked if they would participate. Only one person refused.

Data collection

The data were collected through in depth interviews held during working hours in various office areas at the plant. Most interviews took between forty five minutes and one hour.

Findings

The sample

■ The sample contained 9 male workers. No women made themselves available. The age range was evenly spread from between 25 to early 50s. Two were between 25 and 29, 2 between 30 and 34, 3 between 35 and 44 and the remaining 2 were over 50.

■ Four participants were currently team leaders and 2 were former team leaders. Another was both operator and line repairman. That is, he repaired finished engines that failed testing. One participant was the shop steward, who also worked as an operator. The final participant was an operator with no special duties.

■ None of the sample was a 'new-comer' to the industry. In terms of experience, 3 had been at Engine Makers for 6 years; 3 for 9 years; 1 for 15 years while 2 for over 20 years.

■ Six members of the sample were born in Australia. The remaining 3 were respectively born in England, Sri Lanka and Croatia. Among the Australian born, only 1 had 2 parents of Australian birth. Among the other 5 Australian born, parents were from Lebanon, Italy, Egypt, Croatia and Turkey. Given the backgrounds of parents, the sample has a range of ethic associations.

■ Most of the participants were in conjugal domestic situations as 7 lived with their wife or female partner. Of this group, 4 participants had children, and 3 of these participants were supporting parents. One had 3 children; all others had 2.

■ Of the 7 in relationships, 4 had partners who also worked full time and 2 had partners who worked part time. 6 of the sample were therefore in a double income situation.

■ All participants in relationships were either buying or had paid off a home. Incomes did not vary much as team leaders received just over $40 000 per year and operators receive over $35 000. There had been little 'over time' for several months.

■ Participants were not disadvantaged through lack of education. Two had left high school after year 12; and 3 in year 11; 4 in year 10. All had completed or started the *Vehicle Industry Certificate*. Further, 2 also had finished apprenticeships—one in aircraft fitting, the other in upholstering.

■ Parents of most participants had been manual workers. Only 1 participant had a university-educated father with a professional occupation, that being, school principal. Fathers of 3 participants had been tradesmen. Among the others, the father of 1 was a truck driver/owner, while the occupations of the remaining participants' fathers were machinist, demolition worker and bus driver. The remaining participant claimed he did not know his father's occupation.

■ Six participants were from families of two working parents. The mother of one participant had been a school principal. Other occupations of mothers were nurse, secretary and factory worker. Mothers of two participants worked as cleaners.

Physical environment

Sixty-five people work on the line and testing area in teams that add certain parts during engine assembly. One team leader describes his team's contribution as, 'whatever bolts to an outside of an engine—exhaust manifolds, solenoids, various brackets, harness brackets, coil packs'. In each team there are a number of assembly and sub-assembly jobs. The workers refer to their teams as zones e.g. Zone 1, Zone 2 etc. All workers, regardless of seniority, wear a light blue shirt and trousers. As with workers at most large automotive firms, union membership is about one hundred per cent. Senior shop stewards have their own offices in the plant and dedicate all their time to union matters.

The supervisor—that is, the line foreman—described the engine line as 'very labour intensive'. There were no robots and any computers were not visible. To observe the line, one simply saw workers putting parts onto engines with their hands or air-powered tools.

The shift begins at 6.20 am and finishes at 3.00 pm. There is a single shift and participants claimed that there had been no overtime for several months. Team leaders arrive half an hour earlier to prepare for the shift and receive wages for this extra time. Workers have three breaks: lunch, which is 30 minutes, and morning and afternoon tea—both 10 minutes.

Work orientations

All participants took a long term view of their employment with Engine Makers. Some expressed strong loyalty to the company and were thankful for secure, comfortable employment in a large firm:

> I know that this company has been good to me. I come in and do my job and no one ever complains about what I do. I just follow all the rules, and no one's got any complaints. See that's how it's to our advantage, to work in a big company…at the end of the day, we go home and 'that's it'. We don't worry about nothing. That's what I hope to do anyway. Then come back the next day and we've got a job here that actually pays the bills. (Operator A)

> Obviously, we're all in it for the money. I'm not denyin' that, nobody would and 'the more, the better'. But if you just come for the money, 8 hours a day and that's all you're here for, it's not worth being here. You've gotta get something out of it, you've gotta get some job satisfaction. At the end of the day, you gotta walk out the door happy. (Team leader A)

When asked about his idea of being 'happy' at work, he emphasised the need for stimulation, learning experiences, a sense of accomplishment and growth:

> Somethin' to stimulate your mind. Somethin' to say you've done a good job that day—you've achieved target, you've had a big problem; at the end of the day, you've solved the problem. Something that expands your own learning, that you're just not stagnant—you've gotta get something out of it. (Team leader A)

All but two participants claimed they enjoyed making friends at work, indicating that social solidarity may be strong. Given the interdependence within the group's organisation and their extended period together, the high level of solidarity is not surprising.

Tasks

The assembly line tasks are narrow, in that they are small sequences of actions, which operators repeat until they rotate:

> I'm putting on the front cover. I have to do up three bolts, put the suction pipe on and then put the front cover on, and put the bolts in the front cover and then pass it along. (Operator B)

> Well it's pretty basic. Probably anybody can go to a job and perform the task. We've got all the Standard Operation Sheets (SOPs) and we usually go

through the jobs with an operator. They go through the sheet and it shouldn't be a problem. (Team leader B)

Alternatively, another participant described the workers as 'skilled labourers'. He identified operators' skill as their versatility in manual tasks—a skill not held by everyone:

> I'd like to think that we're all 'skilled labourers'. I'm pretty good with my hands. Since I was a young fella, my dad was a mechanic, my brother was a panel beater and painter and I've done all these kind of things as I was growing up, so it (autowork) doesn't seem like a great deal to do, you know. But some people, they're not so gifted with their hands, you know—to do things, like operate guns and put in screws and all these kinds of things. They put the things on the wrong way around. (Operator A)

When asked if it is possible to compare the skill of the operators to tradespeople, he answered negatively. He claimed that tradespeople, such as maintenance staff had superior skill because they 'repair things on the line', and require understanding of hydraulics and pneumatics—principles that allow an appreciation of how the line works and give them some power over it. Conversely, operators just 'make sure they're puttin' in good parts' and remain aware of safety hazards. The participant has a notion of higher skill based on knowledge and control of machines or processes. Operators simply function as part of the process, interacting with the machines.

Other participants also considered that by working at Engine Makers, they had acquired knowledge and experience that other manufacturing firms recognise. These included knowledge of lean production, communication skills and experience in leadership.

Kaizen

Some writers focus on *kaizen* as a procedure through which workers continually refine their standard operating procedures to reduce job cycles times i.e. maximum time to execute a task once (Fucini and Fucini 1990: 37; Graham 1995: 105; Garrahan and Stewart 1992: 6; Reinhardt et al. 1997: 130–1). However, team leaders claimed that it was unusual for worker operators to make improvement suggestions to Standard Operating Procedures (SOPs), even though the practice has sanction. Operators usually just accepted SOPs from engineers, although there was some negotiation between engineers and team leaders.

The suggestion scheme, which is not compulsory, is another *kaizen* process. The scheme motivates employees with small payments and prizes. Each suggestion earns a $20 payment and 'points' toward prizes like televisions. A team leader considered that rewards for suggestions were substantial incentives for operators to be more attentive:

> You might notice a socket's worn. If an operator notices it, I'll write that down and I'll 'put it in' for him—they're keeping an eye on their job and taking ownership of their operations. If you can make an extra hundred bucks a week, just from putting in a few suggestions, well then I think that's a good idea. (Team leader C)

Most other participants were cynical about the suggestion scheme, perceiving that management often failed to implement submissions, due to lack of time or unwillingness to spend money. Participants also considered that management delayed in paying rewards making employees generally indifferent to the scheme.

Just in time (JIT)

As they had to complete over 250 engines every shift for the final assembly line, participants were aware they were part of a just-in-time system. However, participants did not consider that JIT created problems for which the engine line should take responsibility. Following is a quote from a team leader who placed responsibility for problems on other staff such as the parts chasers—i.e. forklift drivers—and maintenance crew:

> Some parts chasers are still trying to adapt to it and they are having problems still trying to supply the parts. You might wait five or ten minutes and that stops the line, basically, and makes it difficult for us. The maintenance guys are under a bit of pressure. If they don't get that machine goin', then we don't get parts and we don't assemble engines and it goes down the line. No engines— no cars. (Team leader B)

Operators simply understood JIT as a rule requiring forklift drivers to deliver parts bins, one at a time as needed. They felt no stress due to the absence of inventory. Rather, they were positive about JIT as it facilitated more physical space. They saw the pressure as being on the forklift drivers.

> Most of the time, it's fairly good. As soon as that actual bin finishes you can have another one. So that's what they call a 'just-in-time'. So the stockman (forklift driver) can't just fill up and put so many things 'there'—a couple of days worth, because that takes up so much room. (Operator A)

Participants therefore just focused on making their daily quotas, perceiving that JIT was the responsibility of others. Hence, they did not see JIT as a source of stress or mental challenge as held by MacDuffie (1995: 61).

Teamwork

The range of team activities was well defined. There were two-minute meetings every morning—usually on safety issues; rotation of tasks between members; and the appointment of a team leader who took responsibility for preventing disruptions to production. There were no regular *kaizen* activities particularly with regard to decreasing idle time in job cycles as noted by Adler (1995: 215–16) and Graham (1995: 105).

Given this range of activity, all participants were supportive of the team concept. Generally they considered that team responsibilities gave operators 'ownership' or responsibility for their zones and their work:

> Yeah, I think it's a good idea. I think it promotes ownership within the section. People will take care of certain aspects within their job, where before, you walked in the gate you left your brain there. (Team leader C)

Also, participants perceived that teams provide support for individual workers and a pooling of knowledge and skill, thereby extending the potential of each team, if not the entire line.

> It's a better than before. Because we working together. We helping each other. And always, the more people who is involved inside is easier to solve any problems. That's a true you know, you can't deny it, 'cause we participate together. (Operator C)

The team leader role offers extra support to operators. Previously, operators depended only on their supervisor, who might be elsewhere on the line when needed, but now the team leader is close by and can give advice and make decisions. The position is also one of seniority to which operators without trade qualifications can aspire. Hence it is an opportunity for career advancement and learning. Team leaders were required to take responsibility for organising rotation, relieving workers on breaks, training new people, submitting members' suggestions, fixing minor machine problems. A team leader therefore has a varied job that offers more stimulation through responsibility, personnel management and problem solving:

> Bein' a team leader, it's not too bad. You got a bit of authority, and it's not like you're on the line all the time, so you're lookin' at always, getting' the numbers out, quality, how people do the job, you know, try to work with the people, so they have a good day and they have a smooth run. (Team leader D)

Team leaders also represent a 'grey area' in the hierarchy which can make their positions difficult. Although hourly workers, they are responsible to management for their team's production, safety and personnel management. They are operators with supervisory and management roles. If their teams do not function satisfactorily, they face pressure from the supervisor; and if they make unpopular decisions they will face resistance from within their teams:

> I have no disciplinary roles, my job is as a mentor, trainer, diplomat. That's how I look at my position. If my people are happy and they give me what I need at the end of the day, then management are happy. So as a team leader—we feel like we're in 'no mans land'. We've basically gotta, 'butter up' the operators, so that we get maximum effort from them with the minimum amount of fuss. And we've also gotta keep management off their backs, when we don't make production. (Team leader C)

Training

All but one participant had a vocational qualification that is available throughout the industry—the *Vehicle Industry Certificate* (VIC). The VIC requires 200 hours of on-the-job training and 200 of class training. Through on-the-job training, workers qualify to do a number of tasks and attain the flexibility necessary in lean plants. The classroom training is about general factory processes and problem solving. It includes elective subjects about the processes in workers' own departments.

Only a single participant did not want more training. The rest wanted to gain more skills and qualifications through training either on or off the job. They hoped for stimulation, further assets in the job market or a basis on which they could move upwards in the company.

> Well obviously I'd like to further my training. If anybody goes and does any courses—anything relating to engines, operations manufacturing, engineering—they might get a chance to actually apply for a position one day. That's what I'm hopin' for. (Team leader B)

Two participants felt motivated by wasted educational opportunities at school. The following quote is from a team leader who had just finished a TAFE course in computer networking and was hoping to move into a suitable position:

> I'm always looking for more qualifications. Schools are important. Today without school, I mean you're nuthin'. Goin' full time study, I'd do any time. I realise now after so many years, quittin' school early and what I did wrong and if I had the time now, I reckon, I'd make an 'A-Grade' student. (Team leader D)

Eight of the nine members of the sample had completed the *Vehicle Industry Certificate* (VIC) which attracted a range of views. Some participants saw it as an insubstantial program and felt that it offered no real training. Others were positive about its scope and value for autoworkers:

If you go and do the VIC, you're required to do a number of jobs that are around the place, so obviously people are more flexible in that way. (Team leader B)

Workers receive part of the overall pay rise as they complete each stage of the course and gain recognition for having more skills. Those who were negative or ambivalent about the course felt that its only value was the extra money. However, one team leader believed this arrangement was positive because it associated a reward in the form of a pay increase for every new unit of skill or knowledge:

> It's directly linked to your pay level. So the more you learn, the more you get paid. The more skills you get, especially with problem solving, how to identify different sockets; guns; what gun is used for a particular job; what tools are used for a particular job. (Team leader C)

Engine Makers also offered adult apprenticeships and traineeships in engineering, when they needed such staff. To apply, operators sit for exams in maths and literacy. Participants claimed to know few people who had entered these programs. They also considered that the scholastic requirements excluded some operators:

> I haven't been to school since I was 15 years old, now I'm 40 whatever, so it's a long time, you know. (Operator A)

Another avenue of training for participants is through studying in their own time. This was possible for participants with limited responsibilities at home, because they work little overtime. One team leader recently completed a TAFE course in computer networking. Also, the line supervisor indicated that he was prepared to give discrete assistance to anyone wishing to study, in the form of limited leave. However, he was not prepared to make this an official policy because he believed that it would be open to abuse.

In late 2002, Engine Makers sent team leaders to Japan in preparation for their work on a new assembly line. The purpose of the trip was to view and use the technology of the new line at a Japanese training centre. This is consistent with the common practice in Japanese owned/managed plants in the US of sending team leader to Japan for orientation (Fucini and Fucini 1990; Besser 1996: 62; Graham 1995: 58). Hence some team leaders are getting the benefits of special training, special knowledge and the opportunity to advise management on the purchase of technology and organisation of plant and workers.

Career paths

According to the assembly line supervisor, operators with adequate ambition and abilities had a career path to foreman or even beyond. Operators could enter adult apprenticeships, and go into an engineering qualification, which would qualify them for supervisor or management positions.

Most participants however, believed they had little chance of progressing past team leader. As previously stated, participants felt that the engineering traineeships were rare and required levels of maths they did not have. Participants also perceived that all senior jobs were filled for the long term:

> They tell me there's only two options—if someone dies, there's a job available— or if someone leaves. But usually if someone's got a good job—they don't leave. So basically, there's nuthin' comin, nuthin' happenin'. (Team leader D)

Entry into a supervisor's position required a university qualification of at least a diploma. Engine Makers do not offer any official assistance to operators or team leaders for university education. Hence, they would have to study in their own time to gain the educational prerequisite to be a supervisor. Previously, Engine Makers offered its own, 'supervisors course' but have suspended this program, perhaps because few such positions will be available in the near future.

Despite their lack of qualifications, two participants, both team leaders, had recently acted in supervisory positions. Engine Makers therefore, trust some team leaders to perform at higher levels. They have at the same time, blocked their path to entering that level permanently.

Regardless of the perceived obstacles, most participants were anxious to progress in their jobs. Almost all wanted to either gain promotion or have an opportunity to work in the new engine plant, which will utilise new manufacturing technology.

> I just done a 4 month stint as a supervisor, it was only actin', but it was good experience. It was a lot more stress, a lot more hassle. I could probably handle going up to that level if it came at me. (Team leader A)

> I've still got 15 years of work in me. And this plant that they're building over there, is gonna be the most up to date plant in the whole of Australia, I guess. So, it would be really good to get in there, you know. Do just about anything to get in there. (Operator A)

Limitations

As the study used a convenience sample the findings are not representative of the perceptions of all workers on the line, because the participants were not randomly chosen. The findings are also not representative of engine assembly lines in other factories. The researcher notes that other automotive firms have different cultures and shop floor practices that are likely to affect findings of similar research.

Conclusion and implications

Basically, participants were satisfied in most aspects of their jobs. They enjoyed stimulation through extra duties that offset the monotony of assembly work. Team leaders in particular, had a varied work life.

Notably, almost all participants wanted more rewards than simply good wages. They wanted mental stimulation, the satisfaction of having performed well and chances for promotion and further training. Several factors may motivate this social attitude. First, extra responsibility—team leadership, repair, shop stewardship—may have given participants a higher appreciation of their own ability and the experience of intrinsic reward. This may have created extra confidence and desire for more work satisfaction and ambitions for promotion and training.

Also, social norms about the importance of achieving success and status may have been significant. Three admitted to being disappointed about underachieving at school. The two with trades qualification, may have also wanted to regain their previous status. The aircraft fitter mentioned that he grew up in a working class town where he was told at a very early age that he would be an 'engineer' and he had accepted this destiny. In describing his initial experiences as an operator he admitted to feeling a drop in status. Therefore his motivation to become a team leader and perhaps a supervisor one day could be related to a desire to regain his former status as a worker with recognised special skill.

Another factor may be the long term relationships that participants shared with Engine Makers. Fucini and Fucini wrote that at Mazda, Flat Rock, 'the company viewed the employee–employer relationship as a 'marriage' not a 'casual date' (1990: 57). Participants in this study may see their relationship to Engine Makers from the same point of view. They consider they and Engine Makers have a long term mutual commitment. They see the 'marriage' as an equal partnership where both they and the company should grow together. Participant's ambitions may then be symptomatic of a contemporary, perhaps post-modern view on worker/company relationships. The relationship is based on mutual commitment and workers feel that as the company gets long term rewards, so should they.

The research found a tension between the orientations of participants and the training and promotion structures in the firm. In relation to promotion, participants perceived that career paths were blocked because of lack of opportunities. Some were anxious to move 'sideways' into more satisfying work such as that offered on the new assembly line. However, there seemed to be few opportunities even for sideways movement.

If this sample is representative of the entire assembly line it demonstrates a new challenge to human resource staff at Engine Makers as operators have a significant grievance about lack of opportunities for personal development. Ironically, by devolving more responsibility to the lowest level of their hierarchy, Engine Makers may have stimulated social factors that have created a push for upward movement in the firm.

Bibliography

Adler, Paul S. (1995), 'Democratic Taylorism' in Steve Babson (ed), *Lean work: empowerment and exploitation in the global auto industry*, Wayne State University Press, Detroit.

Babson, Steve (1995), 'Lean production and labour: empowerment and exploitation' in Steve Babson (ed), *Lean work: empowerment and exploitation in the global auto-industry*, Wayne State University Press, Detroit.

Berggren, Christian (1992), *The Volvo experience: alternatives to lean production*, Macmillan, London.

Besser, Terry L. (1996), *Team Toyota*, State University of New York Press, Albany.

Deyo, Frederic C. (1996), 'Introduction' in Frederic C. Deyo (ed), *Social Reconstructions of the world automobile industry: competition, power and industrial flexibility*, Macmillan, Houndmills Basingstoke, Hampshire.

Ford, Henry (1922), *My life and work*, Angus & Robertson, Sydney.

Fucini, Joseph J. & Suzy Fucini (1990), *Working for the Japanese: inside Mazda's American auto plant*, Free Press, New York.

Garrahan, Philip and Paul Stewart (1992), *The Nissan Enigma: flexibility at work in a local economy*, Mansell, New York.

Goldthorpe, John H., David Lockwood, Frank Bechhofer and Jennifer Platt (1968), *The affluent worker: industrial attitudes and behaviour*, Volume 1, Cambridge University Press, Cambridge.

Graham, Laurie (1995), *On the line at Subaru-Isuzu: the Japanese model and the American worker*, Cornell University Press, Ithaca.

Ingrassia, Paul and B. Joseph White (1994), *Comeback: the fall and rise of the American automobile industry*, Simon and Schuster, New York.

Japan management association (eds) (1989), *Kanban: just-in-time at Toyota*, Productivity Press, Portland, Oregon.

Macduffie, John Paul (1995), 'Workers' roles in lean production: the implication for worker representation' in Steve Babson (ed), *Lean work: empowerment and exploitation in the global auto-industry*, Wayne State University Press, Detroit.

Meyer, Stephen (1989), 'The persistence of Fordism: workers and technology in the American automobile industry 1900–1960' in Nelson Lichtenstein and Stephen Meyer (eds), *On the line: essays in the history of auto work*, University of Illinois Press, Urbana.

Ohno, Taiichi (1988), *Toyota Production System: beyond large scale production*, Productivity Press, Cambridge, Massachusetts.

Parker, Mike and Jane Slaughter (1995), 'Unions and management by stress' in Steve Babson (ed), *Lean work: empowerment and exploitation in the global auto-industry*, Wayne State University, Detroit.

Rinehart, James W. (1996), *The tyranny of work: alienation and the labour process*, 3rd edn, Harcourt Brace & Company, Montreal, Canada.

Rinehart, James W., Christopher Huxley and David Robertson (1997), *Just another car factory: lean production and its discontents*, Connell University Press, Ithica.

Williams, Karel, Colin Haslam, Johal Sukhdev and John Williams (1994), *Cars: analysis, history, cases,* Berghalm Books, Providence.

Womack, James P., Daniel T. Jones and Daniel Roos (1991), *The machine that changed the world,* Harper Perennial, New York.

Appendix B: A table of random numbers

To use this table of random numbers it is necessary to pick a starting-place. One way of doing this is to ask someone to pick a number between 1 and 32 (in order to select a column in which to start) and then to pick a number between 1 and 50 (to select a row).

Once a starting-point is selected it is permissible to move in any direction (up, down, to one side or diagonally) as long as the movement is systematic.

Let us assume that the task is to select a sample of 30 from a population of 90. The elements (persons, tests, laboratory animals or whatever) in the population would be numbered from 1 to 90. The task is to select randomly 30 of the 90 numbers. Let us assume that your starting-point was row 19 column 30. Since you are selecting two-digit numbers it makes the most sense to use the numbers in columns 30–31. Hence the first number is 06. If you choose to move down the column the second number to be selected is 41. When you reach the bottom of the column start at the top of columns 28 and 29 and work down until you have selected 30 numbers. This will comprise a random sample of 30 from a population of 90.

A table of random numbers

Row	1	2	3	4	5	6	7	8	9	10	11	12	13	14	15	16	17	18	19	20	21	22	23	24	25	26	27	28	29	30	31	32	Row
1	2	7	8	9	4	0	7	2	3	2	5	4	2	6	7	1	6	8	5	9	1	3	5	4	0	3	6	6	7	6	5	1	1
2	2	2	6	0	4	1	7	7	3	8	7	3	6	7	9	4	2	1	3	8	9	0	3	4	9	0	2	6	3	0	9	8	2
3	9	1	6	6	3	9	4	9	1	0	5	1	5	2	2	7	5	2	5	3	4	1	3	9	5	8	1	3	8	2	9	2	3
4	7	0	5	5	9	2	7	5	7	8	0	8	8	5	0	6	0	5	9	0	5	7	4	5	2	0	6	1	6	4	2	0	4
5	4	7	3	6	6	3	9	8	2	1	7	9	7	6	4	2	4	9	6	0	3	6	3	5	3	9	9	1	8	5	1	3	5
6	8	2	0	2	8	7	7	6	0	2	2	3	1	1	1	6	4	8	5	2	2	3	4	2	2	6	5	2	2	4	9	6	6
7	0	8	7	5	3	3	6	4	2	6	8	3	1	6	5	0	0	5	5	7	8	1	0	1	2	9	1	4	3	4	7	6	7
8	9	4	1	9	0	8	4	6	6	8	6	3	3	2	2	3	7	4	7	5	1	5	7	6	3	7	9	4	5	5	3	5	8
9	5	0	0	6	7	4	0	0	0	1	9	5	9	9	1	8	1	4	7	4	9	8	7	2	4	3	0	8	6	4	2	7	9
10	1	9	5	4	1	5	2	6	2	9	4	1	1	5	8	4	4	4	6	1	8	7	8	6	4	8	7	4	4	0	5	8	10
11	5	6	4	4	1	8	7	2	8	3	6	1	5	9	8	6	2	2	9	1	9	0	4	8	1	0	1	3	5	3	4	4	11
12	7	9	2	5	1	9	7	9	3	1	8	6	8	7	7	6	6	5	0	3	8	1	1	2	4	7	8	9	1	7	5	2	12
13	3	3	3	5	9	5	1	4	0	8	2	5	6	3	5	4	6	5	7	2	6	7	8	9	9	9	8	0	9	1	5	3	13
14	1	9	0	4	0	0	9	9	5	7	4	1	5	9	4	7	6	4	8	2	6	4	4	1	8	8	1	5	4	3	8	0	14
15	5	4	4	7	2	0	3	7	9	1	0	9	6	2	9	7	4	7	6	1	1	6	1	2	2	9	5	8	4	4	8	6	15
16	2	9	8	2	5	5	5	9	3	2	0	4	9	0	6	4	4	2	1	5	7	3	6	5	5	4	5	7	9	6	6	4	16
17	9	7	6	2	6	7	7	3	3	3	1	7	5	0	9	6	1	1	3	9	2	1	1	0	0	1	3	7	7	3	7	3	17
18	5	8	2	4	3	3	0	8	5	3	5	7	5	8	3	5	9	3	4	5	4	6	3	9	2	7	1	1	4	9	1	3	18
19	4	3	4	9	5	0	3	6	2	9	7	4	6	2	5	6	9	8	3	6	1	4	0	3	5	9	7	1	8	0	6	9	19
20	1	1	9	8	4	8	0	6	7	0	9	7	9	6	9	9	4	0	6	0	0	5	9	6	5	1	4	2	0	4	1	9	20
21	6	9	1	8	3	3	7	5	9	6	6	7	7	6	0	4	5	3	4	5	7	3	0	6	1	0	3	0	0	3	5	0	21
22	7	0	0	3	8	1	3	4	7	9	5	2	6	9	9	7	3	2	5	0	2	3	5	3	9	7	4	8	9	4	1	5	22
23	3	7	2	0	8	1	5	6	9	0	1	7	8	9	6	6	6	0	7	8	1	9	6	7	4	8	9	6	3	6	5	1	23
24	2	7	0	0	0	6	5	0	6	5	6	0	3	2	9	3	1	7	2	2	8	4	9	0	4	3	2	4	5	5	1	2	24
25	3	0	7	0	7	8	4	9	4	2	8	2	4	7	4	9	6	0	4	3	8	1	7	7	0	9	8	4	6	3	1	2	25
26	6	2	9	3	3	1	7	7	5	2	2	3	4	6	4	2	2	4	7	5	4	4	4	1	7	1	6	7	1	2	6	8	26
27	5	4	9	2	1	4	8	5	7	0	9	6	4	7	2	1	8	9	7	6	1	3	3	4	6	6	5	9	0	7	0	3	27
28	0	3	7	0	1	7	3	8	0	3	6	2	3	1	0	9	5	5	2	5	9	2	0	2	8	7	7	2	0	2	7	2	28
29	9	3	6	6	2	2	0	9	7	2	3	9	2	8	7	3	1	0	7	0	8	9	3	8	8	5	3	1	3	1	0	9	29
30	2	9	5	6	9	9	5	6	9	8	2	8	0	0	4	4	8	8	5	7	2	1	3	4	9	5	2	6	8	3	6	6	30
31	8	5	7	2	9	2	6	5	9	3	9	7	1	8	3	5	6	6	1	2	1	5	5	5	6	1	7	1	5	7	5	9	31
32	8	4	5	7	7	9	9	5	1	4	5	5	0	9	5	3	1	3	9	3	7	8	1	4	0	5	4	1	5	4	4	0	32
33	8	7	9	8	1	8	4	1	4	3	7	7	0	9	1	9	4	6	1	3	8	6	5	9	2	2	8	1	6	9	0	1	33
34	7	3	2	5	1	8	6	3	2	8	5	8	6	9	3	4	5	2	6	1	9	0	6	9	0	5	4	6	8	0	3	2	34
35	8	9	9	0	1	8	8	8	9	5	7	5	0	4	1	1	6	0	3	1	3	0	3	5	8	9	2	7	8	8	7	1	35
36	0	2	9	7	8	8	1	7	6	1	6	7	6	4	2	5	0	5	8	3	2	4	7	7	2	2	6	2	6	8	6	0	36
37	0	5	2	3	2	3	8	1	8	8	1	6	2	3	0	7	3	0	1	2	6	2	6	8	3	7	4	4	3	8	9	9	37
38	2	2	6	8	1	6	9	6	2	6	7	9	1	7	8	0	2	4	8	0	4	7	3	3	8	4	4	8	4	3	3	8	38
39	0	7	8	4	9	5	8	8	0	7	2	1	8	1	7	5	3	0	7	4	1	0	3	2	0	1	2	8	6	5	9	4	39
40	4	8	0	7	0	5	9	9	4	9	6	9	8	2	0	6	4	0	7	8	1	1	4	2	1	6	7	0	7	3	1	2	40
41	9	2	0	1	6	7	2	8	3	9	8	8	3	4	7	8	4	0	5	1	6	8	7	8	3	5	4	5	0	4	0	6	41
42	0	8	8	3	4	0	9	2	2	8	1	5	0	4	8	2	6	2	9	2	1	9	8	5	3	1	0	7	8	5	3	9	42
43	2	0	6	9	7	5	2	8	2	5	5	4	0	7	7	1	7	8	6	8	5	1	3	7	8	2	7	1	9	3	6	3	43
44	3	1	8	6	8	3	5	6	3	2	7	4	1	8	9	4	5	6	8	0	6	4	6	4	1	0	9	1	9	8	1	4	44
45	0	0	8	6	1	7	5	0	8	5	6	5	0	8	2	7	1	1	6	3	4	6	0	0	9	4	7	9	2	4	8	7	45
46	3	3	2	9	4	2	5	3	3	8	2	4	2	6	2	5	2	9	0	1	3	7	6	5	9	1	4	6	0	1	0	0	46
47	8	4	7	4	0	4	5	1	2	1	0	4	2	5	7	7	9	4	6	5	8	3	3	3	1	0	3	7	7	7	8	6	47
48	0	2	4	3	0	2	0	7	2	8	8	0	8	4	1	6	0	2	3	5	9	7	5	1	3	6	3	2	8	7	5	8	48
49	4	6	5	6	3	0	4	5	2	0	1	5	2	7	9	5	3	0	2	2	1	6	1	1	0	0	9	1	6	1	7	7	49
50	3	4	8	3	4	5	8	7	5	9	7	1	6	3	9	9	0	9	4	2	5	8	9	5	3	3	3	6	4	5	2	0	50

Index